BIBLICAL ECONOMICS

Apostle Steve Lyston

Lyston
Consultancy & Enterprises LLC

DEDICATION

This book is dedicated to all those who are willing to be connected to the Spiritual CEO to solve problems especially in economics; because the failure that has occurred globally is a result of mankind no longer wanting to connect to the things that God has created for them to prosper. It is unfortunate that, today, mankind is more interested in connecting to the forbidden and unclean things for solutions – which brings disaster, loss and failure.

This book is also dedicated to those who want something different from the normal secular economic theories that have brought the world to the economic state is in this era.

If you are one of those who yearn for change, this book is dedicated to you.

THANK YOU

To the Father, the Son and the Holy Spirit – the President, the Chief Executive Officer and Chief Operations Officer and the Ultimate Economist in Whom there is no lack – I Give Thanks!

To my family, for standing with me – beside and behind me – Thank You!

A Special Thank you to The Gleaner Company Limited (Jamaica) for carrying my articles over the years.

TABLE OF CONTENTS

INTRODUCTION

As each year begins, many leaders worldwide give their usual speeches on the expectations for that year. Many make statements for change that make you wonder if we are all on the same planet! Wishes and luck don't bring change – it is through Divine Favor and a willingness to obey God's instructions, change can and will come!

The World is missing out on the number one energy source – the Holy Spirit – Who gives the greatest knowledge and wisdom. He is THE KEY to a thriving, healthy economy and having an intimate knowledge of Him and how He function and what He requires of us can solve our energy crisis, bring growth and birth new vision within the marketplace. The success of many politicians and leaders of the past is that they used to acknowledge the Holy Spirit as the One Who gives power to get wealth!

Many times, the Holy Spirit will give instructions to help nations, individuals and organizations – and it has nothing to do with religion. Because of pride, they reject it and then they find themselves in a quandary and scrounge for solutions. Please note that Amos 3: 7 says, *"Surely the Lord GOD does nothing, unless He reveals His secret to His servants the prophets."* That means He will unveil, disclose His plans for nations as long as we are in a holy fellowship with Him; even when judgement is pending and can be averted through repentance, God always reveals it to His true servants. (Genesis 6: 13; Genesis 18: 17 – 18; Daniel 9: 22; John 15: 14 – 15)

Church Leaders that are crying out for change have abandoned the Holy Spirit from their environment, and as such have created a market driven and secular environment. As a result of them doing things in their own strength and 'knowledge', rather than in accordance with the will and instructions of God, the Church now appears to the World as a powerless entity, there only for rituals and to be 'used as needed'! For example, there are people – including Christians – who are flying all the way to Australia to seek healing; there are those who engage in New Age and occult practices in order to be helped and healed. The local churches are there and are supposed to be manifesting the power of the Holy Spirit – the greatest source of Energy – so that the people can be helped and healed!

The Holy Spirit is God. He is not 'Tongues'! He created Life; He brings order, gives insight, empowers and illuminates. The success of scientists in the past was their dependency on Him for discovery and breakthrough. Now we have scientists and doctors who refuse to acknowledge the help that the Holy Spirit gives them, so now they are creating more problems for mankind as many of their tests have brought negative repercussions and have wreaked havoc on the peoples of the nations!

The Holy Spirit is so important, that Jesus needed Him in order to function fully while He was on earth! Surprisingly, there are many Theologians – some of whom advise governments - who don't even embrace the Holy Spirit, when He is within the Godhead and the source of Wisdom. So, if one is not pulling from this All-Powerful Energy Source, from which other source would one be pulling?

The Holy Spirit is in everything! He is a Person and He can be grieved, offended or blasphemed. He exercises so many functions in our daily activities. He reveals, He teaches, He witnesses, He intercedes, He commands, He testifies, He brings conviction to the world! Even when we lie or do something wrong, He nudges us! (Romans 8: 26; Matthew 12: 31 – 32; Acts 5: 3; Ephesians 4: 30; John 15: 26)

Whether we are Christians or non-Christians, cult, secularist or atheist – whatever we are, He is the very breath you breathe and if He doesn't show up for 'work' one day, that's it for you!

There are many other names by which He is known based on His function in our lives. He is the Spirit of Promise and He is Truth! He is often symbolized by Fire – the Fire of Purification and Illumination. He is also symbolized by Wind – the Wind which brings Revelation and Change! It is the Wind that exposes and reveals truth! We feel the effect of the Wind, we see what it does, but we don't see it! Furthermore, He is symbolized by Oil, Seal and Water. You are encouraged to engage in your own research.

When Pastors, Politicians and Leaders of every kind, allow the Holy Spirit of God to direct and guide them, then we will see success and change this year and beyond!

CHAPTER 1

WHAT IS BIBLICAL ECONOMICS?

So, what is Biblical Economics?

A formal definition and explanation of Biblical Economics is that it is *"the application of Biblical Principles in the decision-making process of any individual, business or nation regarding the most efficient and effective use of their limited resources in an effort to satisfy the unlimited needs and desires that come about as a result of human existence."*

Biblical Economics not only speaks to issues affecting the economic stability of a nation, the issues affecting, influencing and governing every organization and individual in a nation, but also encompasses solutions for every issue within a nation.

Biblical Economics embraces the fact that God created the Garden with everything that man needed and wanted even before He created man. The satisfaction of needs and wants are at the foundation of the principles of economics. Inherent in the whole concept of Biblical Economics is the idea that God did not originally create man to labor, having given man all the necessary resources and the capacity for distribution of those resources. Further, that it was man's poor decision to divert from God's instructions and listen to a voice other than His in order to satisfy a need or want, that give rise to economic woes and the need for the restoration of God's original plan of true prosperity for man.

Simply put, Biblical Economics is the study of how effectively people can use all their resources in decision making. It embraces the principle that economics involves more than just money, wealth and finance, but includes the proper management of human resources - the gifts, talents and skills of human beings – which the secular society has failed to do. They instead focus on the wealth aspect.

The Bible is a wealth of information on every issue of life and is filled with solutions and hidden treasures of valuable clues and information that when unlocked, can cause individuals, organizations and nations to live and walk in true prosperity, health, wealth and wisdom.

Biblical Economics is about the choices made on a daily basis according to Deuteronomy 28: 1 – 14 and Joshua 1: 8

Biblical Economics is the original blueprint for economics at any level, and the only authenticated Economic Theory book – The Holy Bible – to manage an economy – what they call Macroeconomics or Microeconomics.

The Bible outlines everything that affects mankind – the dos and the don'ts are all written in it. When we don't follow it, there are always economic consequences for both individuals and nations. In it is outlined different forms of government, starting from the Patriarchal government, teaching about the father as the Head. It also teaches the Principles of Taxation, how to treat the Poor, even Immigration Laws, how to treat Aliens, about Birthright Laws, Interest Rates, Real Estate Laws, Criminal Laws.

Every economic principle is outlined in the Bible for us to follow, and because we have neglected those principles, there is a global shift that is coming, that will have an impact on the global economy. Only those who make the change for Biblical Economics will stand. For example, the majority of the sustenance of man comes from the ground – food, housing, precious stones and minerals, trees to facilitate our breathing process, water (which is fast becoming a scarce and precious item). Where water is concerned, we are headed for a global shortage.

Agriculture and Rearing Livestock are the oldest professions, and man should never lose that. However, because of greed, man has diverted and has focused on other kinds of resources including fake items.

Biblical Economics is the study, through Biblical application, of how people use their limited resources in an attempt to satisfy unlimited needs and desires that come about as a result of human existence.

What Does Biblical Economics Entail?

Biblical Economics not only speaks to issues affecting the economic stability of a nation, it also speaks to issues affecting, influencing and governing both secular organizations and the Church as well as issues affecting you.

Biblical Economics, therefore includes issues such as:

- Economic issues and strategies
- Distribution of Resources
- True Prosperity of Household, Business and Nation
- The Value and Impact of knowing Times and Seasons
- Tithing, Seed Time and Harvest
- The Importance of Godly Leadership
- The Natural and Spiritual Connection

11

- Understanding the Holy Spirit and Business
- The Importance of Prayer, Worship and Fasting in Business
- The Impact of strong families on a nation's economic success
- Economic Growth and Development Biblically
- Different kinds of Famine and how they affect Individuals and the Nation
- What to do during a Famine
- Generational Curses, Foundational Cracks and how they affect a nation

This is not an exhaustive list of topics but it gives a general idea of how much is encompassed in the principles of Biblical Economics.

Is Biblical Economics Necessary?

The Bible is a wealth of information on every issue of Life. It is filled with solutions and hidden treasures. It is the handbook on which each person, each organization, any nation, can rely and be prosperous, healthy, wealthy and wise.

Nations, businesses and business people are not seeking to find solutions to the problems that have been overwhelming them, particularly over the past three decades.

Individuals are seeking various sources and methods of increasing their wealth in order to achieve a better life and keep up with rising costs of living. Everyone at every level is seeking a solution of some kind to make a better life and to acquire as much as they can to live at least comfortably, if not, luxuriously.

Every solution that any person, institution or nation is seeking to find, can be found in the Bible. The world is in such a terrible state today and God is the only One holding the solutions which can be found in the Word.

Ultimately, when someone is face down and there is nowhere else to turn, the only place left to look is up.

The World's Economics

Each day we realize that many of the nations' leaders around the globe seemed to have a vision for their nation – but without the people!

Jesus showed us that building the people is the most important factor in order to build nations! He took untrained, uneducated men and transformed them into world changers!

When the building of roads, a sky scraper and human sexuality become the number one vision for a nation, then there is a serious crisis. When billions are being spent to open Abortion Clinics, while they fail to spend it on Education, then you know we have a problem. Abortion, spiritual or natural, is the number one cause of the global crisis we are now facing.

Many of the good politicians that had a vision to make significant changes never made it. They were wiped out because of Abortion.

We are now seeing a major attack on our boys as a ploy to wipe them out because of their purpose. Why not empower our boys? Many of them have within them solutions for our problems. So many speak about women and children – but the boys are being neglected! All that is being done is the building of more prisons.

God created man to rule and to lead. What the political scene needs are real men with backbone to stand up and do what they have been purposed to do!

Have A Purpose!

Everything God created has a purpose. You have been created with a purpose and a mind to accomplish greatness! No human mind should be wasted. Remember that no-one can fulfill your purpose for you. Your purpose is greater than going to church to warm the bench as usual! Likewise, the church's purpose is not to focus on erecting buildings as a part of the 'pretty building competition'; it is to empower and build the people – that is primary! The building is a secondary issue. (Matthew 28: 18 – 20; Luke 4: 18 – 19)

When the church fails to do that, then we have all manner of 'rights' groups with wrong motives rising up to deal with issues that would have been handled by the people if they had been built up and empowered.

The reason you are alive and have survived stillbirth, abortion, accidents, rape, robbery, miscarriage is to fulfill a purpose. Everything that happens to your life – good or bad – is a key to your life's purpose.

Some of the scientists, inventors, and those who are considered great men – whether or not they believed more in the Creation than in our Creator – they fulfilled a purpose God had for them. Today we are beneficiaries of their fulfilled purposes.

In days gone by, there were physical efforts by leaders at all levels to DO MORE to bring positive change. Today, in light of technology, they see no need to make an effort to bring change to a nation's situation. They sit back, press buttons and push paper, and they make no move to go out physically to see and know what is happening within or to their nation unless it is 'press-worthy' to do so; or for deriving personal pleasure.

The moment God created us, He put in our dreams, visions and assignment, as well as the path we must walk and even the people who are to be around us, in order for us to be great! Now remember that the devil tries to imitate everything God does, so he puts around us the wrong people, to influence you to think the wrong way, and even to marry the wrong person; and wrong decisions give rise to other wrong decisions being made.

You can't discover your purpose by working two jobs for survival. In a case like that, you will become spiritually bankrupt. Spiritual bankruptcy comes about when we fail to get into God's Presence. Whether you believe it or not, whatever you spend time with most often, you become just like that. Nations are now refusing the good things that would bring about positive changes and instead embrace and support those things that do not! All they seem to do is borrow loans as an alternative when God wants us to be debt-free. God wants us to be debt-free. When we are not debt-free, the lender dictates the terms, the policies, how, where, when and what we do and can impose their own beliefs on the borrowers. When we are debt-free, we are truly free!

Regulate the Regulatory Agencies

In order to create more jobs, reduce poverty and give small businesses the opportunity to grow and be effective in their nation, we need to look seriously at regulatory agencies.

Many times, regulatory agencies have been set up with a mandate stating they are protecting the poor, setting rates, protecting consumers as well as setting license and compliance criteria by which organizations must legally operate. But oftentimes, they are not set up in the interest of the 'small man'. In fact, they are the biggest hindrance to economic growth. It also hinders persons from coming forward with new ideas such as alternative methods and options for healing, communication, higher returns on investments as well as solutions for energy! Regulatory organizations shut out small businesses and small business owners and those who desire to enter the market while they protect the big businesses and their owners from competition, even giving them exclusivity!

Airlines

Within the Airline industry, regardless of the season and the price of petrol, they can increase the prices to their suit, sometimes out of the reach of many of their customers. It cripples small businesses causing lost opportunities for such organizations. Lost opportunities have the potential to cause serious losses and bring failure and poverty. Furthermore, the baggage fees being charged by most airlines when consumers have paid their hard-earned money for airfares, is without conscience.

Tele-Communications

There should not be a monopoly in this area; it should be left wide open to attract healthy competition while offering nationals the opportunity to choose based on their needs.

Developing nations are often excluded from entering the markets of the first world and even from receiving the benefits other nations receive because of the imbalance evident in regulatory agencies. They impose mandatory re-tooling and policy changes on the developing nations before they can enter the first world markets, and by the time they get these things done, these nations they have run out of funds and have lost valuable opportunities.

Regulatory issues have even affected the first world nations through zoning laws and other 'red tape' which have stifled the small businesses! In certain areas, faith-based organizations have already been zoned out! Faith-based organizations often provide jobs and help the community.

If there is to be change, growth and economic recovery, this issue must be addressed. Markets need to be opened so that prosperity can return and new players can enter. Even in the area of Real Estate, there is too much red tape and there are too many problems - from calculation of taxes to mortgage rates and building permits.

There is the need for the persons in the regulatory agencies who are unafraid to stand up and uphold the right – standing up for proper business practices and principles.

Things That Can Spur Economic Growth

Reform and regulate these agencies to deal with the economic challenges ahead. For example, Food, Energy and the Financial Sector are critical areas that affect every individual; so reform and regulation will prevent serious food shortages ahead. It will also prevent market disasters and help manufacturing companies and small business to the benefit of the nation.

Remove Duty and Taxation from Solar Energy Equipment and Increase government investment into this area of Energy so that low-income persons can afford to access Solar Energy for their homes.

Stringent measures must be put in place to monitor landlords who are charging exorbitant rental and leasing rates, so that low-income families can afford to have a place to stay, or a small business owner can lease office space and still run a business.

Real Estate Appraisal and Evaluation companies need to be closely monitored to prevent abuse.

Small businesses should be given a 3-year reprieve from paying certain taxes so that they have proper time to build a foundation and be successful to the benefit of the nation's economy. High energy costs, high bank interest rates and so on can kill a business in the first year.

The economic changes that will be coming about will come through small businesses. Thus, we need more small business associations to be formed, especially for those small businesses operating for over 30 years as well as to guide the young entrepreneurs.

Global Shift in Banking and Insurance

There is a global shift taking place taking place in the banking and insurance sectors and it's happening very fast. Some don't even recognize until it hits them. These changes taking place will cause many more to become poor and homeless. It is critical for Christians to know Times and Seasons, and what to do as it will become worse. Many may laugh or scoff, but they will see. Many are quick to condemn scammers, but are silent when it comes to the "legal scammers."

Insurance companies are often quick to increase premiums and they are doing this at a rapid pace. Miss one payment, and the policy lapses or they cancel it. Let's say you are sick, need surgery, but you had an auto accident. They will try everything in the book to not give you much. Furthermore, you will get another increase on your insurance premium.

Many health insurance companies have a group of persons with which they network, who offer the cheapest service. Then without your knowledge or realization they adjust your policy benefits and instead of getting the agreed medication they force you to take generics which give you little to no help. Many are dying without justice and these insurance companies are goliaths and seem to operate with their own laws. No politician even dare to challenge them.

Every organization must practice business with morals, grace and mercy. Many people are crying because of the injustices that exist within these organizations and until the decision-makers begin to feel it themselves, they will not know what it is like so they cannot empathize and make a change.

The Banking Sector

Banks have been overcharging people for years. They have been exploiting their own people. Now, you cannot even transfer from one account to another without a charge. If you put a Manager's check in your account, (a check that was purchased with money – so that money is guaranteed) they hold it for two days or more. If there is a direct deposit (salary) to your account and you owe money somewhere, your whole salary is taken so there is nothing left in your account or in hand - you are not even able to purchase medication. Essentially, you are left to die.

Banks charge you an overdraft fee even where they do not allow the payment to go through that would have put you in overdraft.

Very shortly, in fact it has already started, you will see rapid increases in the charges for bank statements and credit card statements. They will increase selling our information to bigger banks in Europe. Many accounts will be closed and as soon as that starts happening, they are going to have contracts in place to force us to agree to them imposing a penalty if we decide to close our accounts before the "appointed time." So either way, high fees would inevitably be meted out to you.

They charge withdrawal fees and impose withdrawal restrictions on customers and that will be increasing quickly.

Mortgage payments will be skyrocketing which will force many into illegal activities to try to alleviate the oppression. So ultimately, the banking system will force people into illegal activities. The safest place up to this point are the Credit Unions, but they will be coming under pressure to put laws in place for people to be working for a long time before they can become members.

On a global level, if there is no serious coming together to address these issues, then poverty levels will rise, there will be high co-pays for surgeries, lab work, dental work and insurance premiums across the board. This will potentially force a lot of people into cremation instead of burying their dead.
We cannot continue on this path.

Maybe we should, with prayer, consider purchasing land and holding on to it. Should people begin to increase insurance coverage on life, property and business?

I am not giving financial advice, so please seek proper financial advice from a financial professional. The picture is on the wall and this is an urgent call for heads of state to no longer ignore the problem that exists in the insurance and banking sectors.

No Shortcuts to Being A Millionaire

Locally and globally, there are many tears that have been shed and much pain felt because people have been deceived out of their life savings, and even Christians have suffered even greater loss. Anyone can be deceived, and Christians are not exempt.

Deception comes as a result of a person's ignorance of a matter, and manipulation by others who have the knowledge but selfish motives. However, mistakes and deception cause us to be wiser in future endeavors. The shadow always comes before the real thing!

When ideas are presented for investment opportunities, we must read all the fine print and look more deeply than the surface to avoid deception. We must carry out investigations and engage in serious prayer – never be too quick to invest in something that offers high returns in a short time, substantial rates of interest on your investments and a quick trip to *'Millionaire-ship'*. *There are no shortcuts to becoming a millionaire!*

You must seek legal advice from those who are driven to satisfy their customers, not driven by money and profit-making. We must carry out searches on those from whom we are taking legal advice and also on those presenting business ideas for investment to us.

1. Always remember, you have the right to negotiate any deal being presented to you.

2. Let no one bully you into taking advantage of the deal 'NOW! NOW! NOW!'

3. You must check out the level of risk involved in all pyramid and any other investment schemes being presented to you.

4. Never put all your eggs in one basket – no matter how good it sounds and how sound it seems, never put you entire lifesavings in one place.

Church and Investments

There are many asking if Christians should invest. The answer is YES! And it is clearly supported in Luke 19: 13 – 27 and Matthew 25: 14 – 30. Jesus outlined that Christians should do business until He returned; but He was speaking about doing so on the individual basis.

He gave the Church all the resources they would need to avoid deception. Corporate gathering is for Prayer and Worship – not to carry out business transactions in the Temple. (John 2: 13 – 16 & Matthew 21: 12 – 13)

Church and Marketing Opportunities

It's no secret that investors, among others, try to use the Church as their Target Market for various schemes, and most times they target the Pastors as the Leaders of the Flock to sell the ideas to their congregants.

No member is obligated to comply to any investment supported or promoted by their leaders. Investment is an individual choice that should be approached with great wisdom – preferably Godly wisdom.

Any product being presented to you for investment purposes must be thoroughly investigated and be found to meet all the legal, physical and spiritual requirements. Further to this, you must know the source of the product and the destination of the proceeds. You wouldn't want to be supporting a product that is not in line with your beliefs.

Utilizing Your Spiritual Gifts

There are three main gifts given by to the Church to prevent deceptions. They are called the *Revelatory Gifts*

(1 Corinthians 12) – *Word of Knowledge*, *Word of Wisdom*, *Discernment of Spirits*.

Word of Knowledge – It is a supernatural gift that reveals facts of those things that are presented to you – both past and present. It is more powerful than a lie detector test. (Exemplified in John 4; 2 Kings 5)

Word of Wisdom – It is the supernatural insight of the future. This gift allows you to put plans in place to avoid deception.

Discernment of Spirits – This is a supernatural gift that helps you to distinguish good from evil! It helps you to identify motives – whether good or bad. (Exemplified in Acts 5)

These gifts help you to make the right decisions and examine what is presented to you. It helps you to examine and analyze the motives of individuals and organizations, and it also can be used to reduce Crime and ultimately save lives!

The next time something is presented to you, whether secular or religious, utilize the resources that are given to you to acquire and maintain your blessing.

Too Rich To Be Poor

The greatest resources we possess to bring global change, take us out of debt and create jobs, are our gifts and talents. Each person was born with gifts and talents. They have within them the solutions. Do not look to politicians to solve your problems.

Most make the decision to satisfy their status quo and create a legacy.

The gifts and talents given to you are paths to your success. Those with natural abilities in the different areas attract greater success and greater financial reward.

The more the world experiences global financial meltdown, the greater the demand will be for gifts and talents. It will be the greatest exchange of wealth we have ever seen. The world is running out of ideas and solutions – even Hollywood. The demand for the names of Hollywood and for brand names is diminishing and do not carry as much clout as it used to. The greatest wealth is normally found in poor areas where the society is neglected. Check to see where most of Jamaican musicians and sports personnel are from; many of them bring positive attention to the nation. Take for example Bob Marley, Shelly Ann Fraser-Pryce and Usain Bolt, they are known worldwide and bring positive attention through their natural abilities.

It is surprising that many countries, including Jamaica, do very little to bring out the gifts and talents of an individual. They always jump on the bandwagon when they do well. Even companies that should do not help, but after the fact they want to capitalize through marketing endorsements.

Gifts and Talents

It is difficult for John Q. Public to walk into a certain level of wealth; because he is merely working to pay taxes and bills.

Our gifts and talents are for building. Not everyone is a builder. Some can make people smile/laugh, some people write books for all ages and poetry, some can cook, some have good business sense, some can effortlessly make money because they were made with these gifts, and some have the do excellently in trade and finance. (Luke 19: 11)

Check to see which dormant gift you possess. You are accountable to God for all the gifts and talents He has given you. It is our responsibility to honor God with the gifts and talents He has given us and never depart after God has established you. Many have done so. (James 1: 17 – 18; Deuteronomy 8: 18; I Timothy 4: 18)

Oftentimes, it is not the job gained through academic success that brings you fame, it is your gifts and talents.

Ideas

For stakeholders to help to nurture the gifts and talents of and individual, we need to revamp the Education System and genuinely help those who have the gifts and talents. We need to look at institutions such as the Montessori and Technical High Schools.

One of the roles of the Economist is to look at the Human Resources and its management recognizing that nations have been building the system instead of investing in the Human Resources. No country must spend more money on building roads or purchasing ammunition or servicing debts than they are spending on developing the Human Resources that nation possesses. Sadly, within many Churches too, more is being spent on building the edifice than the individual.

Old/Abandoned buildings can be utilized as an Arts and Cultural Center for Arts, Music, Dance, Playwriting and other such activities. Persons utilizing the services could also be taught the management aspect of the various Arts industries. This could also be used as a vehicle for inner city to pull out their gifts and talents. Build state of the art studios on that premises and encourage them to express their talents positively. This has the potential to reduce crime.

Where applicable, divest government-owned bus lines and set up a government-controlled regulatory or compliance agency to ensure rates remain affordable and fair to the general public. Jamaica, for example, should divest their Bus Service, the Government of Jamaica should then set up and operate a Regulatory and Compliance agency. They can get into different forms of transportation when they can lease to the Tourism Sector. The savings that will come from that can be used to empower the Youth.

Instead of purchasing several new police cars, recruit more police to ride bikes and teach them to ride properly. Logistically, it is better, because you will reach into various areas more quickly and the money saved can be channeled into Education.

It should be mandatory that all foreign investors give back a portion of what they have profited in the country, to the development of sports and education within the nation from which they profited.

There is great wealth within the nation by way of the invaluable human resources it has and we are too rich to be poor.

Be A True Millionaire

There is nothing wrong with wanting to become a millionaire. But there is a price to pay. It requires proper planning, proper investing and hard work, especially for those who do not inherit wealth.

Too many become poor in pursuit of millionaire status, having gotten caught up in the various schemes and scams, only to become worse off than they were before.

We are living in a time when money has become the god of the world and has consumed the minds and hearts of many. As a result, there are many "investments" in the world that have caught the attention of the people, but they are in fact scams.

There was a time when people would engage in a "partner", pooling their money together and each cycle, a different person would get their draw. People would use this money to help buy their house or pay for their child's school fee, or to deal with serious/important personal matters. Nowadays, "partner" doesn't work anymore, because as soon as they collect the money they are gone! I know people who joined a partner in years gone by and to this day they are still waiting to get their draw.

Putting your money in the bank will not allow you to be a millionaire. Contrary to popular belief, the lottery is not the way to go either. It causes people to become poorer and cause many families to break up. How many people win the lottery?

Today many are excited to see certain laws being passed to legalize marijuana, so much so that shops are being set up to sell it. Who is buying the bulk of it? The Poor!

Better Way to Invest

God gives us dreams, visions and talents. We need to begin to bring forth that vision and that talent God has us. Lack of money should not be an obstacle for you to start your business. If someone gave you US$500, how would you invest it to turn it over, make a profit and reinvest it? Think carefully.

1. *Always have multiple streams of income*. Have your eggs in more than one basket. There are many ways you can reduce your expenditure – clothes, entertainment, brand name electronics - and the excess. Use a simpler or less expensive phone rather than high end phones.

2. *Always tithe*. Thing release revelation and new insight. Lack of tithing or not giving to the poor has

resulted in many businesses closing down; and more will go. Tithing will also bring protection; and prevent you from paying extortion.

3. *Invest in Farming*. Food and water will become like gold to many.

4. *Invest in livestock and invest in your children's education*.

Learn A Trade

Academics has its place; but know that we are in a time where a trade is in high demand and many things are going back to basics.

Learn how to sow and begin to make your own clothes again. Make clothes that would do well in climate change and begin to export to other countries. It will be colder on the other side so capitalize on that. Make pillows, sheet sets, curtains, toys and so on with positive quotes and sell them. These will prove profitable in the future.

Begin to build music studios, tracks, rhythms and beats and sell them. Every rich person in the Bible were either investing in livestock or farming of some kind of agriculture. All the fruits, leaves were created by God for a specific purpose – not only to feed but also to heal us. In society today, many are sick and are paying out a lot of money without being healed. You can be a millionaire when you begin to utilize the things that God has created in the earth. This is how wealth transfer will take place.

Don't be one to sit down waiting for handouts or looking for politicians to solve your problems. God has given you common sense in addition to the gifts and talents you have within – use them. If others can do it, you can do it too.

Remember, no one listens to you when you are poor. Begin to work hard and climb the ladder.

The Poor Should Think Like Millionaires

Without a doubt, the poor are in every facet of society but are being neglected by many, especially by Politicians - they no longer see the poor as worthy of attention. Different countries are passing laws in an effort to ultimately "exterminate" the poor.

For the poor to survive and come out of poverty, they will need to begin to think like millionaires, and that goes beyond wishing that they had money. Every choice they make has to be tied to tangible profit; that includes voting – determining to whom we should give/allow power.

Things Which Affect the Poor

Here are some of the things which affect the poor:

1. Lack of Knowledge of how money or business work.

2. Disobedience to God's Word and instructions.

3. A negative mindset – when the mind changes, the contents of the pocket will begin to change.

4. Complaining in the midst of problems rather than trying to determine a solution or seeking God.

5. Inability/reluctance to read God's Word or any book that brings knowledge/understanding.

The Thinking of The Rich

1. The rich reads everything – even foolishness.

2. They use problems to make money.

3. They think long-term in order to make choices

4. They will not sell their birthright (as the poor would)

5. They do not make choices without being able to get something back in return – even when they vote. (Tax write-offs and so on.)

6. They will sacrifice short term pleasure for long term gain.

7. They will work hard and empower their children to be their successors.

The Poor vs. The Rich

The poor will go to school to learn how to get a job. The rich go to school to learn how to be the employers and how to invest.

The poor put their money in the banks and get practically nothing in return. The rich borrow loans with the money of the poor, buys houses and rents it back to the poor.

The rich exercises more "faith" than the poor do in starting business. The poor are afraid to step out.

The rich don't tolerate liability, they fight it. The poor settle with liability and continue to make mistakes and repeat cycles.

The rich think outside the box, while the poor stays comfortably within the box.

The rich will pick up the coins and re-invest them. The poor will walk past the coins looking for the dollar bills.

The poor often function like crabs in a barrel while the rich will network, even with their enemies, to make money.

The rich values time – and to them time is money. The poor often waste time and money.

The poor gets stuck in a 9 – 5 job, has a poor credit score and pays high interest rates on loans; while the rich invests and get their money to work for them, they build corporations and use their corporation as security and maintain their credit and security.

The rich are shielded by their corporate organizations while the poor have no such covering.

The rich don't worry about crime because they use the crime situation to make money. They invest in prisons, build gated communities, while the poor sit in the midst of the crime, complain about it and continue with their daily routine.

The Millionaire Mind

Every poor person should read in order to begin changing their mindset and outlook, (Luke 16) so that instead of wasting time and resources and being on the verge of being fired, they can rise up to be a Debt Collectors, Negotiator, Modifications Experts.

There are many who in their own minds consider themselves poor and are yet wasting the God-given gifts and talents they have been given to convert into billions. Often it is only when a person's back is against the wall, they will be able to think like a millionaire.

It is difficult to be a millionaire with a 9 - 5 job. God gives us ideas so that we can be entrepreneurs. The picture that you paint of yourself, that is what you will be. We are too rich as a people to be poor individuals.

The poor need to cut some of the things they can do without – false hair, brand name items and so on.

Stop thinking poverty! It is all in the mind.

CHAPTER 2

A NEW ECONOMY, BY HIS SPIRIT

Imagine if nations and organizations allowed themselves to be led by God's Spirit? The nations would not be tapping into the unclean things as a source of solutions, or to gain income.

Any nation or organization built on the carnal things, will surely lead to death and debt, while those built by the Spirit of God will experience growth, peace and prosperity and debt free status

Building by God's Spirit and His ordinance, will allow us to understand the mind of God on a particular situation. He will also open one's eyes, give them the solution, visions and dreams to transform a nation, He will give them and create a new economy. It is so sad to see Jamaica and other third world nations selling their birthright for a few dollars because they refuse to build by God's Spirit, which will surely bring them into enslavement. When one refuses to build by His Spirit, they become blinded to the things that God has created for their nation or their organization. The fact of the matter is that the wealth is always within and is contained in human vessels.

God wants to pour out of His Spirit upon four categories of people - sons, daughters, old men and, young men! But the outpouring He will do within the nation will only take place where there is a need and a desire for change. In order to have a new Economy, there needs to be a new heart, and a right spirit within each person starting first with the leaders.

By His Spirit we:

1. Discern Times and Seasons;

2. Identify the needs and the desires of the people,

3. Determine market conditions and areas of opportunity

Unless companies change with the change, then many companies will miss the moment and be caught off-guard.

I write for the regenerated mind - those who are willing to see beyond the status quo and think outside the box. I write for those who want to see change and are willing to step out boldly and do what was never done before in order to get the results they have never seen before but desire to have.

We are in an era that regardless of one's political affiliation, one must be willing to embrace the truth regardless of who brings it forth. Without a new mind and way of thinking and a willingness to embrace Divine help, a person will not be able to discern even when good presents itself. (Jeremiah 17: 5 – 6)

Over the years, political Administrations have changed, leaders have changed but regardless of who is in leadership the nation is still failing, simply because the way of thinking remains the same. Even those who passionately criticize have the same unchanging mindset! Systems can't change unless the minds of those people change. Why do you believe that when problems arise within a nation – Crime, Youth Unemployment, Poverty – the only thing we can do is to legislate laws to deal with the problem; while we ignore the real problem (and possible solution) and instead create laws to try to fix that issue?

There is no longer any difference in political ideologies – they are all looking to the same direction for rescue – *China*!

Farmers

It is God who has the power to bring a bumper harvest to our farmers. Only by His Spirit does Germination, Growth and Harvest of a seed take place.

A farmer who is versed in his field, has the capacity to forecast what will take place in an economy. The keys and solutions can be found within Farming and Raising Livestock.

So if our Economists, International Lenders (IMF, World Bank) could take a leaf from the books of our farmers – spend some time learning about how they do what they do. They would be better managers and decision-makers. They would understand the term *'gleaning'*, how to deal with the poor, and not to allow nations to have two classes now – the 'haves' and the 'have-nots'.

They would understand the workings of an Irrigation System and the fact that such a system would represent the Economy, and that water represents God's Holy Spirit; thus, in understanding the symbolism of it all, they would then recognize that without God's Spirit no economy can thrive.

Let us recognize that the best solutions for our current situation are found either in us or in the earth – the trees and the seed.

The more we remove God's principles from the Marketplace, the more problems will develop.

For all struggling businesses, ensure that you capitalize on the great opportunities that are coming in the fourth (4th) month. Don't look at the physical/natural situation and step out by faith!

Capitalizing on Kingdom Economics

The world's way of Economics has become obsolete in this era. None of those principles work and modern economists have no solutions and only make statements after the fact. There is a paradigm shift and it is critical for God's people to shift with the shift.

The Kingdom Economics principles benefit all if applied by all – regardless of religion, race or any other factors. They work because that is how God intended it to be.

The former way of dealing with losses was to either file for bankruptcy, divest/merge, impose higher taxes on the poor or close. It forces one to borrow from other countries with clauses that have the potential to dictate how the already sovereign nations must operate (thereby nullifying the principle of sovereignty) – determining who you should employ, with whom you should do business, who should be in strategic positions in the nation and even determine what percentage should be given to the public sector in wages and some don't go beyond 5%. They will also want to determine your parameters for downsizing in your organization. This is where politicians now become ineffective. Furthermore, they also will want to determine guidelines for our education system and health sector which is anti-Christ.

It is critical if we want to be financially stable and debt-free – whether we are rich or poor – to begin to capitalize on Kingdom Principles to deal with the challenges ahead, create jobs and move away from this obsolete, deceptive, manipulative spell casting that WILL come to naught.

Keys to Note

The first key and most important key in Kingdom Principles is *Daily Obedience to God's Instructions.* (Deuteronomy 28: 1 – 14)

Learn about Tithing and the various Seasons - particularly the three main seasons which will bring us increase. They are *March-April* – Passover/Resurrection; *June* – Pentecost; *September-October* – Tishrei/End and Beginning of Agricultural Season). Remember, the earthly banks only extract from us and give us nothing in return. This will open gates/windows of opportunity, investment strategies and will unlock ideas. Begin to protect your ideas (intellectual property). Seek professional advice to help you with that.

Learn about the different levels of increase - 30, 60, 100, 1000 as well as the 4-fold, 7-fold increases and know-how and to what they apply.

Invest in People

Invest in people – gold, food, water and livestock – which are basic substances for man's survival.

For the economists and critics who don't believe God is real or still speaks - while praying, the Lord asked, "What if you had a major disaster – a war breaking out in the United States of America (USA) or an oil explosion in Russia, or a shaking on Wall Street, or riots in various nations or if a major earthquake hitting Italy? How would it affect countries like Jamaica and smaller/third world nations especially with the threat by the Trump Administration of tariffs to be levied on steel and aluminum?" I am sure countries would begin to distance themselves from the USA. The small businesses, and courier services in the USA and neighboring regions would feel the heat. Tourism and Immigration would also be negatively affected in the USA; and because many remit monies overseas from the USA, it will trigger a recession and suffering especially for smaller countries. Then we might see countries forfeiting on debt repayment and create another level of suffering. It is better start to renegotiate with the international lenders to restructure those loans before it is too late. Nations must have contingencies in place for these happenings.

A major appeal needs to be made to get everybody involved in farming and stockpile 10% of everything – whether it is bought or homegrown.

God created the economy before He created man. That being so, we need then to revisit and study God's prescribed order on how individuals and countries must operate, in order to have a solid economy. The further we pull away from the Kingdom Principles for governing, the more problems we will encounter. For example, foregoing a day of rest in order to grow the economy will not augur well for us, it will instead do more damage. Also, implementing systems that would go against God's laws and precepts will affect the economy negatively.

Media houses need to reduce their advertising costs to small businesses and not-for-profit organizations and help them to grow in that area, and they will have loyal clients.

Farmers need to begin to donate 10% of their increase/harvest to the poor – shelters, places of safety and even to feed the security forces of the nation – and that will bring them (farmers) further increase in their yield.

The government needs to have dialogue with the people right away to chart a new economic direction as the old ways are dead.

Deception and The Fight for Economic Dominion

All eyes are watching the happenings taking place in the Middle East, particularly in Egypt. Egypt, Ethiopia and Libya are critical in the End Time in the area of Economic Dominion.

There are mysteries to be unlocked and wealth to be revealed – gold, silver and the secrets of the ancient pyramids. Daniel 11: 43 reveals to us that regardless of the systems in place, there are precious resources within these countries that whoever controls those resources will have economic dominion and unlock the secrets to the wealth.

If Biblical Prophecies are being fulfilled, then all eyes should be on Japan, Russia and China who it is said will join together. They will have a tri-lateral agreement to balance economic power.

Here are some serious questions to ask:

1. Is Biblical Prophecy being fulfilled regarding economic dominion or is there an undermining force behind the scene fighting for the wealth?

2. Is it that the era of oppressive force – the Pharaoh-style leadership coming to an end beginning with Egypt? Exodus 3: 19 – 21.

3. If that is the case, are we about to see a great wealth transfer to the poor? Are we about to see gold and silver change hands?

4. Will financial institutions now be begging persons to take loans and write off debts?

5. Will we now be getting favor from the oppressive rulers?

6. Or, will we see natural disasters interrupt and delay the plans of subversive elements?

This opens the door for other questions. Daniel 12: 4 reminds us that knowledge will increase. So,

1. Will we see even greater breakthroughs in technology and science?

2. Will there be increase in global migration in order to seek economic solutions and business opportunities?

Politicians, Businessmen and the people of the nations must work together to turn around their countries and be loyal to their own brand and believe in their people. Everyone in a nation must support the local businesses, and the local businesses must give back to the communities. If we don't function this way and look for quick fixes, it is going to open the door for deception. At the same time, we have to be careful - there is also the possibility of changing from one Pharaoh to a more oppressive Pharaoh!

There will be many seeking for a better life and prosperity but it must be done through the wisdom of God. There is no quick fix to turning around a nation's economy. Quick fixes only bring deception!

The time has come for all parties within a nation to make the necessary sacrifices, to turn around things. There needs to be compassion, integrity and all decisions being made must genuinely take the poor and the family into consideration. (Nehemiah 5)

Signs of Economic Deception

Look out for people who will come with great economic plans to turn the nation but are really after our resources and our businesses, not to help us. Your businesses may be struggling, but you have gold and a great deal of potential!

Watch for people who will give great gifts and promise great political power. If they undermine their leaders (whether those in power or the opposition) then approach you telling you that you are the next party leader, CEO or head of the organization – beware! Any promotion that you receive that is not of God will come down!

Remember, beliefs play a significant role in decision-making. Everybody makes their core decisions based on what or who they believe and trust!

Every decision that a person makes must have long term benefits, short term gain brings pain!

When making decisions, you must make them taking into consideration the effect on you and your family, and also how that decision will affect others when you are no longer in authority. Remember, every law implemented and every business decision made must be done with betterment of the people at heart. Never implement anything that will be used against you later.

Increasing the GDP God's Way

Proverbs 29: 18 says:

"Where there is no revelation, the people cast off restraint; but happy is he who keeps the law."

When society lacks revelation/divine insight from God, such a society will head in the direction of anarchy.

Regardless of how that revelation comes, whether through prophecy, dreams/visions, or prayer, without it, the people will run wild – they will perish, crime and violence will skyrocket and the society will delve into a downward spiral.

As a nation, we must learn from the mistakes of other nations. For example, we see what is now happening in America's schools because they have legislated God and the Bible out of the schools and the economy, and that has opened the door for everything else to enter – to the nation's detriment. Interestingly the nation of Jamaica has safer schools, so maybe we need to embark on a campaign to invite other nations to school their children in Jamaica. By the way, gun control doesn't solve or even alleviate the problem. It will simple change hands but the weapons will still be used.

Increasing GDP and Jobs

Everyone's cry is to increase the GDP (Gross Domestic Product) and create more jobs. That will only happen as we put God's system and principles in place. Turning an economy around only comes through the fresh oil that will be poured out on the nation (Psalm 94: 10) and as a result of the former and latter rains that will be released upon the nation (Joel 2). Only then will the replenishing take place. God will pour out within the young and the old to bring their visions and ideas to the forefront.

Jamaica: A Case in Point

The time has come for us to think outside the box. The traditional ways of growing an economy are over. We need non-traditional ways. What colonialism has taught us is that sugar, banana and traditional tourism are our only sources of earning as a nation.

First, Jamaica needs to bring its airline back. Then, we need to:

1. Learn from the Informal Commercial Importers (ICIs) also known as *higglers*. All we need to teach ICIs is proper packaging.

2. Stop giving tax relief to the foreigners and give it to the locals instead.

3. Focus on our youth for ideas and solutions - even those below the age of 18

4. Focus on our bushes and fruits – we have good health-sustaining plants and fruits.

5. Export our teachers and nurses. We have the best in the world. Stop degrading or looking down on them. In addition to this, we also need to see a budget where education, health and welfare are top priorities.

6. Cut down on importing cars and let our people begin to assemble cars.

7. Cut the security budget and use the money to train people if we want to increase GDP – it's not about building infrastructure, it's about building the human being first. (Isaiah 62: 1 – 2). Crime will reduce and GDP increase.

Furthermore, if over 70% of the sustenance of man comes from the earth, why not focus on those areas? When the poor get the opportunity, then they will start their businesses and that will help the GDP to increase.

Building

Anytime God is going to increase a nation He pours out in the vessels – the people – who are prepared. Even if we pray for God to pour out and bless the country, it will go to naught if there are no prepared vessel, and that is why the focus must be on building more schools, training centers, sports facilities and also on helping university students with scholarships and school fees if we want to see the GDP increase. We need to build from the inside out not from the outside in.

The only loans we should be borrowing are those to equip and invest in our people. We must do things God's way, not Marx's way! Many countries, in extending their borders, want to apply the pagan principles – as in Amos 1: 13. We cannot do that as a nation. Furthermore, we need to stop shifting the blame to everyone else when something goes wrong and begin to take introspection. We need to stop voting along party lines and begin to vote in the interest of the country. God's way of building on increasing the GDP means that He builds the person first before He focuses on anything else. We are doing the opposite.

If the rich is benefiting from the current economic climate while the gap between the rich and poor is widening, then something is dreadfully wrong. Building more prisons or turning our schools into prisons are not the answers. We must apply God's principles to increase our GDP, not any other method.

Train Locals to Increase Gross Domestic Product (GDP)

Ultimately, Economics in its simplest form has to do with the choices we make. The masses may not generally understand economic terms and definitions and as a result, some have taken the opportunity to confuse the masses with terminologies without an attempt to properly explain what it is all about.   In truth, Jamaica's problem over the years has been wrong choices.

Successive Administrations have been divesting the nation's resources and assets, taking poor advice from foreigners who only know about Jamaica's economy from a distance and then are making the comparison between the nation and Singapore!

Divestment is a trap, and if we continue to divest, Jamaicans are going to become trapped in their own country! Furthermore, if that happens, some of the amenities that Jamaicans now enjoy at home will be no more!   Is divestment taking place for the personal gain of a few; or are they divesting because of laziness?

In many previously authored articles, it was expressed that the nation has refused to train its local people, which can in fact increase our Gross Domestic Product (GDP) and stabilize our dollar if that is done.

What each Ministry should be doing, particularly Tourism, Agriculture, Water, Health, Education and Finance, is tailor-make programs to train the communities.   These programs should be so designed that everyone can participate.   It should address issues such as Parenting, Having Children Out of Wedlock, the Role of a Father, Conflict Resolution and Small Business Startup.   There should also be topics such as Community Tourism and the Negative Effects of Crime; Human Trafficking and Pimping. All these Ministries already have personnel who are not being effectively employed.   We need to move the people away from the 'Eat-A-Food' mentality.

The moment we begin to empower the people, explain terms and terminologies in simple language and helping them to understand how Economics works, how they contribute to the whole process.   We need to employ programs that teach both adults and young people, how to resist the 'drugs man' coercing them to drop off 'packages' within the schools.

Simple Things

Teach people how to resist corrupt politicians issuing cash to shut people up!

Double the size of the army (which will increase employment) and use them as undercover personnel.

Have regular transfer of bodyguards.

The Banks and Credit Unions also need to go into the communities and train people concerning Saving and Finance. Our people are not saving! Furthermore, there are those who have nothing to save, so they need to have community seminars on how to change that! They should open accounts for families within the communities free of charge for one year.

The Banks and Credit Unions also need to give 10% - 14% interest on all Savings. They can do it! This will cut out Ponzi-type schemes, as well as minimize money laundering, and will be a win-win situation! The people are not benefiting from the Banks. The Banks also can start opening accounts for newborns of all married couples and put the first $1000 for them toward an Education-focused account.

All Savings accounts should be free which will increase Savings.

The Government needs to have an Electronic Benefits Transfer System – where those of low or no income and especially the elderly poor can deal with basic needs – Food, Medication, Water and Light. There also needs to be a flat rate on water and based on the number of people in the household. Don't tell me that in the land of Wood and

Water we can't have water at a flat rate. What needs to be done is that we need to build more tanks/reservoirs to harness that resource before foreigners get the water. We can do it ourselves especially if we double the army and use the Engineer Regiment to carry out that task.

The General Consumption Tax (GCT) on the masses needs to be reduced and increase the taxes to the tourists especially in the tourist areas. If we are serious about what we are about as a nation, there is no way tourists should be enjoying lower taxes than the citizens and residents of the nation.

We need to have aggressive programs that fully involve our youth and children significantly to engage in planting/replanting trees/flowers regularly and community clean-up programs. Allow the youth to become involved in environmental change for the nation's future.

Finally, why does such a small nation have so many car/used car dealerships? There needs to be regulation of that industry!

Did IMF Become Jamaica's Savior?

Our nation's Government, the local business community and even the Church have all been praying for the nation. They have been praying with great fervency for the nation to pass 'the Test' or to get a deal! But while we must pray for our nation's growth, development and economic success, the question now arises – 'When did the IMF become our savior?'

Proverbs 22: 7 states, "*The rich rule over the poor, and the borrower is servant to the leader.*"

It is not wrong to borrow money, as long as we can generate the resources to repay. However, if those capabilities are ever diminished, the borrower will learn (to his dismay) the truth the above statement.

As a nation, we have just celebrated Jubilee. However, the word 'jubilee' means 'to set free; to release of all debt.' Having celebrated that, then if we go back into bondage and into debt, then we have not been truly set free; we would certainly not be free of debt and it means there was no real JUBILEE!

Does the common man really know or truly understand the policies of most international lenders? Oftentimes, international lenders focus on the numbers. They don't have real on-the-ground information with regard to the real state of affairs, the culture, the real effects of what is happening within the nations, nor do they care about that.

The policies of the international lenders are not in favor of the growth and prosperity of local businesses, nor of the improvement of the quality of life of the people of the nation; particularly for Third-World countries – and Jamaica is deemed as such. The policies and decisions of international lenders are dominated by First-World ideas and points of view. Furthermore, very few realize that shareholders consist of a few dominant First-World nations that pay into the organization monthly and so they call the shots.

Let Us Ask A Few Questions…

1. *What if the vision of the international lenders and the direction they are headed are in direct conflict with the vision and direction of our nation?* Keep in mind the issues of politics, religion, labor laws, health, morality, education and its costs, interest rates and food distribution and pricing.

2. *What if their policy and involvement in divestment is hurting/negatively affecting the nation they say they are helping?*

3. *What about trade liberalization policies? Do their policies favor international investors while diminishing the competitive edge/advantage of local businesses?* As strange as it may sound, local businesses would become a thing of the past as the nation would become dependent on international organization and imports.

Jamaica's advantage over the years has been its Real Estate. We have done well and has weathered the storms – literally and otherwise. The depreciation of Real Estate in our nation has been slow (which is good), while other nations suffer in the area of Real Estate! It is critical for our people to hold on to their land and assets.

Blame Is Not One-Sided

Both political parties have blundered over the years by divesting both our local and international assets for practically nothing, and now we are paying the price. International lenders believe we cannot manage. But if we are to bounce back, divestment must cease!

As a nation, we must look to farming in an effort to prevent price hikes. We must begin to cut back on expenses. Food and water are going to be the most important things.

Cut back on the number of roads being built, because we cannot put all our hopes into Tourism. Natural disasters and one bad review can wipe that out in a minute.

All politicians, if they want the country to bounce back, they need to lead by example and take a 50% pay cut. Take a leaf from Nehemiah's book – Nehemiah 5: 14 – 19.

1. Cut high executive and consultancy payments, and put in a wage freeze for high income earners.

2. Teach the people to fish and stop the handouts – the cash programs.

3. Look at the logistics of some of the national infrastructure, and begin to focus even more on small businesses.

4. Give small local businesses a 3-year tax break.

5. Start looking into Term limits for politicians.

Will the IMF Be the New Boss?

Undoubtedly, when a nation fails to seek God for its direction and guidance, then that nation is going to find itself in a constant state of severe oppression.

We can't grow and develop a country – a nation – when all that the nation does is borrow! When someone borrows, there are also stringent requirements that go along with it, which will hinder that country from making the necessary changes to bring the country into growth and prosperity; and the creditors call the shots. If this is the case then know that the hands of the authority of the day will be tied if they are to attempt to bring the country on a path of prosperity.

Proverbs 24: 3-4 says, "*Through wisdom a house is built, and by understanding it is established; by knowledge the rooms are filled with all precious and pleasant riches.*"

The Knowledge of God:

1. Brings in the necessary revenue to fill government coffers,

2. Reduces our debt

3. Reveals creative ways to begin to export

4. Creates Employment

5. Bring back the country on a path of sustainability without going to the IMF

These are the things to look into, because going into an agreement with anyone or anybody/organization can prove difficult for the nation in times to come.

1. Will our local companies have a competitive advantage/disadvantage?

2. Will we see more imports than exports; items such as water, fruits, agricultural produce?

3. Will we see more school dropouts and changes in school curricula?

4. Will we see more foreigners being placed in strategic positions?

5. Will we continue to see the dollar slide and foreign currency become more prominent than local currency?

6. Will we see a decline the number of work permits and visas being given to locals?

7. Will we see more financial regulations and compliance adjustments that will wipe out the poor?

8. Will we now be forced to grow our children in a manner opposite to what is scripturally required?

9. Will the government be forced to pass more laws which oppose Biblical Principles, with respect, for example, to issues such as gambling, under the guise of growing the economy? We are already seeing the effects of having neither of the two days of worship being respected.

10. What plans are being put in place for redundancy payments in the event of sudden company/organizational shut-downs?

In 2011 Jamaica refused to follow Canada and USA by voting on a resolution with Israel and Palestine - Jamaica's vote was opposite to the direction of the Scriptures.

This example shows that Jamaica has clearly moved away from being a Christian nation, to becoming a secular state!

Local Industry

Without a doubt, local companies have a great deal of work to do now; and it is important for them to recognize that this is more than a political issue, this is about the nation and its people and their growth and development for a better future!

They now have to come up with creative and new ways to export' and they have to begin focusing on new territories such as Latin America, Asia and Africa. The profit they used to make locally is going to diminish, so they must expand their view and recognize the importance and significance of the global market.

The years ahead are going to be critical. They will need to understand the Time, Season and the global demand.

They must also train our local youth to drive the vision for and into the future; not drive them away!

Furthermore, if the local media houses do not come up with a plan to service the local market together, and launch out into different areas, they are going to be wiped out and suffer the same fate as our national airline! The way in which they operate now needs to be revisited. What they believe is newsworthy today, will change tomorrow and tomorrow is not far away.

It is imperative for locals to buy up the land now and those who already own land, hold on to that land! Even if the land you own is a 'gully-hole', don't sell! All those who own land in the rural areas, start visiting it; fence your property and keep it pruned. Secure the springs and rivers on your property. Plant Bamboo and other trees.

Currency

All stakeholders must come together to protect the currency. When the currency devalues, only the wealthy traders and the foreigners will have an advantage. If it continues in this manner, our homes, vehicles, asset of any kind, will not value much and only foreigners will receive any kind of economic benefit. Then we will see more of our land go into the hands of foreigners and the nation will lose its valuable resources. Human trafficking and prostitution will increase.

If there is no unity, will we see the end of an era for some longstanding local companies?

Live in God's Economy

Many are going through problems left, right and center! Some are on the verge of giving up, others want to commit suicide. Even teens are falling under the pressure. Globally, it is not a rumor, it is a fact we see firsthand. Every category is being affected - Lawyers, Doctors, Teachers, Pastors, Laborers - even some bankers who desire to live right are feeling it now! Many say – "we have fasted, prayed and given and things are getting worse!" People are asking the question - 'why am I doing all the things I should yet things get worse, while my neighbor does not and it seems they are prospering?'

But as God-fearing people, we can't live the way the world does. We have to build our lives on God's economy and totally rely on Him.

The fact of the matter is that the world's economic 'successes and rewards' are coming to an end! They have run out of ideas and they are on the last round. Economists can't even make a proper forecast!

Many of us are being pressed to the limit, but remember that it is through the fire that we are God's people birth - which means - in times of hardship our hidden gifts, creativity and potential are revealed to us. God wants to and is going to bless His faithful ones, but He wants us to be debt free. Only when you have become debt free do you experience true freedom. We must be wise with the resources God is going to give us. We have to start getting rid of the credit cards and start reducing what we owe.

He wants to bless us so that we can be the new lenders. Recognize that when we give to the poor we lend to the Lord. Lenders call the shots and they decide the interest rates. There are those who are poor that we have neglected but we need to feed them! (Proverbs 19: 17)

God is calling us to seek Him more deeply. Many are too busy; hence they cannot receive what the Lord has in store for them. He wants to give them greater insight for their lives. He wants them to be inventors and unlock the inventions He is waiting to give each one!

God is raising up new millionaires, entrepreneurs with solutions and new ideas. The world is bankrupt of solutions. The world cannot do without the Kingdom! Even Pharaoh needed a Joseph.

Your suffering also brings wisdom. Impatience is what brings us into debt and problems most times. With this, God is teaching us patience and giving us knowledge, wisdom and understanding at the same time. There are too many crafty people lurking out there waiting to rob you of your inheritance.

Many times, we will lament and say *"God is late"*. But He was before time, in time and is on time!

Your suffering can also give you a greater revelation of Who God Is! There are different attributes of God - different sides of Him for us to experience. If we had no problems His varying sides and attributes would not be revealed to us. Some in their sickness have found Him to be their Healer! Others experienced His provision in their time of lack have found Him to be Provider!

When one faces problems and there seems to be no way out - high debt, bad credit scores - He can be the God of Favor to such one. His favor qualifies you when the odds are against you. Even if you may be facing eviction, or your business is being auctioned or if you have been denied a student loan - there is always a ram in the bush! Sometimes we go through hardship for the Glory of God. But recognize also that we go through problems in order to increase our faith. When our faith increases, our favor will increase. When our favor increases, our vision will increase. So too will our power and money!

Certain blessings and breakthroughs will never come until we overcome temptation. What would you do if you are faced with a financial crisis and everyone denies you; not because you are unqualified, but because they want sexual favors in exchange for what you need? Will you trust God's favor or will you yield to the temptation? Interestingly, the request for such sexual favors is prevalent - particularly demanded of job seekers!

Do you believe that regardless of what someone is saying concerning the economy, that God can bless you despite all that? (Psalm 68: 9 & 19)
We go through hardship because God wants us to launch out into the deep. In the deep is where uncommon, rare and precious treasures are found. Oftentimes we don't launch out in the deep until we face hardship.

When you launch out into the deep, a great catch and good partners await you.

Your suffering is there to change your mindset - your way of thinking about things and situations. A logical mind is an enemy to faith, as are doubt and unbelief. Faith brings the invisible to visibility and is your Title and Deed to your desires.

Your suffering will allow you to move from different levels of faith in order to achieve greater things in life. Ezekiel 47 speaks of the four dimensions of faith.

1. *Ankle-level Faith* is weak faith, just enough for salvation.

2. *Knee-height faith* is the kind that engages in more prayer and total dependence on God for breakthrough - submitting to His will and ways.

3. *Waist/Loins-level faith* will bring great miracles in your life. It is the Procreative part of man.

4. *Total Immersion in Faith* - God must be totally in charge of your Body, Soul and Spirit for progress.

Remember, regardless of what you are going through you have a right to eat the fruits of your labor! Your way cannot be like the way of the world!

CHAPTER 3

CHOICES DETERMINE ECONOMIC DIRECTION

If we are going to change the economy of a nation, it is critical for us to start within the household.

Managing an economy goes beyond managing money. One of the failures in Economic Management is the focus on the money and finance mainly, while ignoring other salient areas such as Time Management, Labor, Human Resources and Family. Many organizational and national leaders also fail to focus on these areas.

The issue of Family is one area that has been sorely neglected. The decisions concerning Economy have not taken Family into account. The Bible, which many are now attempting to advocate its removal from the marketplace, is the best Book to teach us about managing an economy. It is difficult for any entity to manage an economy of any size without the principles embedded within this Book.

The Bible tells us to teach our children within the home how to manage the resources. It teaches how to avoid the wasting of resources. It teaches us about Labor and Management, and utilizing Human Capital. (Matthew 20; Matthew 25)

How can we change the economy or mindset of a people if we do not start teaching our children from within the household how to manage simple things such as water, light, toilet paper? Most people will be quicker to give their child a Tablet or iPad within the school than to enroll them in an Ecology Project or have them taught to engage in Farming! If we are going to change the economy of a nation, then we have to be willing to accept the fact that God created the Economy even before He created Man. Hence, all that is needed to sustain Man already exists! (Genesis 1 & Genesis 2)

The next thing we have to teach them is that sin affects the economy – reducing profits and changes the original plan; bringing with it lack and poverty! When God created the Universe, it was not His desire for Man to struggle through thistles and thorns. The source of Man's sustenance was never in food, but in God Himself!

Choices We Make

Managing an economy is about the choices we make on a daily basis. Choices determine your future. For example, whomever you marry is a choice, so we must think carefully on that issue. The choices we make when we vote determines the economy of the nation. Do we vote for the sake of popularity? Do we vote for a party because our family votes for that party? Do we send our children or attend a school/college because it is popular or because family member went there? OR do we go where God directs us even if it is unpopular? (Matthew 6: 33). Furthermore, do we purchase goods because of their brands? Are we willing to try an unknown or unpopular brand, even if its quality proves to be better? Do we invest in something because everybody else is doing it?

Recognize that following the crowd isn't always right!
While we know that choices drive Demand, and that
Demand drives Supply and Sales, it is important to see
things as God sees them. We do that by seeking Him and
reading His Word to understand His Principles.

For example, *'economics'* in simple terms, is *'the study of
human decision-making - how to choose in order to get what is
needed or wanted, as well as what to do when what is needed cannot
be had / accessed.'*

Realize that the choices we make on a daily basis must:

1. Benefit the Family

2. Positively impact Health and Education

3. Improve the Quality of Life

How about being good stewards of what is in our care?

Contrary to popular belief, Man is accountable to God for
the decisions he makes on a daily basis, especially with
resources! There are billions that go to waste on a daily basis
because Man refuses to seek God on how to manage the
resources.

Psalm 127: 1a says *"Unless the Lord builds the house, they labor
in vain who build it ..."*

The areas of Education, Sports and Entertainment – which
are in fact part of Human Resource Management – were not
being properly managed all this time. This has contributed
significantly to the high levels of unemployment, lack of
vision and an unavailability of opportunities at all levels
locally!

Nations are now suffering because of the wrong choices they have been making. As a result, debt and borrowing continue to rise. We are borrowing when we should not be and we are giving away our land in the same breath!

For changes to start, we can all be economists by starting to make the right choices within the home. When we start to make the right choices on an individual level, then the collective benefits will be seen.

Four Elements for Economic Development

Economic Development is the number one priority for every nation at this time. Many countries, however, are now struggling with the current system of economic development. For example, the Textbook Syndrome is no longer feasible at this time. We must now focus on Biblical Economics and Kingdom Principles in order to have a balanced economy. It is imperative for every government that wants to be successful to focus on four (4) main areas:

Health   Trees, Leaves, Herbs,

Water   Wells, Rain, River, Catchment Areas, Coconut Water

Energy   Wind, Sun, Solar, and Hydro Power

Agriculture   Food, Farming and Trade

Ninety per cent (90%) of man's substance comes from the earth. Everything was created from water! The earth was created from water. That means the economy is created from water itself. Water also represents the Holy Spirit and so we could surmise that same water is vital to economic development, then economic development cannot take place without the Holy Spirit.

If we are going to have an economic revolution, particularly in the Third World countries, then transformation leaders have to create a vision to develop and market the natural resources that already exist. (Revelation 22; Ezekiel 42; Genesis 1). If they don't move quickly, First World countries are going to take away all the resources we already have.

What nations need to do is to merge Agricultural Ministry with Health, and merge Water with Energy. Once we have a plan, train and equip the people, then we will be on the path to success.

For a balanced economy to emerge, we must follow the original plan. Everything was created with four (4) main areas or divisions. For example, within a person you have the Brain, Skull, Neck and Face which forms the Head. The Brain houses Intellect and Information systems. The Neck provides boney support for movement, The Skull encompasses the Brain and the Face contains distinguishing features between different individuals. So, in order to be successful, each nation has to be willing to be different from other nations, identify and follow the economic blueprint that is specific to them and their economic situation.

Within each person is a set of solutions for economic development! So, the government needs to create an information database to listen to the various ideas for economic development.

While Macroeconomics focuses on the behavior of the market and other areas such as unemployment and inflation rates Microeconomics focuses on the behavior of the consumer. Since the consumers possess the capacity to bring solutions for economic development, then there needs to be more focus on the Microeconomics.

Built on Fours

On the fourth (4th) day of Creation, God made two (2) great lights – the Sun and the Moon; and God gave light to govern – the sun by day and the moon by night! Then God separated light from darkness. For success, every government must separate from the dark things in order to experience growth within a nation. Every leader must have *four* set of characteristics for success. The characteristics of the:

Lion   - Dominion and Kingship

Ox   - Must be actively concerned about the welfare of *all* involved

Man   - Rule with compassion and mercy

Eagle   - Vision for the future; able to see ahead and know which area to focus on for economic development.

It is critical for leaders to understand the Times and Seasons for Economic Development to know when to:

1. Implement
2. Invest
3. Divest
4. Restructure

These areas are going to be critical for any nation choosing to move forward!

1. There are four (4) seasons

2. There are four (4) Cardinal Directions

3. Interestingly, Budgets and Taxes are always presented, tabled, implemented in the fourth (4th) month.

4. There are also four (4) basic functions for money and levels of Faith.

The government needs to focus on four (4) things:

1. Keep power equal and have proper checks and balances
2. Provide National Security

3. Have Economic Equality

4. Pass Laws that will benefit the people and provide economic stability

I believe every Transformational Leader should put systems in place to have a national audit to include the Central Bank/Treasury, so that when there is a change of government to clearly outline what will be handed over to the new government. We need to see a Profit and Loss Statement that the common man can read and understand. In Nehemiah 5: 14 - 19, Nehemiah requested such an audit. In fact, he believed that self-sacrifice is necessary for moral leadership and he led by example. Previous governors had lived richly at the taxpayers' expense, but Nehemiah refused to do so. Many of our politicians today would do well to take a pay cut.

Steps to Rebuild the U.S. Economy

All eyes are again focused on the United States of America, but they now have to focus on strengthening the areas that allowed them to become a strong nation in the first place.

Helping humanity and feeding the poor is something the United States of America has been good at doing. They always put themselves in the position to assist weaker nations and peoples. (Psalms 41; Matthew 25)

The United States of America is the only nation that has placed on their currency the statement, 'In God We Trust'. Hence, they have to rebuild their economy according to the principles of the God in Whom their forefathers trusted. (Psalms 127: 1)

While there will still be political instability, God allows different people in different sectors to come forward with the spirit of Daniel. America should now bring the focus to small businesses in order to begin rebuilding their economy. Their greatest resources are in the ground and they should focus on the ground – food, water and energy.

Immigration Reform

This is what will bring a great blessing to America – AMNESTY! Biblical Principles support it. When the United States of America calls for an Immigration Amnesty then their Tax Revenue will increase, sales of Real Estate will increase; healing of families will take place; schools will benefit; crime will immediately reduce. They also need to encourage foreigners to invest particularly in Real Estate, by reducing the Property Tax. When Property Tax to foreigners is reduced, that will revamp the failing Real Estate sector.

In addition to that, when there is an Amnesty, therein also lies the potential for America's military force to increase.

Family Values

The United States of America must now increase their giving to Faith-based and other NGOs in an effort to rebuild communities – particularly in the area of Youth Development; they are the future. There needs to be proper mentorship of the Youth.

A greater focus must be placed on effectively helping NGOs and Faith-based organizations that help those with disabilities as well.

All-Round Re-Focus

The state of a nation's social, moral and economic well-being is directly influenced the state of the churches within the nation. (Haggai 1 & 2) The Church in America needs to get back to basics and focus on rebuilding.

America should never take its eyes away from Biblical Prophecies. Thus, they need to equip and build their military now more than ever, have the best communications and weapons to deal with future challenges and threats. (2 Chronicles 26: 14 – 15)

The nation also needs to do more and better for their veterans. They have to remember that the enemy within can be greater than the enemy outside. The veterans still have a great deal to contribute to nation-building.

The United States of America need to rebuild their Space Program. Never rely on another country – Biblical Prophecies cannot lie.

The United States of America need to continue with Free Health and Free Education for those who cannot afford it, and put systems in place for foreign students to have an easier opportunity to stay and build what they have learnt.

The United States of America must embrace and invest in the 'small' man – those who are considered the rejects of the society. The shelters have become treasury of wealth. Many who have solutions they are seeking are there.

Let there be an easier process with regard to Visa restrictions concerning African countries and smaller nations. This would be balanced with the adherence of such individuals to vaccination processes and health guidelines and requirements.

The United States of America need to cut out the zoning and tax restrictions throughout the nation that are killing businesses and making it more difficult and complicated for smaller businesses to exist and flourish.

There needs to be a group that will stand up to the banks and influence them to cease plundering businesses, homeowners and the poor. The banks are some of the greatest obstacles to economic change and growth. It is a stronghold in the nation. Law makers need to stand up to the banks.

The Church Should Lead Economic Revival

With all that is happening globally, and especially with the reports out of Venezuela that the people are now eating dogs and cats for survival due to extreme hunger and lack in that nation, without a doubt there is a global disaster coming! It is going to affect the Caribbean, and that includes Jamaica.

It is the Church that should lead the economic revival, and it is imperative that we begin to teach people the Biblical/Kingdom principles for survival. We have the skills, the talent and the anointing to transform the nation and we need to stop looking to the politicians or the private sector to lead that charge. Many of them do not have a clue of regarding the timing and strategies that are necessary for what we face now. We need to focus on food and look at cost-cutting if we are to be viable in the international marketplace. Likewise, we need to teach the Secular that Kingdom Principles – God's Principles - are the only way toward true success.

The Church needs to unite quickly and move because, when people are hungry, they do not think about denomination or doctrinal beliefs. We must stop competing with and begin to complement each other. Food will be the order of the day!

If every building that is owned by a church was being fitted with solar panels, then millions would be saved and could be channeled and utilized to create employment, to help the poor, reduce poverty and increase economic development and sustainability.

Every Church needs to install wells or erect tanks for water storage. Churches also need to erect fuel tanks for storage of petrol.
When the Church is truly functioning and walking in economic empowerment, only then will others respect the Church. Neither politicians nor the private sector truly respects the Church. Having a few rich people in your congregation or even in your denomination does not gain you the respect of others. The time has come for the church to actively engage in things like Farming! We need to cultivate vegetables and begin to understand and also utilize the bushes/herbs to bring healing and rescue the Health Sector! (Ezekiel 47; Revelation 22) We need to recognize that pharmaceutical companies are not in the interest of the people.

The Church needs to buy land and hold on to those lands. That is the only way there will be wealth transfer for the next generation.

Debt Reduction

The only way the Church can be free is to be Debt-Free!

It is the responsibility of the Church to teach the community about making good financial choices and how to be debt free. For example, teaching the people to stay away from Credit Cards; scrutinize every Bill they get so as not to be overcharged.

Furthermore:

1. Teach them not to use the Debit Cards to pay Bills when they will be charged a fee; but instead to pull out the total and then pay the bills by cash!

2. Cut down on purchases of phone credit and on using minutes (depending on the phone service you employ) – talk less and seek God more! The phone companies are making huge profits through the sale of phone credit for calling overseas and on minutes to make local and long-distance calls and most of them are not giving back!

3. Only purchase what is necessary! Look for quality, not brand name!

4. Stay away from Loan Sharks!

5. Avoid taking out a second mortgage unless you are starting a viable, inspired, God-given business.

6. Sow your way out of debt and when God gives you a debt write-off, extend it to others! If major companies want debt write-offs, then they will need to write-off the debts of the smaller companies or individuals who owe them

The Church needs to understand that it holds the power to empower the people! Politicians will not bring change, and there is going to be global disappointment regarding politicians globally!

Only through the Church will the change come! The Church has to restore families and we need to teach them how to survive and to deal with what is ahead. There are some serious economic civil issues and famine ahead in some countries because of the principles and practices that have been carried out over the years. In order for the Church to have a voice they have to stay clear of political handouts. The blessing that is coming to the Body of Christ is not about Ponzi Schemes, Pyramid Schemes, Get-Rich-Quick Schemes or anything of that nature. It is about Diverse Vision, Inventions and Ideas for the Body of Christ.

The Anti-Christ Platform: The Economic System

Revelation 13: 16 - 18 says: "*He causes all, both small and great, rich and poor, free and slave, to receive a mark on their right hand or on their foreheads, and that no one may buy or sell except one who has the mark or the name of the beast, or the number of his name. Here is wisdom. Let him who has understanding calculate the number of the beast, for it is the number of a man: His number is 666.*"

It is very critical in this season for us to understand the book of Revelation. Many Pastors and individuals are afraid to read this book but it is *relevant!* Signs, seasons and symbols are critical in the Book of Revelation. The Mark of the Beast is not only a mere matter of a chip being placed in your forehead. It is a system that both corporations and merchants impose. They will join with political leaders and they will impose laws and decrees which are anti-Christ - meaning against Christ and the Word of God! Once you refuse, they will try to starve you of food and funding (grants, food stamps etc.), and they will lay sanctions on organizations or nations that will not agree!

The anti-Christ will come through the economic system and the Beast represents an incarnation of political and social evils especially sexual immorality.

The number 6 symbolizes carnal flesh image, the carnal nature and the number of Man. That means a world leader will rise that will be empowered by Satan, and Daniel 11: 37 says:

"He shall regard neither the God of his fathers nor the desire of women, nor regard any god; for he shall exalt himself above them all."

The right hand represents allegiance, power and honor.

1. To whom will we have allegiance in the end-time?

2. To whom will we give honor?

Every single person will have to decide! Many are doing it already for money and power.

According to Daniel 11: 37, the anti-Christ will have no desire for God, women or the Church! Money and power are the only things he will worship. The anti-Christ will change definitions and make new decrees! He will glorify sin and call it something else.

Revelation 13: 7 lets us know that believers globally will be persecuted and beheaded and be forced to accept unclean lifestyles and false religions.

Revelation 13: 4 - 5 reminds us that men will worship the anti-Christ to get power. He will be an orator - powerful speaker, but he will ridicule and blaspheme Jesus and the Bible! There is a difference between 'anti-Christ' and 'The Anti-Christ'! The 'anti-Christ' is used to speak of systems and/or people against Jesus Christ and who are fore-runners to the main person of the Anti-Christ. The Anti-Christ is one who will reveal himself to be and bring the solution for all the world's problems – purporting equality for all!

Each time you see the word 'Beast' in the Bible, it symbolizes animal characteristics in behavior. The anti-Christ will have Satan's help and will have demons and fallen angels to carry out his bidding! Many leaders will sell their souls for power and money and to be rich! You are going to see a lot of organizations coming out of the woodworks supporting spiritual fornication and adultery! They have to do it to establish their dominance in the marketplace.

The Book of Revelation speaks about Babylon; and Babylon is a system without God! Babylon is coming from the spirit of Nimrod. Study Revelation 18 and you will see his rebellion against God.

Revelation 8: 3 - 4 says: *"For all the nations have drunk of the wine of the wrath of her fornication, the kings of the earth have committed fornication with her, and the merchants of the earth have become rich through the abundance of her luxury." And I heard another voice from heaven saying, "Come out of her, my people, lest you share in her sins, and lest you receive of her plagues."*

Any believer or individual who calls him/herself a Christian, who supports or is a part of the Babylonian System in any way, God is calling them to come out; otherwise they will be receiving the same judgement as those who engage in the Babylonian System.

Each believer has to look within him/herself and seriously ask the question - "To whom am I pledging allegiance?"

Recognize that believers can get caught in the Babylonian system if they rebel against the Lord! There is no way in the world anybody can serve 2 masters!

Let it be known that Jesus is not coming back as a Savior, He is coming back as a Judge!

1 John 2: 18 reminds us: *"Little children, it is the last hour; and as you have heard that the Antichrist is coming, even now many antichrists have come, by which we know that it is the last hour."*

CHAPTER 4

BAD ADVISORS MESSING UP GOOD LEADERS

We have watched over the years until now, many leaders with good intentions get to the point of ruin because of bad advisors. If there is going to be change, then there is the need for new natural and spiritual advisors. Many of the current set of advisors locally and globally are either distracted, corrupt, selfish and do not desire any good for the leader under which they serve. We now need those in the back to come to the front – whether in Politics, National Security and even in Business. We have been recycling advisors throughout every Political Administration. Unless there is a gradual shift, many leaders are going to 'bite the dust'.

There are advisors who, as long as they are not affected by particular situations including system regulations, taxation and so on, they do not care about the kind of advice they give. In the Bible, there were advisors to Nebuchadnezzar, Nathan to David; there were also bad advisors who cause their leaders to die.

In 2 Kings 12:8, Rehoboam rejected the advice of the elders regarding taxing and it caused a revolt and the death of his Treasurer.

In order to choose good advisors for leaders, we cannot choose from our list of school mates, church friends or lobby group leaders. Furthermore, being academically successful does not qualify them for the role of Advisor. An Advisor:

1. Must have a heart for the nation

2. Must have mercy and compassion along with Godly wisdom.

3. Must be loyal to the leader. (They cannot be advising their leader and the enemy or competitor at the same time.)

Advisors should know Times and Seasons and when to implement certain measures. They must be in touch with the people and with what is happening on the ground. Advice should not be given based solely on historical data or forecasts or advice based on numbers, because the wind can change in a minute.

What we need are Advisors with a heart for the poor. We need plans put in place for people to begin to till the ground (Proverbs 28: 19).

Furthermore:

1. Broaden the tax base so that the wealthy pay the greater portion of Tax.

2. Reduce Sales Tax and Consumption Tax.

3. Lower or no tax for Small Businesses in their first three (3) years of operation.

4. Flat Rate meter system on water for the poor.

5. Waive the tax on Solar Systems so that the poor can afford to access this benefit

6. Competitive and Lower Insurance rates on Motor vehicles
7. Reduce or remove certain bank charges so that the poor can save (Proverbs 21: 20; Proverbs 22: 3)

Advisors on Immigration

Every country has a right to protect its borders and protect it from those who would want to come in and destroy. However, before any country decides to impose stringent measures, they need to read the Bible carefully.

The Bible specifically states that there are blessings for nations who open their borders for refugees – even Jesus Himself was a refugee when He took refugee status in Egypt. Additionally, there were even cities of refuge built for the rehabilitation of murderers.

What nations need to do is to begin to rebuild the Spiritual walls that were broken down as in the Book of Nehemiah. Any nation that shows mercy and compassion to refugees and undocumented personnel will receive great blessings from the Creator Who is the One Who gives power to get wealth.

It would be a blessing for nations to begin to call an Immigration Amnesty so that families can contribute to the nation by paying taxes, joining the military and the real estate market explode. This will also allow those countries not to be isolated.

It will also prevent certain allies to come together for evil.

Both politicians and the Business sector need advisors who are in tune with our present environment if they want longevity – particularly those within the Caribbean and Latin nations. They need leaders who will begin to capitalize on, preserve and rise to be dominant globally.

The Times and Seasons have changed and a new wind is blowing. It is no longer business as usual.

CARICOM Needs A Vision

Habakkuk 2: 2 – 3 says, *". . . Write the vision and make it plain on tablets, that he may run who reads it. For the vision is yet for an appointed time . . ."*

Without a doubt, CARICOM (Caribbean Community) is going to be under the microscope, with the global happenings – economic problems, crime, violence and the works. The Caribbean islands are positioned strategically to be a force to be reckoned with globally. But the Caribbean islands, because of a lack of vision, selfishness, greed and pride, are reverting to and are embracing enslavement! Even in the dispute that exists between Trinidad, Jamaica and the problem with Barbados, they must realize that it is a distraction to further divide and conquer the potentially powerful group of Caribbean islands. The fact is that regardless of where exactly in the Caribbean we are from, we are all always regarded as 'from the islands.'

What other countries – developed countries – are after is the resources that God has given the region. The fear our Caribbean people generally have for God is not appreciated by the other nations who refuse to embrace God.

CARICOM is going to go through a shaking which will wake them up. They need to seek for a plan for the entire region, not to focus on individual islands. We are blessed with sunlight, herbs, water and we have precious minerals and metals, in addition to the exquisite fruits and goods! Furthermore, the music is world class! So the question becomes, "Where are the visionaries?"

In order to put plans in place for the next generation, one of the weaknesses of CARICOM is that they do not push the Youth! They themselves fight for power and neglect the development of the Youth in the region.

Our next question is, "Where are the inventors to bring about those inventions that will reduce our energy costs, utilize our climate?

In the area of sports, people need to come together and plans put in place to capitalize on the kind of environment we experience as well as the abundance of talent and resources that exist in the CARICOM region.

Competition

There is competition and there is competition! The islands of the CARICOM Region are competing against each other, while there is no concrete vision in place' to generate employment. The only thing that is being given great attention is Borrow, Take Grants, Divest the Assets. Nothing is sacred and everything is being 'given' away. VIP Passports are being given away. CARICOM is now losing its identity.

First, they need to tell the people that there are conditions for borrowing and the people need to know what the conditions are. There is no such thing as *Free Money*, even as they are given grants! Grants are tied to criteria issued by the country that gives the grants. Some of these criteria are dissolute, and further to that, the CARICOM would need to pledge to these nations, and vote for them where required even if they disagree.

It's going to come down to four nations with which they will have to pledge. Unless there is a drastic shift in CARICOM, it is going to break up; which will go against the very vision that some of the forefathers tried to create for the Region. They need to open their blind eyes and wake up!

Unity

Every sector within CARICOM – Schools, Church, Banks and the Private Sector need to come together and create a vision for the region if they want to become and stay vigilant! They need to begin to garner and harness witty inventions for the development which must be led by them and nobody else.

Each time they come out to say they do not have any money for this or that, it is LAZINESS!

Many major investors that come into CARICOM are using the group. They are using our money and our resources and are making huge profits and pulling the profits away from the islands.

1. We need bankers within the region to help our farmers and manufacturers as well as our school leavers. We need to get people to plant again – teas, herbs and bushes for different cures!

2. We need VISION! Our vision must outlive generations. Visions must be inspired by God.

Our vision must empower the people to put them into action.

Prayer is what keeps one's connection to the giver of Visions. Hence, those who are removing prayer from their administration or organization will become Vision-less. They must build on the Solid Rock!

Vision must be about building the people - that must be first priority. Building roads and major infrastructure without building the people will bring disaster.

All the Caribbean countries already have the necessary resources to build their own logistics hub. What they need to do is rally around the Latin and African nations as trading partners.

CARICOM needs to wake up before it is too late!

We are in a season where management styles and leadership styles are under scrutiny and in some cases need to be revisited. While praying, the Lord said to us that Management and Leadership styles – whether business, church or politics – we will see one of the greatest reformations take place and some will rise and some will fall subject to their style of operation. The Lord further said to us – many people are flying high and they have not prepared a safe ground to land. The question is, if God is not the navigator, how and where will they land?

There are several ways to look at this. Many people are on a high and it seems they have everything under control – as if everything is going their way. But they may find themselves crash landing at the end of the day if God is not their navigator.

It is critical to know which management styles to employ in a nation during the various seasons. Leaders must know what the people of varying classes and levels in their nation need. The people need leaders who speak their language and understand their pain and their issues; one who will motivate them and reach them at any level they are at. They need leaders who understand the struggles they are going through and can encourage them. That is why leaders cannot be absolute and rigid; they must be willing to change, grow and allow for growth.

Leaders must also show mercy and compassion, particularly if they want it to be extended to them. Many times, when things occur within our society, many leaders behave as if they are righteous and perfect, and fail to understand the actions of individuals at times, to their detriment. The two most powerful commandments for anyone to employ are – *"'You shall love the Lord your God with all your heart, with all your soul, with all your strength, and with all your mind,' and 'your neighbor as yourself.'"* (Luke 10: 27)

Regardless of the day of worship or anything else, these are the two greatest commandments. Anything that is put before God, or negative treatment that is extended to our neighbor – whether your co-worker, family member, church brethren, staff, boss, and so on, means that we are not following those two commandments and if you are not following those commandments, then you cannot talk about any other commandments.

There are people who will preach to us about keeping the commandment, yet they spend more money on their dog than they would on the person who takes care of their children and household. They treat their secretaries like nothing and then present themselves to the public like angels.

Manage an Economy

If we are going to manage an economy, the people's welfare must be the number one priority, because neglecting them after begging their votes in order to maintain power is wrong. If the same effort we use to gain power was being employed to help the people, the nation would be much further advanced. Likewise, if the churches were using the same effort it used to erect buildings to empower the people, the nation would be in a better state.

Solutions for the Sliding Dollar

The government needs to shut down the black market that allows the officials, elite, extortionists and drug dealers to make exorbitant deals, while the poor are met with stringent measures to perpetuate hardship. Jamaica is larger than Grenada, and at the time of writing this book, the Eastern Caribbean (EC) dollar was EC$2.67 to US$ 1, and has been so in that range for many years. This sliding dollar issue is creating major and negative impact on the poor.

Today's Focus

The main areas of focus should now be the renewal/restoration of each person's mental and emotional health, as well as a change in the overall way of thinking of our people. Additionally, the spiritual health of our people undeniably affect how we function as a nation.

We need to lift the quality of life that each and all persons live in the nation. We need to help our small businesses. Some have been in business for years and now have to shut down because of the high utility costs. Some can no longer compete with foreign companies because of the environment in the business sector. We are putting our own people out of business, the ones who are willing to keep the money circulating within the country as opposed to the foreign entities, that make the profits here and pull it out of our nation and into theirs.

Following God's Instructions

Regardless of how foolish an instruction may seem, the key to overcoming certain obstacles in your life is to simply follow the instructions – whether spiritual or professional. God will never give you an instruction which goes against His Word.

Many times, people are going through problems and God gives them simple instructions. Some may start the process and then become inconsistent and ultimately discontinue, while others may just ignore the instructions altogether. There are others who start the execution of the instructions but as soon as they see a little light in their circumstances, they abandon the instructions to run after the light and then because they did not follow through on the instructions, the problem returns and they are back at square one.

When problems come up, the Lord does not always use the same method to bring the solution to your situation. Not every problem requires long prayers and prophecies to get you past the problem. Some solutions come in the form of instructions from God that must be followed to get the complete breakthrough/victory. This is why the Lord has given the gifts of Word of Knowledge and Word of Wisdom – for direction. Again, God is not going to give you instructions that are opposite to or go against His Word.

When you go to the doctor you must follow the instructions given on the prescription in order to get the full benefit of healing. In legal matters, you must follow the instructions of the lawyer in order to be victorious in your case. In the same way, when you go to the servant of God for Spiritual counseling and advice, you must also follow the instructions given. In all cases – Doctor, Lawyer, God's servant – there is time that was spent to get the necessary instruction for you to follow for your benefit; and it cost the doctor years of study and continuing education; it cost the lawyer their years of study and time to stay up-to-date with current laws in order to advise you well, and it cost the servant of God, time spent in the Presence of God, and in the Scriptures and maintaining a holy lifestyle to receive and maintain the anointing to hear from God and give you the right instructions for your situation. Your obedience to God's instructions bring peace, prosperity and the fulfillment of your purpose and also creates miracles. You will never move forward past your last act of obedience.

(Deuteronomy 28: 1 – 14; Proverbs 14: 12; John 14: 21; Joshua 7: 10 – 13; 1 Kings 17: 15 – 16; Hebrews 11: 11; Ephesians 6: 5 – 8 and 2 Kings 5)

When things are not going right in your life, check and see which instructions you did not follow. What if the leprous commander Naaman did not obey the instruction to dip 7 times in the Jordan? What if he had allowed his pride to cause him to disobey the instructions? You will never be a good leader until you learn to follow instructions; and here is the big key – you do not have to understand his instructions. For example, a person may be acting in a movie and the director gives an instruction on how to play a part. The director sees the vision for the movie much clearer than the actor does, so the actor only needs to follow the director's instructions. Likewise, when your boss gives you an instruction on the job, your role is to follow the instructions as long as those instructions do not go against the company's policies and guidelines. You are not the boss and you are not privy to what the boss knows concerning the organization's vision.

Remember, you can be given an instruction – both Spiritually and naturally – just to see if you are willing to follow instructions.

Recurring problems happen because instructions are not followed. Political and governmental failure and defeat comes about when they refuse to follow instructions. Ministerial failure comes about when people refuse to obey the instructions given by God and the leader above them. Life becomes easier when we follow God's instructions and waste is reduced and eliminated. The world would be a much better place if we only learned to follow instructions. Discipline starts with following instructions. Our victory begins when we obey and carry out the instructions given.

Give Us Vision Lest We Perish

Vision is inspired by God, and when a nation suffers – crime, violence, poverty, high debt or hopelessness – Proverbs 29: 18 reveals that when a society lacks any revelation from God or Divine insight, such a society is headed in the direction of anarchy.

The vision of a nation, company or organization (spiritual or secular) is given to the leader of the organization and this person is the visionary. The Visionary is the person who will outline the vision to the organization or to the people of the nation who will clearly and accurately communicate to each individual the vision of the nation and how they will fit in it.

The problem we have in the society has come about because the 'neck', 'hands' and 'feet' have a different vision from the 'head'/visionary. This is what brings about division, rebellion, undermining and even conspiracy within and outside the organization/nation.

The problem is this: everybody wants to lead, but in reality, everybody can't lead. What many do not realize is that they have to be faithful to another man's vision before God entrusts them with a vision of their own. There can be no growth unless everyone works toward realizing the vision of which they are a part.

Write the Vision

1. The Vision must be documented on paper. (Habakkuk 2)

2. The Vision must be inspired by God.

3. The Vision must be birthed with prayer and with the knowledge that there is a time and season for it to be birthed.

4. The Vision must be one that deals with the demands of the people. It cannot be short term, it must be long term.

5. The Vision must have core values.

6. The Vision must be built on the Solid Rock, not on sand.

Most of the problems that the local and global leaders or organizations have been experiencing is as a result of the fact that they will come up with a manifesto and then abandon it when they get into the seats of power. Or, they will attempt to build on the vision of our forefathers, but sadly they don't realize that the visions of the forefathers are dead and they must have a God-given vision of their own. For example, Moses' Vision was to deliver the nation of Israel out of oppression, but Joshua's vision was to carry them into the Promised Land. Although Joshua succeeded Moses, the Visions were different because the paradigm shifted and the circumstances changed.

Furthermore, we are not helping the Vision of an organization or nation when we employ or take on someone just to give them a job. We must look determine if they are the right fit for and can contribute to the Vision.

In the era of Moses, God fed the people with manna, but in the era of Joshua, they had to fight, because what they had to overcome had changed. There was a time the people would be given the fish, but there comes a time when you have to teach the people how to fish.

The majority of the people within the nation don't know the Vision of the nation. Each time an election comes around many do not even know why they are voting. They vote for a leader and then they turn around and curse the leader.

Everyone must ask the question: Why does my organization exist? What is my organization to accomplish? Is my organization relevant to this era? Am I in reverse, neutral or drive? Can the infrastructure of my organization deal with the vision? Is the Visionary or the organization flexible for a paradigm shift?

No vision can be successful unless you have the right people to build, and they cannot be political. The vision must capture the things that are affecting us. We cannot rid a nation of crime by purchasing more bullets. The economy cannot be fixed by reducing the debt unless, they decide to deal with the real issues from the root.

As it stands today, the Vision of our forefathers have become irrelevant and obsolete in light of the current issues that are affecting business and the economy. Saying so is not an expression of disrespect to the things our forefathers achieved within and for the nation. On the contrary, it is recognition that what they did was successful for the era to which it applied, and that we too need to seek for what applies to this era.

God, give us *Vision!*

Bad Advisors Causing Global Failure

Proverbs 15: 22 states: *"Without counsel, plans go awry, but in the multitude of counselors they are established."*

Regardless of the plans and vision one has, success or failure will depend on the advisors/counsellors with whom one surrounds oneself.

Much of the global failure we see today is the result of the bad advice given by poor advisors in seats of influence. Leaders have had short tenure simply because of the poor advice they have received.

Nathan was a good advisor to King David (2 Samuel; 1 Kings). He gave advice based on God's will and purpose. He was not there to get rich or seek fame and popularity; he never compromised nor was he afraid to speak the truth. Many advisors today have wrong motives and treat their role as a mere paid position rather than the serious and important function it regarding nation building and global success.

Regardless of the capacity within which they give counsel – religious, political, legal, financial, business operations and so on – they must have one thing in common – the fear of the Lord! (Psalm 25: 12 – 15)

Through the fear of the Lord comes wisdom, knowledge, guidance, spiritual prosperity, posterity and have a Divine Confidant Who will reveal secrets to you in order to give good advice and solve problems.

Leaders in every capacity need advisors who will not be 'yes-men', ones who will not compromise and will tell them the truth even if it is not what they want/like to hear. For example, many leaders take advice that go against God's laws and precepts, including making decisions and/or passing resolutions against Israel. (Joel 3: 2, Genesis 12: 3; Ezekiel 39: 6 and Zechariah 2: 6 – 8)

Oftentimes we are concerned about who opposes us but the enemy that is within is greater than the enemy without!! If the persons in your inner circle who are advising you believe that they are more qualified than you are and harbor secret ambitions/hidden agendas, then they will advise you to your downfall!

Never take advice from those within the occult, false prophets, apostate Christians, diviners, magicians or soothsayers! Once you take advice from them, it will bring defilement on yourself and on the people! (Exodus 7: 11; Genesis 41: 8; Leviticus 19: 31; Leviticus 20: 6, 1 Chronicles 10: 13; Isaiah 8: 19, Isaiah 47: 12 – 13.

Always check the motives of your advisors! Haman was a bad advisor to King Ahasuerus (Xerxes). He had bad motives – to conspire and lie to the king so that the king would depend solely on his advice, and to rise to power himself. He lied against good advisors (Mordecai) and sought to eliminate an entire race because of his personal prejudices. He misled the king! Thankfully, there was an Esther!

Oftentimes these bad advisors have the sole goal of blocking those who will come with the truth!

Good advisors teach those they advise to please God first – God will please the people!

Every leader must first have a relationship with the Chief Advisor – the Holy Spirit! (John 15: 26). The Holy Spirit is our Advocate, Comforter, Helper, Intercessor and Teacher.

Every advisor must know the times and seasons! Many leaders make decisions in bad timing! Some try to get the favor of man in order to get victory, meanwhile, they are falling out of favor with God! It is not what man says that counts, it is what God says!

A good advisor must be wise, discerning, and able to put plans in place for future famine, disasters and so on. (Genesis 41: 37 – 57)

Nothing happens in the earth without God revealing it! God has been speaking to many leaders in dreams and visions to prevent certain happenings within a nation – whether it be health crisis, economic crisis or even election loss; but there is none to interpret! Why are their dreams not being interpreted?

The purpose of dreams and visions is to:

1. Provide God's answers to our questions

2. Give instruction in the things of God

3. Warn us against unseen danger

4. Guide us away from wrongdoing

5. Keep us away from pride

6. Save our lives

There are many negative happenings globally. Many leaders are making many mistakes and billions of dollars are going to waste.

Our leaders have been getting bad advice and have been employed bad advisors.

In Daniel 2, had the king not threatened to destroy them and their household if they did not carry out their roles, he would not have seen the light and understood what to do from there.

If leaders want to be successful, they need to take a good look at what has transpired over the years with the same old advisors throughout the years – regardless of their field. So, if we want to see change, first change the advisors!

CHAPTER 5

BIBLICAL PRINCIPLES TO SOLVE THE NATIONS' PROBLEMS

Regardless of the Economic Goals a nation has, it is extremely difficult to achieve them if the family is broken. Unless the institution known as Family becomes a priority, those economic goals will not be achieved. It is therefore necessary to begin effectively dealing with Common Law relationships and children being born out of wedlock – it brings a bastard curse on the nation.

We cannot achieve the movement from poverty to prosperity by ignoring moral values nor by dishonoring Biblical Principles, which are God's laws to govern a nation. Deuteronomy 2: 1 – 14 specifically teaches us that blessings belong to us when we adhere to God's laws and precepts. It is not about a few cash-rich countries that will get us on the path to prosperity as they invest in our nation. They are going to get out more than they invest. Meanwhile, the next generation will have nothing to get.

A few years ago, while in prayer, the Lord revealed that because the nations refuse to practice Biblical Principles, it affects everything including their economies. Many Third

World nations including Jamaica are looking to wealthier nations and people to bail their nation out, but they must recognize that their sovereignty is going to be at stake. The Lord also revealed that we would see many single term Administrations throughout those nations, and also that the poor would be the ones to feel these woes the hardest. He said the land and infrastructure would be at risk, so Deuteronomy 28: 15 – 28 is being fulfilled in our midst.

Biblical Principles teach us that nations should have a fair distribution of resources; and that can only take place when people look to God, Who will teach us how to distribute the resources. (Mark 6: 41). We must look to God for help and we must give thanks for the resources and divide it all equally and fairly. We must ensure that we are accountable for the fragments within the nation.

Even when a nation budgets to spend a certain amount, it is only when we commit it to God, can we see it work according to plan. No politician can deal with the needs of the people, only God can. Only with God's wisdom can Job Creation be a genuine reality that gives work to idle hands instead of floating around the same pool of 'already-employed-individuals'. It is easy to write a financial plan, but are you getting the backing of Heaven?

Regardless of how small our resources are, when we commit it all to Him, He will turn it around. Nothing is too small to create a financial flow. Remember the five (5) loaves and two (2) fish.

Before any physical or financial renewal can take place within a nation, there has to be spiritual renewal first. Then we will have blessing and restoration on the land; fertility will replace death and barrenness, and, spiritual and natural rain will fall and flow in the nation.

Biblical Principles speaks against the divestment of a nation and/or its resources. For years nations have been warned to cease, because all these things would bring reproach on the nation. Many politicians may not care because as far as they are concerned, it is "In Today, Out Tomorrow!" We cannot speak of growing an economy when we do not practice Biblical Principles – tilling the ground and farming must be our number one focus, for Job Creation and Sustainable Development. Management of human resource, which includes talents and gifts, must be at the forefront for economic and social development. If we look at the budgets for Third World nations, those areas are sorely neglected.

Biblical Principles supports higher taxes for the wealthy. Everybody cannot be paying the same tax rate. Nations are assessed based on their ability to pay in several international circles. There should be some sort of assessment scale that allows those at the lower end of the pay scale to pay a lower tax rate and a ceiling set for those at the higher end of that pay scale. Furthermore, putting leaders in strategic positions needs careful spiritual guidance before they are selected.

The most critical areas that nations will have to deal with are Job Creation, Education for those 5 – 17 years of age, Migration, Crime and Violence, Humanitarian Relief, Poverty Eradication, Housing for lower income persons, Extensive Food Program and Occupational Safety and Health.

The concept of Biblical Principles is not about dealing with just one set of persons, it is applicable to all for the benefit of all. While many continue to ignore the principles and are looking to man and to other nations, we are about to see many countries plunge into famine.

Gatekeepers Within A Nation

It is critical for us to understand the importance of gates and gatekeepers within a nation. If we are going to have true reformation and change, then we are going to have to adjust, rebuild and repair.

Who Are The Gate-Keepers?

1. *Police*
2. *Soldiers*
3. *Security Guards*
4. *Customs*
5. *Immigration*
6. *Corrections Staff*
7. *Church* (The Fivefold Personnel – Gatekeepers for spiritual and natural things)
8. *Governmental Institutions* (particularly Finance, Foreign Affairs and Tax Office)

The Gates and Gate Keepers within a nation are important, as they control the access to a city or a nation. The Gate must be manned and the Gate-Keepers must be taken care of. For example, they should be given incentives such as Tax-free/Tax exemption benefits, to motivate them. (Ezra 2: 42, 2 Chronicles 9: 17 – 22, Isaiah 62: 6 – 10, Nehemiah 11: 19, 1 Chronicles 26: 1 – 2, Nehemiah 3)

Focus on Internal Security

Oftentimes, we focus on Internal Security but neglect External Security. For example, those coming in under the disguise of 'tourists' or ex-patriates and contractors, what are their mandates and motives? What systems are in place to monitor their movements? Are they a part of the negative activities we see daily? Who monitors the contractor(s) and those engineers building the roads? What are they doing?

No gatekeeper can be effective unless we allow God to build.

Psalm 127: 1 says, "*Unless the Lord builds the house, they labor in vain who build it; unless the Lord guards the city, the watchman stays awake in vain.*"

Oftentimes organizations are negative toward God's principles, people and in fact, anything to do with God, including devotions and prayer.

The Gates in a Nation

The Sheep Gate

The purpose of the Sheep Gate is Ministry to God's people. Teach, Educate, Empower and Feed the people. If the people are not being fed with God's wisdom and knowledge, then we will fail. Furthermore, compassion must be shown. Good leaders – shepherds – must motivate the people. Sheep feed best when they know the shepherd is close by to feed them. They feel secure. (John 10: 2 – 3). Shepherds must not only care about themselves, but they must care about the Sheep. The management is the Shepherd, the staff members are the sheep. It is about more than money. The sheep need that personal touch from the Shepherd. That is why Pastors have to lay hands on the sheep. A Shepherd must be a Counselor and must spend time with the sheep.

The Fish Gate

(Nehemiah 3: 3) This is Ministry to the Unsaved. All the gatekeepers are called to minister to the Unsaved. One word of encouragement will reduce crime. When the organization begins to create an environment for spiritual empowerment, then we will begin to see change. We must restore the Sheep Gate before the Fish Gate. Healthy sheep will produce healthy lambs through the evangelism. This ministry includes training and equipping. What if all our prisoners began to be equipped Spiritually? A transformation would begin, budgets would be cut and most of them would change and not return to the prisons. When people go to prison, they should come out rehabilitated not remain the same as they were before or get worse. Only the Gospel of Jesus Christ can bring that about, not New Age practices.

The Old Gate

(Nehemiah 3: 6) The purpose of this gate is Foundational Principles and Truths, Moral Principles. Truth never changes from generation to generation. When we try to remove the ancient landmark which our fathers have set, then we will have problems within the nation. New truths are coming in with which we have been compromising. For example, doctrine, theology and philosophy, which are not in line with Biblical Principles (Proverbs 22: 28 Proverbs 23: 10, Hebrews 6: 1 – 3, Acts 2: 41 – 42)

The Valley Gate

(Nehemiah 3: 13) Its purpose is the Ministry of Compassion. We must always to meet another person's need. Kindness and meekness are mandatory. Helping a fallen brother, who has emotional, financial, mental, domestic challenges must have a support system in place to help staff who are the gatekeepers. This will prevent bribery.

The Dung Gate

This deals with the Ministry of Cleansing. Its purpose is to provide the inhabitants of the city with a place where they can dispose their garbage or waste. If there is no place for disposal of waste and garbage and to allow for repentance and change, people will become sick. Sin makes one sick.

The Church cannot be exempt from the nation, neither can Christ be excluded from the nation.

The Fountain Gate

This is the Holy Spirit that would bring Revival, Refreshing and Restoration. When the garbage such as unforgiveness, bitterness and hatred is emptied out of our lives, then the Holy Spirit – Who is the Fountain Gate, will manifest, and we will begin to get solutions, and rivers of water will begin to flow out of the lives of the people, and a time of refreshing (Acts 3: 19 – 21) will take place. The economy will also grow and our borders will be secure. God does nothing without His Spirit. (Zechariah 10: 1, Hosea 6: 3, John 7: 37 – 39, Joel 2). Prayer and praise change the environment.

The Water Gate

The Ministry of God's Word. Only through God's Word can cleansing take place naturally of spiritually. No nation or individual can survive without water. The Spirit of God moves when the Word of God is declared. Both the Spirit and the Word work together. (Numbers 31: 23, Numbers 33: 9, Deuteronomy 8: 15, 1 Corinthians 10: 4) So, we truly cannot lead without the Word.

The Horse Gate

We need Burden-bearers to carry heavy burdens. There are burdens – problems that are too difficult to carry. There are some problems man cannot solve. We need intercessors to continue to pray for God's counsel, God's will and God's ways. The carnal man cannot solve the spiritual problems without the Holy Spirit. We cannot solve the problems with our intellect and without God. The burden must be lifted from the flesh to the Spiritual.

This one dictates a Final Restoration coming. Christ is coming back. There is a perfecting that is taking place now in the Body of Christ. He is coming back for a church without spot or wrinkle, so we must be ready. (Revelation 7: 2, Revelation 16: 12)

We Need Solutions Not Prostitution

Anyone within a nation who wants to legalize prostitution should be considered an enemy to the nation's progress. Who in the society would want their sons and daughters involved in prostitution? What we as a nation should do instead is to create opportunities for our people to be employed and learn a skill, motivating them to respect their bodies, their value and maintain dignity.

Many of those involved in prostitution will be the first to tell you that they do not want to be involved in it; but they engage only because they are desperate to survive and often have no other support system. Many are single mothers, others some are members of prominent churches.

Many leaders in society are too lazy to take the step and come up with solutions to create opportunities for the people. They are, instead, quick to come up with answers that call for very little effort on their part and does not do much (if anything at all) to truly advance their people and nation. Some leaders pretend as if they care about our women and youth or are championing gender issues, but from time immemorial until now, they are using the women and children as a front and they do not really care about them. Some are in it for what they can get out of it themselves, not because they truly care about the welfare/well-being of the people.

Our leaders and our people should be getting together to discuss how to bring out the gifts and talents within the nation for sustainable development and to create hope, rather than debating whether or not to legalize/decriminalize activities which degrade, demoralize and diminish the value and dignity of our women and youth especially.

Decriminalizing Prostitution

Legalizing/Decriminalizing Prostitution will open the door for greater hardship and abuse even rape and murder in the nation. STDs (Sexually Transmitted Diseases) will increase.

The influential men/women of our nation who engage in the services of Prostitution will then have a freer hand at legally coming after our young ones and there is nothing that we would be able to do about it legally.

There are men of influence who cannot have a good erection and demand unprotected sex from the young girls (or boys).

The dons, pimps, extortionists and drug dealers will now be allowed greater power to run our nation amuck.

Women's health issues would spiral downward since you cannot truly put a block on/stop those with STDs nor guarantee protection, because once they/their time are paid for they are 'owned'.

All we would be doing is strengthening the sex industry, increasing the levels of immorality and degradation of our women and youth, increasing kidnapping/sex trafficking and the total breakdown of our health industry since there is not a stipulation regarding those with sexually transmitted diseases and women's health will be at greater risk. Furthermore, our high school students, who do not see job opportunities anywhere else, will now look at this as an outlet and all that would happen is when they are of no use to them or are not 'marketable' for their purposes later in the industry, they discard them, push them aside and leave them to die without hope.

No nation can be built without morals and a sense of civic pride or dignity. Without those elements, the people of the nation are on a path to self-destruction.

A 2007 Dutch government report stated a highly significant drop in the emotional well-being of and a great increase in the use of sedatives by prostitutes after the legalization of Prostitution.

No leader would want to cash in by legalizing prostitution in taxation. Government must provide real alternatives and opportunities for our women and youth. In legalizing Prostitution in any country – I guarantee you will see a heavy influx of women from other nations being brought in because they would be deemed more 'marketable' and more affordable.

There is so much talent within our nations; so many untapped skills, ideas and solutions. Is the legalization of prostitution the only solution nation leaders can find in order to improve their nation's economic situation? Should they make the people the products for sale rather than creating opportunities for them to create new products and bring true growth and development?

Solutions

1. Teach our people to live within their means.

2. Effectively teach our people to save and budget.

3. Banks should eliminate 50% of the charges they currently levy on the public and encourage savings.

4. Increase the Minimum Wage Amount.

5. Conduct a survey throughout communities to identify the number of unschooled children existing and get them schooled.

6. Reduce Sales Tax significantly.

7. Hotels and Doctors need to give major discounts to families – particularly where the parents are married.

Our leaders need to earn their salaries and provide good/proper opportunities for the people of the nation they *serve*.

Invest In Your Nation

The more we refuse to invest in our own people – local staff, local businesses and the youth – the more our sovereignty is exposed to risk of decay.

Very shortly we will see most of the strategic positions within the public and private sectors being taken by expatriates. If that happens, it would mean that our country's leaders have failed. The number one criterion of our country should be to put laws in place to create an atmosphere of growth and prosperity. For example:

1. *Laws dealing with the protection of our Dollar*
2. *The Reformation of our Justice System,*
3. *Constitutional Issues*
4. *Campaign Financing*
5. *Term Limits*
6. *Dual Citizenship*
7. *Energy and the Removal of Monopolies*

Before the nation can encourage international investors to come in, we must first create a local environment conducive to the survival of local businesses. It means we will need to first invest in our own people!

Everybody is looking for solutions, but solutions will be forthcoming when those above are willing to listen to the suggestions of their own people.

Many times, organizations spend millions in consultancy services external to the organizations when there are those within the organization and the nation – depending on the company – who can give solutions. Oftentimes after the External Consultancies have given their 'solutions', the same internal staff who they previously overlooked, are the same ones who have clean up the mess. The country is in the state it is today mainly (but not only) because of the misappropriated advice of the international consultants to the business community.

Companies need to identify faithful and committed employees and train them to deal with the demands and problems the organization and its leaders encounter. Always train a mixed set – that is – persons from all levels. Oftentimes leaders focus on training those managers or senior personnel who are not necessarily engaged in the operations while they neglect to train the line staff involved in the daily operations.

Sometimes, government ministers are sent to international seminars, summits and/or training sessions instead of sending persons below them who are actually driving the vision and operations. In other instances, leaders are sent for training when they are close to retirement, and the information and training leaves when they do and those left behind don't receive the full benefits of such training. Even in the Security industry, oftentimes the training is given to the commander of the division; while there is no investment being made in those on the frontline/on the ground.

The Success of Every Manager

For change to take place, we must start by investing in our High School students. There are many things they can use the high school students to do and cut wastage while giving them the experience for their resume. In order to adapt to the changes, we must be willing to do so.

With the political system as it is, there are very few young people who are attracted to politics. If we are unwilling to change, unwilling to invest in our youth, unwilling to embrace the ideas of those who are on the ground, so to speak, then how can we expect our young people to want to play a significant and vital role in this area or in any industry for that matter?

The criteria for selection of persons for political representation ought to be revisited. The main bases for qualification or selection are academics, how much money a person has and the potential they possess for money-making.

Very few people know who the Key Grip in any movie is, or what the stuntman in a movie looks like. But when the movie is number 1 in the Box Office, it means they have done an excellent job and they have played a role in making the movie a success. It is so also for the local media houses! Sometimes people are awarded for being the Best Journalist, the Best Photographer, but what about the Cameraman, the Production Personnel, the Technicians and Editors and Lighting personnel? They too must be recognized.

The success of every manager is not solely as a result of his or her academic qualifications and intellect, but also on extent to which they invest in their support staff members.

Even in the Church, many recognize the Pastor, Bishop, Elders, but neglect or ignore those who sweep the floors, clean the bathrooms and keep the sanctuary clean. They not only should be recognized, but we must invest in them.

We Need Veracious Nation-Builders

We need veracious nation-builders, not those voracious for attention and personal gain! We need people who genuinely and honestly desire to restore the nation in a balanced way – not just on an economic level. We need those who wish to bring the balance of the Spiritual, social, economic, legal, familial and other areas; recognizing God as the Head of our nation, Who is the Creator of all things; and knowing that the earth is the Lord's and the fullness thereof.

The nation is certainly not lacking in intellect and intellectuals, but regardless of this fact, without the element of honesty then you will not be seen as trustworthy. If you cannot be trusted, then your efforts will be in vain. Veracity is a vital element to restoring and building any nation. How many politicians and businessmen abide by the law of the land? For that matter, how many Church leaders are practicing what they preach? Who pays taxes? Many are talking about lotto scamming; what about money laundering? Laws are being implemented to target one set of persons while the bigger fish are being allowed to escape. How many politicians have there been that have said that they are sorry for not being honest with the people they represent?

The action displayed toward the people of the nation that they are supposed to serve and represent, is the same action they display toward God.

Both political parties over the years – past and present cabinets – need to be truthful to the people of the nation concerning the economy, especially the state of the economy now. This issue affects everyone including the unborn child in its mother's womb.

Many times, the leaders will say that it is not for the people to know certain information. But it is better for us to know so that we know how to plan ahead individually. The country is in a state of captivity because our leaders in every level of society are not being honest. How many businessmen are willing to come forward and admit that they have helped to bring the nation to this state and have been receiving more from the nation than they have been giving back!

The church leaders have found themselves in a position of compromise because they put their favorite political party, their denomination and the name of their church above truth and righteousness. As a result, the voice they ought to have within the nation has been quieted and made inaudible!

Good Intentions

Many past political leaders had good intentions, but they were and many still do today; but they were and are surrounded by people who are not trustworthy. Every leader must have the ability to discern their surroundings and motives.

Each had the opportunity to be the greatest leader, but they missed that opportunity when they chose to reject sound advice. Before we can see change within the nation, the 'spirit of Haman' that has been surrounding our kings has to go. 'Haman' has no respect for the king or the queen. 'Haman' never exemplifies any reverence to God. He was selfish and condescending in his ways. 'Haman' thought himself wittier than the king; and his motive was to take control and to seize the throne.

Abortion Comparison: Jamaica vs. USA

Oftentimes our leaders will try to compare the United States and Jamaica when it comes to policy decisions. But they must understand that both countries have vast differences in size nature and the economy. Jamaica's social system does not support abortion; we have Christian values. Abortion is wrong! Are we moving away from Christianity to paganism?

According to the United Nations, "In 1994 the International Conference on Population and Development (ICPD) outcome document instructed that *'Governments should take appropriate steps to help women avoid abortion, which in no case should be promoted as a method of family planning ...'*" In addition to this, the UN also says that *"Member States have agreed to help women avoid abortion and UN agencies are prohibited from promoting it as a method of family planning"*, and Jamaica is a member state and was an active participant in the 1994 International Conference on Population and Development (ICPD), so Jamaica agreed to do this.

If Jamaica has taken such a decision to amend any law that runs counter to the agreement, the government would be guilty of reneging on this commitment that was made to the international community.

The government can do many things to keep women from making poor decisions and help them to make good choices. Although a pregnancy is unplanned, it does not mean they are or ought to be unwanted.

We need honest mentors to motivate our youth in the right direction, and our nation on the right path.

The problem that exists in America today – the division and different issues have come through the door of abortion – a death culture that has affected the economy and is destroying the family. A nation cannot be built on death. America and other nations that embrace this "death culture" of abortion is destroying its own future.

Righteousness and The Economy

The nations' economies must be rebuilt, and if they seek God, He is willing to give each nation the plans to bring them restoration. They started to focus on the wrong things and big investments none of which were benefiting the nation. What they have also done spiritually, is to open the doorway for more problems, because God will not bless a mess!

No one can build a nation or economy on unrighteousness and prosper. There are consequences when Spiritual Laws are broken. The nation, particularly the leaders must decide at this juncture whether the nation will follow and listen to God or not, because that will determine our direction. Why ask for the solution if you're not willing to listen to the Solution–giver!

God would have shown them the danger of entering into certain agreements that would be devastating to the nation in the time to come; where the Administration of the Party has moved away from moral values. The decisions that they have made to negatively affect foreign policies which are not in line with Biblical Principles, and it is now causing greater hardships on the nation. Unless the Lord builds the house, they labor in vain! (Psalm 127: 1)

The Bible Solves Every Problem

Many people are now challenging the existence of God, His Deity, His Wisdom and even the Word of God.

At the same time, the world is in a crisis; the ozone layer, the economy, world peace and social systems are diminishing daily. Everything seems to be leading toward global catastrophe, all because of man's ignorance toward Spiritual truth!

There are two 'trees' that God uses to speak to man prophetically about Spiritual truth. (Genesis 2: 9)

There are two elements necessary to know the things of God:

1. A revelation of God by His Spirit

2. An appropriate spiritual response by man (1 Corinthians 2: 14 – 3: 4)

Surprisingly, most who want to challenge God's existence, while they may not believe in God, attempt to tap into a different 'system'; just as it was in the Garden of Eden. They are attempting to eat from a different tree in order to find Spiritual truth!

Spirit answers to spirit, not spirit to mind and logic! The Holy Spirit interprets Spiritual things to Spiritual people. The Holy Spirit is the only One qualified to reveal God to man, because He is God! Man can know things about other men, but within himself, he cannot know anything about God, unless the Holy Spirit of God reveals it to him.

An unbeliever or an atheist possesses the spirit of the world. When one accepts Jesus as Savior, he receives the spirit of God. It is very foolish for someone who is an unbeliever to attempt to 'prove' that there is no God, when they don't possess the Holy Spirit of God! For anyone to understand Spiritual truth, and even the Bible, they must be born again through Jesus Christ.
No one who is blinded by the spirit of the world which is in effect darkness, can experience true Light which brings with it true revelation of the things of God and the knowledge of God, and even the purpose of their life and nation.

God can only communicate Spiritual truth to Spiritual men and women who accept Him first. Ask yourself these questions:

1. Can you make a withdrawal from a bank account without becoming a customer of that bank?

2. Can you receive the full benefits of being the member of a club or civic organization without becoming a member/ a part of that organization?

A big part of the benefits of being a Christian – a follower of Christ – is learning about the One Who is our Head, and being able to communicate with Him in the language He has afforded us, one only He understands – Speaking in Tongues!

In answer to the two previous questions, Yes, we can make withdrawals from the bank without being a customer, and we can access certain benefits from a club/civic organization without being a member/part of that organization. How do we get that? Hacking, stealing or corruption of the process! At any cost, it's illegal!

Trying to gain knowledge about God's existence through Kundalini Release and New Age Philosophies are methods of which God is not a part, nor does He support.

Know And Understand The Word Of God

Many will say they know what the word of God is or says. However, *reading* the Word of God is not the same as *knowing it!* How many times have we read legal documents, think we know what it is saying, and then get duped? It means then, that we need legal counsel. There are lawyers/legal counsels, because there is always the potential to misunderstand the words contained in a document.

An unregenerate man knows nothing about God! Only the regenerate spirit of man is capable of proper judgement. Those who have His mind will be able to discern or to understand spiritual truth.

Knowledge of the things of God is more of a Spiritual than Intellectual or Theological nature. God's wisdom sees the world's wisdom as foolish, especially in the area of security, economic and political decision-making. Why are so many countries deteriorating and unable to find solutions? Recognize that everything that was stated in the Bible that would come to pass is now happening!

Many who speak against the Bible are cowards! They know it is true, but because it brings conviction to them and it confronts their lifestyle, they deny it publicly so as not to negatively affect their reputation.

Use the Bible for Values and Attitudes

Why are we alarmed at the breaking down of Values and Attitudes within the society when the Book of Codes, Ethics, Morals and Values has been disregarded and rejected? Why waste more money on research to find out why our children behave the way they do? We have replaced the Bible with Harry Potter, X-Rated Cartoons and other forms of media that teach our children how to perform magic, engage in violence and tolerate un-Godly behavior. Media and Marketing companies engage in borderline pornography just to advertise hair oil, food and drink!

The Family, which is the first line of Government, must get back in position, and begin to train the children. There are Codes of Ethics and Moral Standards in the Bible that work for both Christians and non-Christians.

With the fight to remove the Bible from our society, with what do we replace it? Will it be the Quran, New Age Doctrines, the Principles of Kabballah or Kundalini - what will it be?

Surprisingly, even Media Houses are afraid to quote Scriptures. They prefer to quote from philosophers of all kinds and doctrines of all kinds – Monotheism, Pantheism, Astrology, Gnosticism, Universalism and Spiritualism. All of these "-isms" may lead to Communism!

It is interesting and somewhat hypocritical, that when officials are being sworn in, or when we are taking oaths in a court of law, the Bible is the book on which the hands are placed to make the vow that they are to honor. Do they realize that the oath made with the hand on the Bible means that it is a vow to uphold, not just the Constitution, but also everything contained in the Bible? When people are afraid to uphold what is within the Book, it is the equivalent to perjury and treason – especially when they vow to 'tell the truth, the whole truth, and nothing but the truth so help me God.'

Code of Ethics

There are Scriptures that speak about the Labor Laws, Severance Pay, Firing Employees, Rotation of Workers, through Deuteronomy 15: 13 – 14, Deuteronomy 23: 25 – 26, Deuteronomy 24: 14 – 15, Leviticus 19: 13, Leviticus 25: 43 and 1 Kings 4: 27. The Scriptures also teach us not to oppress employees and not to rob them in their salaries/pay. (James 5)

The Scriptures also tell us that foreigners are to be given labor jobs and the citizens are to be given the management of the labor force. The Bible is also clear on Gender Issues and Human Rights.

The Scriptures speak to us on Environmental Issues, warning us not to cut down fruit trees, what to do with bodily waste, resting the land, dealing with toxic waste, having open spaces for beautification of the town. It also lays down the principles of the 3 R's – Recycle, Re-use and Reduce. (Numbers 35: 1 – 6; Deuteronomy 20: 19,

Deuteronomy 23: 13 – 15, Leviticus 25: 1 – 7; Psalm 104: 10 – 14)

The Scriptures teach us about the Law of Gleaning – a mandate given by God for every business person and every farmer to set aside a part of their budget to help the poor. (Leviticus 19: 9 – 10) Both rich and poor need each other! Certain blessings the rich cannot receive until they help the poor, especially Healing, Divine Revelations and new ideas!

Leviticus 19: 32 speaks to us about how we must treat an elder – calling them dinosaurs, ignoring their deathbed pleas for assistance, robbing them of their pensions or holding on to their pensions so that they cannot even purchase food and medication after they have labored within and for their nation!
Leviticus 19: 15 speaks to us about the fact that we are not to honor the mighty while we bring injustice to the poor!

Leviticus 19: 29 says: "*Do not prostitute your daughter, to cause her to be a harlot, lest the land fall into harlotry, and the land become full of wickedness.*"

Leviticus 19: 35 – 36 and Exodus 23: 7, Proverbs 11: 1 and Zechariah 8: 16 – 17 speak of integrity in business. There should be no selling of old stock for new stock prices, selling inferior products, 'marrying' items, false advertising and deceptive marketing strategies, lying Press Releases and falsifying financial statements.

Leviticus 20: 2 clearly tells us how NOT to treat our children.

So, the Bible clearly tells us that when morality breaks down within a nation, crime and violence, bad economy, poor values and attitudes and low moral standards will result. Joel 1 and 2 tells us the causes and solutions concerning the issues of the nation. The Bible even tells us about Animal Rights.

Application of the Biblical Principles can save us a great deal of the struggles we now endure.

7 Critical Factors for Nations To Address

1. *Leadership* – It is very critical for the leaders of nations today to have a servant-leader quality and style in order to bring real change today; and with the pending US Elections, every candidate's style of leadership should be taken into consideration. The leadership of any nation should rely heavily upon Godly instructions and should display true love for the people within a nation.

2. *Economic* - There will be continued economic instability within the US, the Caribbean and Europe because the wealthy have been allowed to over-exert their authority at the expense of the poor and middle classes. Increase taxes on the rich! In addition to this there should be no taxes on basic food items. General Consumption Tax in countries such as Jamaica should not go above 12%. The banks and their systems have been and continue to be the biggest hindrances to the nation and its growth. Major countries need to begin writing off the debts of smaller countries. Likewise, major companies need to do the same for smaller companies.

3. *Security* - There are too many doors of access open for potential attacks globally due to improper security practices. Total security is highly unlikely without the Lord and the root of this issue needs to be dealt with urgently! Security personnel need to be properly screened for any job description. Therefore, security for Land, Sea and Air Transportations must be tighter. More stringency is required to secure the citizens within a nation. There needs to be an up-to-

date database with all the ex-service men who left honorably so that they can be re-enlisted in the event of an emergency. There also needs to be more training in security management and disaster preparedness.

4. *Health/Water* - There are so many medications on the market that have been causing serious side effects for over four decades. Doctors, Nutritionists and Lab Technicians need to explore the natural things that God Himself made for the benefit of man's continued existence and He has given us plants that can sometimes be employed to cure us. There are medications that need to be banned from off the market immediately to eliminate fraudulent business activities within this field. More tanks and wells are needed urgently. Instead of focusing on Marijuana, government needs to focus on the herbs in general and make an effort to see how they can help in healing for the nation's people. The focus should not only be on treating, but also on curing. Have a program where the focus is on training more paramedics and First Response Personnel. There also needs to be a reduction in the price for drugs to the general public.

5. *Agriculture* – We need now more than ever to preserve our trees because for so many of their fruits are not given the chance to grow and be part of God's beauty and purpose. The trees help to preserve the environment – provides shelter and shade. There must be more attention given to animals that are butchered for consumption to ensure it is properly done. Focus on the usefulness of local plants is just as important as many of them, such as Thyme and Sage for example, can be useful in marinating and preserving meats and fish. Begin to produce more fresh water fish. Also, rent warehouses and store food and water in the event of a disaster. Remove

any taxation from food brought in by NGOs (Non-Governmental Organizations) which would not compete with local entities.

6. *Global Warming* - There is the potential for many of natural disasters to occur in certain countries even beyond the ordinary. These countries will be declaring National Crises/States of Emergency. Disaster-prone areas should no longer be inhabited by people, and there should be underground domes built in the event of heavy rains resulting in floods. Tsunamis, earthquakes and tornadoes will increase. The Disaster Preparedness Committees should seriously re-visit disaster-prone areas, observing closely the kind of disasters that are inevitable and determine how best to reach the general public and prepare them quickly! There should be at least an hour's training via the radio and television, as well as by phone. This should also be a common focal interest within schools and the work force.

7. *Education* - The cost of education to students at all levels must decrease so that the lower and middle classes can complete their studies. Government bodies need to also look into waiving fees for those who are unable to pay until they are working, and have a written agreement - a Document/Letter of Commitment. There needs to be a greater and more active focus on developing the gifts and skills of the youth in the schools. There is the need for more focus on the Technical, Arts and Montessori schools.

Let us prayerfully seek God's coverage, protection and mercy during the 8th and 9th months each year prophetically.

.

CHAPTER 6

CAN CHRISTIANS BE IN POLITICS?

This is a question that many are asking today. Can Christians serve in politics without becoming corrupt and ultimately lose their salvation?

We have seen many Christians enter politics and once they start serving, they compromise, begin to support the things they once stood against and "evolve" as they say. Recognize that man may feel he has "evolved" but God's standards, requirements and principles remain the same.

By speaking with many Christians who serve in politics as well as in diplomatic circles and other influential areas, they say it is very difficult to do so based on the way in which the secular operates. They operate using bribes and corrupt practices, especially when working with many of the influential, international bodies. Once they are dealing with such bodies/groups, to get financial backing or to pass a bill or even to get contracts, they have to do something in return – whether it is sexual favors or some other corrupt practice in order to get the support for their cause/bill/action.

When overseas representatives/managers/clients come to your country or organization to be convinced to support your country/government/bill/action they have to be taken for drinks – usually alcoholic. More demanding characters may require drugs and must be serviced. Failure to comply would mean losing your job/position or hinder your promotion. As a Christian, you shouldn't engage in either of those activities. Further to that, many of the activities would be planned on a Christian's day of worship – whether Saturday or Sunday – and you would be required to attend. Which means for a Christian, they would have to miss going to church services.

Partisan Christian Politician

Many Christians in politics, particularly when there is a conscience vote, are forced to compromise and side with their leader on issues that would come against the Bible, which is the Word that governs every Christian. Otherwise they would be viewed as rebellious, unsupportive to the leadership and anti-social, and be sidelined and unsupported by those within and ultimately would have to walk away and allow one willing to yield to the corruption to take their place. It is all about winning votes at any cost and get the support no matter what it costs you. So their choices are compromise or walk away.

Passing Resolutions and Bills

Even within the political and diplomatic circles, getting certain resolutions and bills passed that will benefit the people of the nation would mean going against your Christian principles while selling out to the real enemy who will come calling sometime in the future. So, for example, they will support and even fully fund your project to acquire the large factory that has been closed for years so you can turn it into the new children's home or community center in exchange for your supporting/voting for their abortion bill or legalizing marijuana bill or some other. They will even promote you as an ambassador or allow you to sit on 'prestigious' boards, or promote you to Senatorial/Ministerial level in exchange for your vote on their corrupt bill/action. They will even "pressure" the government to promote you into a particular government ministry stating that they have "confidence" in your ability to do the job.

Other Christians complain that it is difficult to get jobs in certain foreign services, because the job descriptions are tailored against their Christian principles and so they have to walk away from the opportunity to bring positive change.

Sadly, many in politics feel that Christianity is the only faith that they can be this bold to come against in such a manner. They are afraid of the other religions because of the money or influence attached to them.

Consider this. How do those in Public Relations and Media speak truth when their organizations lie and they have to present the lies as truth? What do they do?

Serve!

If Christians walk away from their assignment, who and the Salt of the earth and Light of the world? If men and women such as Daniel, Deborah, Joseph and Esther all served in government and stood without compromise and God promoted them, why then are we coming with excuses about serving in this capacity, when we have the greatest insight, foresight and solutions? Why are we retreating instead of standing?

Church Must Lead Global Change

Now more than ever the things that are happening globally – hopelessness, crime, and poverty – and it seems that politicians have no clue; they remain quite ineffective. All they are doing is trial and error. We are even now seeing nations signing peace treaties which are only there to strengthen the enemy's hand for the world to become an even more dangerous place.

Most secular leaders are now walking in open deception without realizing. Some of them will even bring God's judgement on the nation, the economy and even remove the hedge of protection around the leaders and the nation.

The question that many are asking, "Why are there so many religious leaders surrounding global leaders and there is no change? Why is that?

In days gone by, there were teaching priests like Hilkiah who would instruct nations and kings on the laws of God - the dos and don'ts. (2 Kings 22: 8 – 14)

2 Chronicles 15: 3 says: *"For a long time Israel has been without the true God, without a teaching priest, and without law"*

It is the Church that should be instructing the secular leaders on how to administer justice, how to have a peaceful nation, how to bring reform, how to help the poor and needy and how to bring about a reduction of crime and hopelessness; so that peace can be maintained within the nation.

If we look through many of the civic organizations and Rights groups, and see what they are doing, we will recognize that they are doing what the church should be doing, but that is because the church leaders have failed.

Light

The Church is Light! God requires everyone (including leaders) that call on His name, to walk in Light and must be a reflection of His light!

The lampstand God commanded to be in the temple was always to be light – thus the light would always be shining on the people. (Exodus 27: 20). However, in 1 Samuel 3: 1 – 3, it is clear that the lamp was almost out and should have been replenished in keeping with the directive of God. In addition to that the same Scripture reveals that the eyes of the leader in the temple began to go dim. So there was no open Vision – they became blind. This is similar to what is taking place in the world today.

However, take a moment to recognize that it was before the light went out, that God called Samuel. So He put Samuel in place before the temple and thus the nation, went plunged into utter darkness and chaos.

The problem that exists within the USA, the United Kingdom, Jamaica and the remaining Caribbean countries, many are blaming the politicians. However, the politicians are not the problem, it is the church leaders; many of the church leaders are not truthful to the secular leaders.

Let it be clear that a person can be a church leader – leading thousands and be very influential, but they don't *know* God! (1 Samuel 2: 12). The sons of Eli were priests but the Scripture says they did not know God!

It is the responsibility of Holy Priests (Pastors/Bishops) to atone for the sins of the nation. They must be led by the Holy Spirit, not by philosophies and opinions! Oil must always be in their lamps; they must always have a fresh revelation from the Word of God for secular leaders. They must live holy! If they don't then they will always lose the battle as did Eli's sons.

Furthermore, if they do not change, secular leaders will plunge into further error that will bring judgment on everyone including the priests!

When a nation fails to serve God, they will eventually serve un-Godly nations.

The Church and Market Demands

Regardless of the product, once there is a value and a need, there is going to be a demand placed on it. So if there is a need within a nation for security and protection or for gaining power, or for employment – regardless of the source, then a demand will be placed on solutions to those needs whether the solution comes from a positive source or not. So, for example, if a person does not believe in God, but they are sick and in need of healing, they are going to search for the healing regardless of the source.

Recognize that the world sees everything as dollars and cents. So making profit and maintaining power are the main, if not, sole goals. So in order to maintain power, they are willing to do anything including evil, as long as the opportunity presents itself.

The Market Driven World

We live in a world that is Market Driven and Competitive and we either get ahead or fall behind. We fight for space in "brand name"'/Ivy League schools; we fight for upper class honors versus lower class honors to graduate. Meanwhile, some join civic organizations, clubs or even sleep with the boss to get ahead. We even have persons auctioning their virginity in order to get ahead.

The Church should not be naïve, but instead create an environment to counteract the evil and people will come to the Church. Jesus is the ultimate App Creator, and He has an App for everything!

The absence of the power of God – which is the genuine and authentic source for healing and peace for mankind, result in the creation of a counterfeit – yoga, witchcraft, idol worship and so on. That propels the people into sin. So a politician or businessperson would not employ a suit-wearing obeah man/witchcraft worker/diviner, to advise Him using the "illegal" sources of witchcraft and divination, if the churches were listening to the Holy Spirit in order to know what to tell them in their search for direction.

What Creates the Market Need?

If there were no opportunities for our youth in terms of employment, they are going to seek after it and if they cannot find it, they are going to create them; and if you try to suppress it without an alternative for them, it is going to worsen and while they are searching, they are genuinely looking for power to protect them and for guidance, because they are not seeing a genuine, authentic representation of God's power to attract them to Him and the Kingdom and repel them from evil. So we as the Church need to shut our mouths, because we have suppressed the healing power, we have quenched and put out the power of the Holy Spirit, rejected the existence and Divine power of speaking in tongues, Prophecy, the Deliverance Ministry and the Manifestation of the Supernatural. This has resulted in our cessation of feeding the poor, creating jobs and have replaced the manifestation of God's power with PhD's, Theology and Philosophies. As a result, we have allowed a market to be created, where people are seeking alternatives. It is as if they are seeking for the generic drugs rather than the original and genuine article. Realize that a sermon without power is simply a bunch of words well put together

– it doesn't work anymore because people need to see the power of God.

Get Back to The Original Brand

We, as representatives of God's Kingdom, are called to empower, edify and to bring transformation. We are called to touch every aspect of society – bankers, politicians, the widow and the youth. We are called to teach the world Kingdom Economic Principles and the danger of making certain decisions without consulting God. We ought to establish training and empowerment centers within our communities. We are not called to simply occupy space and be irrelevant and ineffective. We are the ones to show people the way, teach politicians the dangers of making certain covenants and the impact of those decisions because God gives us insight, foresight and illumination; and it is no longer business as usual.

Light in The Marketplace

Every believer's ethical duty and diligence in the marketplace is to perform as though serving Christ, even as counterparts/coworkers may not be Christian.

Many times, Christians are the most difficult people to work within an organization; which ultimately sends the wrong signals or message; and it turns people off from employing them. (Ephesians 6: 5 – 9)

With the global problems being faced by every sector, including the financial, security and political arenas, and if the children of light don't rise up now, there are going to be some dark days ahead globally.

Matthew 5: 16 says, *"Let your light so shine before men, that they may see your good works and glorify your Father in heaven."*

The children of light should allow their light to shine within their organization, bring solutions for the organization without compromising. The main fact that they are part of the organization means that God has placed them there for a purpose; and if that purpose is not being fulfilled, then that door of access is going to close. Such persons need to ask themselves the question, 'Why am I here?'

Many secular organizations make decisions, which bring great hardship, security risks and/or suffering, while those who know the truth – the children of light – keep silent because of fear. They should not fail to carry out their function in helping society. If fear gets the better of them, then we are going to see anarchy, more job losses, poverty or more human trafficking! More laws will be put in place to violate Biblical Principles and our beliefs – regardless of our faith.

The Christian Boss

The Christian boss should lead by example in whatever area they are placed to manage. They can't be like the secular leader. Their main source from which to draw strength and direction in order to carry out their daily activities and to deal with the daily challenges must be GOD!

Many times, it is said that Christian bosses are worse than the unsaved ones. Christian boss, you MUST show mercy and compassion. You must understand that you are accountable to God, in the same way that God would hold a Pastor responsible for the flock. (Ephesians 6: 9)

Galatians 6: 10 reminds us *"Therefore, as we have opportunity, let us do good to all, especially to those who are of the household of faith."*

We need to look out for each other as Christians, not to become a clique, but to unite so that others will see the right example of the Light!

Christian bosses should not exploit the poor. You cannot be like the secular bosses who gain their wealth by dishonest means. The main reason why the world is going through this dark period is as a result of the fact that the children of Light have compromised for fame, money and power. Now we are reaping the benefits of that. Many have gotten access to make a difference but they have compromised.

The marketplace is crying out for Light! Remember, children of Light must use their money so that God gets the glory; feeding the poor, giving scholarships to children of those who truly need it. According to James 5: 3, we ought not to lay up our treasures for ourselves while people suffer. You have been blessed to be a blessing.

Christian Politicians

Every Christian politician should study Matthew 5: 13 – 16. They should understand that they are Kingdom Citizens and the metaphor of salt and light indicate the citizen's influence for good, as they work in the secular society. Any believer who no longer holds on to the Word of God, is of no use to God or man! Each Christian politician must recognize that they are to be reflectors of light which come from God. No light, if it is the proper one, can be hid! No one who walks in light, should embrace darkness. All should learn from Daniel. With all the plots from political associates, he remained true to God without compromise. Daniel brought solutions and he never bowed to corruption.

When children of Light see themselves as servants of Christ first, then the Spirit of Excellence will come upon us, to help your organization, your first goal is to please God. Then God will please the people.

Every employee must deal with his/her organization with honest, excellent service. Remember that your reward may not come from man in a Performance Appraisal or increase in salary; but in due season God will reward you.

Christians in The Marketplace

Every institution, every place of business, in fact, any environment/organization outside of home and church is considered to be The Marketplace. Christ encouraged us to be effective in the marketplace – to be the Salt and Light. We have the cure and we can show the way and the Truth and give guidance, wisdom and knowledge. A Christian in an organization who is simply working for pay and benefits but is not creating any impact is like a thief. Some of them say they are only going to follow their job description because no one is listening to them. But, what about that part of the Job Description which highlights Use of Initiative, especially when God has given you insight and foresight? In light of this therefore, any Christian who is not creating a positive impact within the marketplace, must re-evaluate their relationship with God. Many say they are Christians, but they have no relationship with God.

Impact

No boss will ignore a good idea. Not even king Nebuchadnezzar! When God grants favor and grace to a Christian to work in a particular organization, it is their responsibility to outline to the organization the weaknesses, the opportunities, the strengths and the threats. When Christians fail to carry out their functions then it creates a negative impact and significant fall out and we are now seeing companies making huge losses, falling out of favor and poised for defeat, meanwhile Christians sit and observe from the sidelines, putting their own jobs at risk.

Oftentimes Christians make excuses regarding secular organizations versus Christians. However, God did not allow any organization to be Christian or non-Christian. He allowed organizations to make a profit to create an impact within the community, so other people can be gainfully employed. A Christian's job in the workplace is not necessarily to preach to anyone per se, but for their light to shine in the organization so that it is clear that their foundation is built on the Rock and that God gives them the power to get wealth. Christians should be teaching them how to make profits. We are Kingdom Ambassadors; and an ambassador speaks on behalf of their kingdom regarding the best and most positive principle to utilize in order to maintain favor and grace. We must positively change negative culture within the marketplace, but most are allowing the negative culture to change them instead.

We are supposed to teach:

1. Godly Values and Business Ethics
2. Good Stewardship
3. Proper Management of the Natural Resources for the benefit of all.
4. Fair Distribution of Resources.

The priority of an organization or of the nation(s) regarding what their focus should be in a particular season.

No Excuses

Governments are focusing on (spending in) the wrong area. How can many nations have immense levels of natural resources (oil, gold, water) yet people are homeless and are eating out of the garbage?

Christians should stop giving the excuse that they are afraid to lose their jobs, and speak the truth about the revelations they are receiving via the positive and negative happenings in the organization. They must always remember that opposition is inevitable. For example, Daniel and Esther who served in various capacities of the political and national arenas. They never compromised because of the benefits available to them, but they kept their leader in line. They were never once fearful because they were confident in God. They saw their workplace as their assignment and we must learn from Jesus in the marketplace and how He impacted it. He was not afraid to approach fishermen, farmers, lawyers, the heathen, politicians, doctors and billionaires.

It is God's desire for organizations to be blessed and for leaders to be successful. A lot of companies are operating at a loss and they are simply looking in the wrong areas for the source of the problem.

Be An Agent Of Positive Change

Wherever a Christian works, their impact on the organization should bring positive change, growth and development. They should keep their boss (or the king) smiling even when other advisors are giving information, they must stand out because they have the right information. If they fail to do it, then their heads will also roll among the others when chopping block time comes.

Christians! Use the Gifts In The Marketplace!

There are many resources that God has given Christians to build nations, organizations and even the marketplace. However, many are spending millions in the wrong places in order to get solutions for survival. The gifts are spiritual resources given to Christians for the *profit* of all. [*Profit* from the Greek term – *'sumphero'* which means **'to** *bring together, to benefit, to be advantageous'*.] (1 Corinthians 12: 7)

Spiritual gifts are not to be buried or hidden in the ground. (Matthew 25; Luke 19) Many church leaders over the years have done a poor job of teaching their members who work in the marketplace – the public and private sectors – how to apply the spiritual gifts they possess, to daily situations they face, and how to use those gifts to build!

Surprisingly, even Christians who observe other Christians using their God-given gifts call them evil or crazy! Yet they listen the horoscope, engage in tea leaf reading, tarot card readings, palm reading and use other mediums and devices to gain information within the marketplace; and all these bring defilement!

The recent passing of the Flexi-Week law is an indication that Christians, wherever they are placed – need to utilize their God-given gifts to advise their employers and to make meaningful contributions. If even God rested from work, then we need also to follow suit. Not adhering to this will not help the economy; it will, instead, destroy the economy. When the dust settles, we will see whether it is mammon or God's Word that will triumph!

It is critical now, more than ever, for those who possess the spiritual gifts to begin utilizing them; advise their organizations on business decisions.

Investment Strategies

It is very critical for those within the private or public sectors to help those within their sectors to understand Times and Seasons; How/When/Where/In What to invest! They also need proper direction when there is going to be Market Expansion, as well as to make other major decisions.

As the globe darkens, gifts and talents will be more valuable than even academic qualifications. God used men like

Joseph, Daniel, Isaiah and Nehemiah to rebuild and reform nations!

Spiritual gifts go beyond religious beliefs. For example, many within the marketplace, God uses dreams and visions to speak to them for decision-making. But many are unable to interpret it or believe it is foolish and ignore the gifts; only to pay the price later! For example, God uses dreams to speak to us for six (6) reasons:

1. To provide God's answers to questions
2. To instruct us in the things of God
3. To warn us about unseen danger
4. To guide us away from wrongdoing
5. To save our lives
6. To keep us away from pride

God is always speaking but are we listening? He speaks even to political leaders and kings – on how to run their Administration.

The following are some of the gifts given to help within the Marketplace: (See page 131)

GIFT	SCRIPTURE	USE
Leadership and Administration	*Romans 12: 3 – 8*	Used for modeling, superintending and developing human capital and systems
Teaching	*Romans 12: 3 – 8*	How to explain and apply truth. There is a difference between the Gift of Teaching and Teaching as a profession. Not all Teachers have the gift to teach. Hence the problems in many of our schools today!
Giving	*Romans 12: 3 – 8*	The capacity to give beyond the normal expectation, supported by a willingness to do so and a high level of humility and grace without the expectation of something in return.
Word of Knowledge	*1 Corinthians 12*	Supernatural Revelation of the Divine will and plan, insight or understanding of circumstances or a body of facts by revelation that is without assistance of any human resource. It involves moral wisdom for right living and relationship. Word of Knowledge is best used in counseling, interrogation by Law Enforcement personnel, the Medical Industry and it solves problems

Word of Wisdom	*1 Corinthians 12*	Supernatural perspective to ascertain Divine means for accomplishing God's will in a given situation. Divinely given power to appropriate spiritual intuition in problem-solving. Gives direction. Best used in negotiation, the diplomatic, political and judicial fields forecasting accurate economic paths.
Discernment of Spirits	*1 Corinthians 12*	Supernatural power to detect the realm of the Spirit and their activities. It reveals the plans and purposes of the enemy and his forces – plots, plans and intent. Best used within negotiations, security, fighting terrorism, new businesses – revealing the persons actions and intents and whether or not they should be trusted. It prevents one from being deceived in a relationship or by politicians' empty promises!

Christians! Focus on The Kingdom!

Luke 17: 20 - 21 says: "*Now when He was asked by the Pharisees when the kingdom of God would come, He answered them and said, "The kingdom of God does not come with observation; nor will they say, 'See here!' or 'See there!' For indeed, the kingdom of God is within you.*"

Many times – even Christians – will ask the question, "What are Christians doing?" or "What is the Church doing?" However, the next time that question comes up, ask yourself, "What am *I* doing?"

There are so many Christians are focusing on the wrong things, such as, the world's ways of doing things, material blessings, their denominations, food, clothing and so much more. However, to be an effective Christian, we must focus on what Jesus focused on as His number one priority. Jesus' number one priority/focus was the Kingdom!

In contrast to expectations of the Pharisees, the Kingdom is not external and physical in the sense of being a political domain, but rather internal and spiritual. The Kingdom is within you and it is presently embodied in Him. Once there is a Kingdom there must be a King, and if Jesus is the King, we have to receive Him as Savior. Then we have to allow His kingly rule, not only in your life, but over your affairs, through your life and by your service and love.

Many say they are Christians, but operate independently of rule and principle. No kingdom can function without laws. God's kingdom functions with order and peace. Every nation has a standard of conduct for citizens to follow. If we are citizens of the Kingdom we have to submit to our sovereign ruler. For example, we cannot be part of a kingdom and do what we please. The world is crying out for the manifestation of Kingdom people to come on the forefront. Nations are failing! Politicians are failing! Economies are collapsing.

Mark 4: 11 says: *"And He said to them, "To you it has been given to know the mystery of the kingdom of God; but to those who are outside, all things come in parables…"*

The secret to growing an economy and turning a nation around lies within the Kingdom people. With due respect, many leaders are now turning to the rich for solutions to grow an economy. It will not work unless you embrace

Kingdom principle and Kingdom people. We are in a Kingdom era and only Kingdom Principles work in this era! The old ways are over! God wants us to have dominion over four areas just as Jesus did – **S.E.E.D**.

Sickness/Disease,
Environment
Economies
Demons

The Kingdom of God is about man looking to God as his Source and his Savior. It is never God's intention for man to live on Welfare, under oppression and loans from international lenders who dictate even the lifestyle that they ought to live. The first thing Jesus did was to empower the poor and to break poverty – moving man from poverty to prosperity which can only be done through Kingdom Principles!

One cannot be part of the Kingdom of God and not believe in prayer, fasting, or the salvation of a soul or be ashamed to identify whom they serve publicly. Many Christians are in positions of influence, but they are not playing an active or significant and vital role in society in any measure; and if you are a part of a kingdom, you are an ambassador wherever you go. Joseph, Daniel and Esther were never afraid to carry out their Kingdom duties.

Matthew 7: 21 reminds us that, *"Not everyone who says to Me, 'Lord, Lord,' shall enter the kingdom of heaven, but he who does the will of My Father in heaven..."*

The question then is, "Are you a part of the Kingdom?" Matthew 6: 33 reminds us to seek God first! As a Kingdom person, are you seeking God first? Your blessing and help are in seeking God first.

Many nations are now turning to drugs, immorality to get help and grants. That is their source of choice. But as

Kingdom People, we seek God first and He then reveals to us the secrets! Furthermore, Kingdom People must unite and help each other – not block and betray each other or tear each other down to get help. It is also imperative for us to know that regardless of what prayer we pray on a daily basis, we must pray that we come in alignment with God's Kingdom and that His kingdom will manifest in the earth – bring peace, joy, integrity, righteous people and a nation where families thrive!

Churches Should Be Wise in Business Dealings

Luke 16: 8 *"And the Lord commended the unjust steward, because he had done wisely: for the children of this world are in their generation wiser than the children of light."*

Every Christian should take note of this parable. How can children of Light allow the children of the world to be wiser? They are wiser because whether they are crooks or not, they are more consistent, more attentive and more diligent with what they go after or are seeking to attain.

Since 2006 the Church has been going through serious financial problems due to:

1. Mis-management
2. Failed Ponzi/Pyramid Schemes
3. Economic Downturn (especially the Recession of 2007)

Further to that, a number of Christians lost their jobs and ultimately their homes in the United States. Based on reports, banks began foreclosing on a number of churches. Many began to lose patience on churches that began defaulting on mortgages and said that churches are no longer viable for business unlike other organizations within the private sector which mis-managed and were given bail-out and other tax write-offs. The Church was not spared.

Reports state that in 2010, 270 mega churches were sold. In 2011 138 additional churches were sold. From then to date the number of churches that have been sold have doubled. Even some of the more popular preachers on television, their church buildings were sold. and to non-Christian individuals who in turn rented it back to the church leaders for exorbitant amounts. Furthermore, it has been reported that over 500 congregations filed for bankruptcy. Meanwhile, many churches have had to downsize locally and globally while most Pastors have had to walk away from full time ministry and re-enter the secular industries in order to provide for their families. Others had to resort to itinerant evangelism in order to survive.

Many Christians became embittered as they wondered if the word of God about prosperity truly worked as they saw the un-saved/un-Godly buying up their homes and church buildings while they could barely find money to buy gas to go to the Church. The main fact that it is taught that in times of famine God's people will prosper further complicated things because many were focusing on the prophecy without making contingency plans for the times and seasons in which they were operating. Sadly, many of the churches were getting into schemes/deals the Lord did not instruct them to enter, when they should have discerned that they were being duped by the world! God is still waiting on all the leaders – in the USA and the Caribbean and even Europe, to repent for misleading the people and for the financial calamity that shrouded the Body of Christ. If wealth transfer is to take place, then this has to be done now!

Many Churches have taken grants from private institutions so that they would not go under, but the criteria that were given with these grants forced the leaders to be muzzled! Some of them cannot even mention the name of Jesus within programs offered! Additionally, some church leaders were no longer looking to God to deliver them, but were instead looking to politicians to bail them out and as a result have had to be politically aligned in order to maintain their bail outs. This shows that the Church is no friend to the world and must seek to be wiser in their dealings and doings.

Moving Forward

The needs to begin to unite and pool their resources together. It is time for us to set up joint credit unions and the churches need to start renting spaces to each other without being afraid of any kind of competition. We are not here to compete we are here to *complement* each other. If in the private sector they can rent space from each other to do business, why can't we? Many churches are being charged hundreds and even thousands of dollars to rent a store front. Meanwhile many church buildings are locked up, opened only once or twice per week while paying maintenance and utilities. So, the property – the resources are not being fully utilized and is thus being wasted. The money wasted in this manner could have been used to build schools and training facilities to empower communities. Sabbath-keepers do not use the facilities on Sundays. Rent the facilities to Sunday Churches – we are serving the same God.

The Church needs to stop allowing the world to milk us out while the people within the churches are suffering. We must be good stewards of what the Lord gives us and allows us to access. We must use our bargaining power and begin to do business with each other! Even the animals do a better job of that. Christian Media are more expensive to do business with than the secular media!

Church, it is time, not only to rise up but also to *wise up*!

CHAPTER 7

WHY BLAME THE POOR?

There are many times in the society when things are not going their way they should, and politicians as well as other business interests, are quick to blame the poor for the poverty that exists within the nation. Meanwhile, other significant factors are ignored, such as who the decision-makers for the nation are and what decisions have been made regarding the nation's resources. We fail to educate our people, yet we are quick to speak negatively about population and birthrates and agree with other external parties that population growth is our main problem. As a result, they try to bring solutions to curb that birthrate.

If we seriously want to address poverty, then why don't we look at the inequality in the distribution of resources? Why not have an amendment to the constitution that will allow us to set term limits for politicians, board members and other advisors? How about the nation having a political system that will not stifle new builders from bring new solutions? Are we willing to have a system in the country that does not allow for a rich versus poor scenario and genuinely deals with equality? Will we have a system where even the poorest among us will have an opportunity to succeed? Will we have a system where financial institutions will cease to reject the business ideas of potential borrowers so that they themselves can find a way to use those ideas for their gain? Will they cease use regulations and cease implementing laws to stop those with inventions and ideas from bringing them to the fore – while they capitalize on it for themselves? Even the Credit Unions are not what they used to be.

The poor are often being met with regulations to bond, bind or shackle them because the politicians and other business leaders in the nation know that once the poor become empowered financially, it would reduce the profitability of the rich. Furthermore, the poor would make better choices at the polls in choosing leaders.

How about lowering the Consumption Tax and increasing the Minimum Wage? Cut out temporary fixes like cutting grass in public places and create real jobs. Put funds into restoring broken families and carry out other more meaningful activities such as Sending Social Workers into Communities, Giving people Milk Powder, Cornmeal and other nutritionally beneficial items.

Why not invest in building more clinics, begin to train more nurses on the community level? Give doctors duty-free concessions on SUVs, particularly if they are working in the rural areas.

Every parish should have a security check point that vehicles must go through with detectors to detect illegal firearms.

For small businesses, utilities are among their biggest costs. Why not set a flat rate or have the government subsidize those items so that they can stay afloat and grow to provide more jobs? The profits will therefore be kept in the country. As it stands, the profits are being channeled out of the country.

Why are the drug lords, extortionists and those silent/hidden partners not being dealt with the way they should be, when their actions interfere with foreign exchange and trade?

Food for Thought

1. Provide Cash and Capital contribution to build more labs and research centers to study our fruits and herbs for creating more jobs and farming opportunities.

2. Begin to write off the debts for the poorer class and in particular for the small businesses.

3. Shift our number one focus from building roads to focusing on family-empowerment.

4. Begin to listen to God's voice for growth and strategy. (Jeremiah 17: 5 – 11)

5. Reduce all or eliminate some bank charges.

6. Cease having two nations where there is one for the tourists and one for the local populous.

7. Have free tuition for tertiary level students studying agricultural science, social work, medicine and geologists and bond them for 5-year bond to serve their country.

8. Have an instant freeze on land/property divestments.

9. There has to be stricter laws governing the prices on property rentals and how companies price the goods that have been sitting at their landing points for over 90 days. Ex-factory prices need to be reviewed.

10. Have stricter laws to streamline the Tourism sector and stop the All-Inclusive Hotels from blocking the members of the local communities from benefiting from the Tourist activities and stopping them from playing their part in building the communities.

11. There needs to be a major campaign to encourage people to get married.

12. Begin to move the zinc fences from the communities in Third World countries.

The responsibility for the poverty does not lie solely on the shoulders of the poor. Others in society must take responsibility too.

Have Mercy on The Poor

Many times, within society, we hear statements about growing the economy. We are told about goals and targets, but in the midst of growing an economy, the poor are not in the equation. They are long forgotten by politicians and business people and even some global agencies that promised to deal with charity and such issues. Oftentimes the advisors themselves have no idea what it is to be poor. They simply make logical decisions oblivious of the realities. Sometimes you will see statements made by various countries regarding poverty eradication. They even have international level conferences where they discuss and make statements to those assembled and based on the statements, you wonder if they know where they are living.

Decisions that have been made to make the investors happy meanwhile the poor are very unhappy, in fact they are dying under pressure.

Sadly, the younger generation are drowning under the debt, burdened by the weight of what the previous generations leave behind. This is not a legacy, this is a yoke.

God showed me a vision where a group of politicians and investors were crossing a river. They were all excited at the prospect of new business deals, but in the midst of all that, the Lord showed that there were two generations. The older generation were trying to catch up but they could not. The younger generation, while in the river trying to cross, the politicians were trying to extend their hands in a simple gesture, but it was only for show. They did not realize, however, that in crossing the river at the pace to grow the economy and please the investors, there were different levels of the riverbed and the children were drowning, and the only alternative was for the Church to step in and save them. The politicians and business people did not even realize what was happening. There are other meanings, however, they will be discussed in articles to come.

One cannot drive an economy at the pace of investors and international lenders. Even when the nation passes the test, the people are failing the test. If we want to see the economy grow, we must put plans and measures in place to rescue the poor.

"1 billion children worldwide are living in poverty. According to UNICEF, 22,000 children die each day due to poverty.

In 2011, 165 million children under the age 5 were stunted (reduced rate of growth and development) due to chronic malnutrition.

The World Food Programme says, "The poor are hungry and their hunger traps them in poverty." Hunger is the number one cause of death in the world, killing more than HIV/AIDS, malaria, and tuberculosis combined."

The Bible specifically and strongly outlines in Proverbs 31: 8 – 9 *"Open your mouth for the speechless, in the cause of all who are appointed to die. Open your mouth, judge righteously, and plead the cause of the poor and needy."* Take a look also at Proverbs 22: 22 – 23, Psalm 12: 5 and Isaiah 10: 1 – 3, which is a very serious scripture.

No nation must have any laws or decrees that would bring any kind of oppression or further hardship on the poor. When God establishes a leader in office, God judges them based on the burdens borne by the poor of the nation. In fact, that is what defines one's legacy or the duration of the Administration and when we focus on pleasing the investors and the poor is forgotten, then it brings serious consequences and curses over the nation.

Solutions

The country urgently needs to revisit the economic policies that are pursuing.

1. Jamaica's Government needs to set up Jamaica Monetary Fund for the Poor (JAMFP). The US and other nations can also do the same. This will assist the poor, for example, with basic items, home furniture, and education, burial and health bills. Provision of Nurses' Aides for seniors - especially for the Disabled (children and adults)

2. Co-ordinate with the Private Sector to donate skimmed milk powder and diapers to the newborn babies of poor families.

3. Have a flat rate on water for the poor.

4. Have a flat rate for electricity in low income areas.

5. Reduction of Sales Tax

6. Increase the Minimum Wage

7. Restore and revamp the Free Zone

8. Build more shelters for the homeless

9. More support for Farming – not only in promoting it as a viable means of income earning, but also in subsidizing the cost of tools/equipment

10. Lower insurance rates for second-hand vehicles

11. Let there be no tax for new companies for the first 3 years.

There is much more we can do for the poor, particularly if we want to see the next generation rise to meet the challenges and overcome them for the growth and development of the nation.

Reducing Poverty Through Giving

Reducing poverty is the role of each person within society. It first starts at the individual level. Then the civic organizations and the Church each have their roles to play. The role of government is to create an environment – putting laws and welfare structures in place – to facilitate or encourage assisting the poor and vulnerable.

The number one reason for the perpetuation of poverty is that as a people we no longer give. There are certain blessings that can only come through giving. Being poor is not an excuse to not give. In Luke 21: 1 – 4 and Mark 12: 41 – 44, the Lord spoke about the Widow's Mite.

Giving reveals the state of our hearts and the level of our love, mercy and compassion. If every individual practices giving, poverty and crime would be reduced. It is interesting that oftentimes, the poor are more receptive to giving. So when God gives us wealth, favor and grace, it is so that we can extend our hands to others. There are people who have a great deal of goods, clothes, food in abundance, while their neighbors are going to bed without food, clothing or even medication.

Jesus drew attention to the fact that the Widow gave even in her state of poverty. A mite then was the smallest and lowest value coin. So it was not the value of the coin that mattered, it was the sacrifice and the level of commitment to giving that was important to the Lord. It is imperative to note that we are not to give and then call attention to the fact that we gave. We must teach our children from an early age, how to give. Psalm 41 reminds us that God will even heal you or raise you up from your sick bed as a result of your giving. People have even been resurrected from the dead as a result of their giving.

God's Welfare

The Law of Gleaning (Leviticus 23: 22) was God's Welfare Program for those who did not own land and found themselves in hard times. They according to the law, could reap the corner of the fields, and gather grain which they would then uses for food. Even our farmers and business people no longer practice giving from their harvest or their business profits. This is the reason our farmers and business men are feeling the heat.

There are many within our nation also that will be spending millions in travelling expenses, despite the fact that there are so many forms of technology today that can allow them to host meetings online or engage in Conference sessions and the money saved from travelling could be used to help the poor.

In order to reduce poverty, executive level staff and politicians can donate a part of their salary to the poor, cutting down on their large entertainment package.

Leviticus 19: 10 reminds us that caring for the poor is a mandate from God – that includes strangers and aliens. Everybody must care for the poor! There are major organizations that make huge profits while people are sleeping right on their doorsteps without basic necessities. Banks have homes rotting away while people are sleeping on the streets. People have homes with several rooms they are not using, but find it hard to board a student.

Giving Breaks Famine

The number one criterion for breaking barrenness, famine and poverty is giving. In order to escape the oppressive systems of international lenders and to free the nation from further recurring interest, giving is the only way out. There are things also that those who are wealthy may need, that cannot be had or easily acquired by natural means, but can be received as they give. Giving is the only thing that goes into your future, creates a harvest and shows us that we have conquered greed. When we give to the poor we lend to the Lord. God promised that He would repay and give back to us with interest. God even outlined that people should not steal, but work to give to the poor. (Ephesians 4: 28) Even when we are putting on dinners and functions, we are required to give to those who cannot return the favor. (Luke 14: 12 – 14)

God will judge nations with regard to giving, as giving is the only way out in this era. Many times, we will pray without getting as a result of lack of giving. So it is time for us to start giving – poor or rich – regardless of your circumstances, and we will begin to see change and the reduction of poverty.

The Poor Responsible for Their Financial Decisions

The poor are forgotten within the society, and the drastic local and global decisions that are being made do not include the input or thought of the poor. It is therefore critical for the poor to make better decisions if they want to see drastic changes.

First, the poor must begin to have a different perception and perspective on things. Mark 8: 23 – 25 reminds us that Jesus had to literally pull the man away from his community before his eyes could open to see the truth. Sometimes you have to pull away from your family, your friends, your culture, the curse and the mindset of the people in order to see clearly and get the right perspective or else you will only see disfigured images. Poverty stems from a state of the mind and the state of mind can bring blindness. The poor need to begin to see like the rich – they make and save money. Oftentimes the poor waste money, spending millions on a funeral and not one cent on self-empowerment. The poor use social network to waste time and money – using data and phone credit gossiping and idling; while the rich use social media to make money.

The poor wastes money on appearance to show a false lifestyle, and the rich sells the things the poor uses to maintain the false lifestyle. Do you see a liquor stores, abortion clinics, payday loans stores, pawn shops, tattoo parlors, bars, or brothels in the wealthy communities?

The poor needs to stop making choices based on emotions and short-term benefits, and particularly when voting. They need to cut down on fast food and popular brand names and buy more things wholesale.

The poor needs to make decisions with their children and grandchildren in mind. The rich have no political loyalty. If the poor continue to be "die-hard" supporters of a party they will become poorer. The poor need to understand that politicians serve only what benefits them. The poor need to look to God as their source to take them out of the financial spiral. This is the time for the poor to get wise. The rich will use the money of the poor to invest it in assets that they will rent back to the poor or sell to them at exorbitant prices.

The poor will take their money and buy drugs – crack, cocaine, marijuana; but where are the crack houses? Certainly not in the wealthy communities. Very few wealthy people are going to spend their money to buy that. Instead, most will either invest it for their children's education, or to set up a business they will pass on to their children.

The poor spend millions on phone cards and credit; millions in witchcraft to fight each other, and refuse to give anything to the Lord who can break the curse they are living under.

They would pay to buy false hair, lashes and body parts to create a false image and in the process, they are empowering the politicians and businessmen who in turn create a credit system that would keep them in debt – and they (the rich) do not use their personal credit for anything.

We Need to Cry for The Poor

Jesus' main purpose on earth was to equip the poor and voiceless for them to have a better life. The poor have been forgotten. Many leaders have been put greater hardships on the poor to increase the rich. Proverbs 31: 8 – 9 reminds us to open our mouths for the voiceless, defenseless, poor and needy. Sadly, even for many churches, this is no longer the priority.

Every church, civil government, family and leader – regardless of political affiliation, will be judged on how they treat the poor. There are many, who because of policies and systems, are now homeless, their families are broken and they are becoming hopeless. Some are treated as if they are

148

prisoners of war according to Micah 2: 8-9. They are laughed at, scoffed and treated with disrespect and dishonor, while people use them to manipulate them and gain power.

The poor need to make wiser decisions.

Breaking the Cycle of Poverty

Poverty is a stubborn issue that affections millions worldwide, and the solution to this problem seems to elude many. There are several reasons why poverty exists, but in truth, poverty cannot be dealt with unless individuals and nations address the spiritual aspects of this issue.

When we disobey God's word (Deuteronomy 28), it leads to both spiritual and physical poverty; causes lack of ideas, solutions and revelations. When the earth tries to generate wealth by omitting God and His principles it leads to economic decline, deception, lack of integrity in the market and brings us into unholy alliances in an effort to gain wealth. We must recognize that we cannot separate the physical from the spiritual - they are connected.

When we build on God's governmental principles, we have His perfection, and economic recovery and success is not in the hands of an individual, but in the hands of the Almighty God!

Jesus showed us in Mark 6: 30 – 44, by using five (5) economic keys.

He **Established Order**
He **Took** the resources they already had
He **Broke** – that is, He divided the resources
He **Gave** – that is, He allocated and distributed the resources
He **Blessed** – that is, He relied on His Father to multiply the resources.

Jesus never allowed political/partisan issues to determine how he allocated the resources to whomever was present; He did what was best with the resources to achieve the best results for all! Furthermore, if God does not bless the resources – regardless of how small they are – then it will all be unfruitful! In addition to all this, He picked up the fragments and used them – allowing nothing to be wasted. The fragments can represent the poor, and even the small businesses and other small entities. He knew that even what seemed insignificant had a purpose and function in the grand scheme of things and should not be discarded!'

Disobedience and Poverty

The root cause of poverty is Disobedience, which results in Crime, Sickness, Lack of Growth, High Interest Rates, Poor Ratings, Market Condition Instability and Job Loss. Additionally, on a national level, we would be in Economic and Financial Bondage to international lending agencies. This means we would not truly own any assets.

Interestingly, the number **50** – from a Scriptural standpoint – means Jubilee. At this time, the lands and assets that were divested or taken from the poor would be restored to them.

Some Keys to Come Out of Poverty

Seek God First – Matthew 6:33. Seeking brings understanding, wisdom, power, capacity and ideas. Not seeking leads us to poverty, failure and deception.

Tithe – Malachi 3: 8–10. Tithing is not for the Pastor to get rich, Tithing is for YOUR BLESSING! It is your obedience to this instruction that will bring your blessing from God! You are obligated both to God (Tithing) and to the Government (Taxes).

Matthew 22: 21 says *"... And He said to them, "Render therefore to Caesar the things that are Caesar's, and to God the things that are God's." (See also* Matthew 17: 24 – 27)

1. **Forgive – Matthew 18: 18 – 35.** Failure to forgive will bring you to poverty.

2. **Learn To Fish** – Do not be totally dependent on handouts! Handouts have the potential to lead you to compromise your value, principles and integrity and ultimately lead you to poverty.

3. **Righteousness – Proverbs 14: 34**. When we walk in righteousness (right ways and right standing with God) it promotes. Sin, especially sexual sins – common law relationships, adultery and so on, affects us negatively.

4. **Faith – Hebrews 11**. One's faith in God will generate the provision and break poverty. It will remove the mountain of poverty. Remember, unbelief creates mountains!

5. **Read!** Oftentimes we don't read and we miss key information and revelation that can move us out of our current state and into financial freedom!

6. **Pray Daily** before you make certain financial decisions. Lack of prayer brings financial deception and schemes.

7. **Cease Unnecessary Spending**.

8. **Cease the Get-Rich-Quick Mentality!** Speak to people with integrity to advise you on financial matters.

Those who desire to see change and success within the nation. Fast for three hours each day asking God to intervene in the affairs of the nation and the lives of its people.

Legalizing Marijuana Opens Gate to Poverty

Ezekiel 34: 29 says:

And I will raise up for them a plant of renown, and they shall be no more consumed with hunger in the land, neither bear the shame of the heathen any more.

Without a doubt, God created plants, herbs and vegetation for the healing of the nation and this is something I have always advocated. Some even believe that Revelation 22: 1 – 2 is making reference to marijuana and that it carries twelve (12) benefits to heal the nation. However, if there are those who want to argue on that basis, they have to be very careful that it will not open a can of worms that they cannot shut.

Legalizing marijuana for medical use of its by-product is a fair issue. However, a general legalization will have major negative effects; including opening the door for Latin American countries to lobby for the general legalization to the coca plant which produces cocaine; and to those in Asia who want to lobby for the general legalization of the by-product of the opium plant which is heroine.

Medically, Cocaine is used as a mild stimulant to suppress hunger, thirst and pain. The leaf does not cause the euphoric and psycho-active effect associated with the use of drugs.

What the nations needs to do is not focus on marijuana, but focus on all the plants /herbs and their positive effects and so nations would give special permits to persons at all levels in the society to cultivate it for medical purposes.

Many will argue that many are being arrested for the use of marijuana, but legalizing it is not going to reduce crime it will do just the opposite. If the nation believes that legalizing it will reduce records that people will receive when they get caught with marijuana, then amend the law and treat the offense in the same way we would treat a traffic violation.

We commend one of Jamaica's Universities – the University of the West Indies and its Department of Chemistry who are carrying out research on our natural resources. and What the nation should do if they want to see change in the economy – or a new economy, is give them more money and resources, to help them be more effective and efficient in what they do.

Addictions

Anything to which a person is addicted whether good or bad, will become your idol or will control you! All things we do, eat or drink must be to the glory of God. (1 Corinthians 10: 14 & 31)

If we want to reduce the number of persons being arrested for possession of marijuana, we need to look beyond the possession of the marijuana, and look also at the conditions that exist for those persons, then have a plan of action to deal with that so a repeat is either limited or eliminated.
Why do they do what they do? Some will tell you that it is because of peer pressure – they want to prove that they are tough enough; some will say they have proper mentor – father or otherwise; some say they want to be wise like Solomon! Others say it is a sexual stimulant, especially when they soak it in alcohol.

Gone are the days when people used to smoke banana leaf. Interestingly, as a child, I saw people give marijuana to their dogs to eat, because the dogs were too passive and they would become the most aggressive and dangerous dogs around. Can we take a hint from this?

Ambassadors and other 'elite' are now going around and are trying to entice nations, to legalize marijuana and destroy the youth because of greed. Many of them proposing the legalization are surrounded by security personnel; so they are not speaking from a place of commonality or true understanding.

Would you go to any medical personnel to be treated when you know they are addicted to marijuana?

1. What about the police and the gunmen when it becomes legal?

2. What will happen to our children in the schools when it becomes legal?

3. What will it do to unemployment levels?

4. Will situations of rape increase?

5. How will we deal with someone recovering from addiction to a different drug, will we introduce them to marijuana as an alternative?

6. What effect will it have on pregnant women and those who want to get pregnant and also on the unborn child?

7. How will it affect our athletes, particularly since 'Third-World' nations are always under scrutiny for performance-enhancing drugs?

8. Will it find its way into the culinary world – in our food and drink?

9. How will it affect the nutritional balance in an individual's body?

10. If this issue goes through the gate, then will we see other issues being put to the fore for legalization – pedophilia, bestiality and so much more?

Remember, anything you are addicted to becomes an idol. Every idol carries a spirit.

Who Will Help the Poor?

"Therefore, because you tread down the poor and take grain taxes from him, though you have built houses of hewn stone, yet you shall not dwell in them; you have planted pleasant vineyards, but you shall not drink wine from them. For I know your manifold transgressions and your mighty sins: afflicting the just and taking bribes; diverting the poor from justice at the gate. Therefore, the prudent keep silent at that time, for it is an evil time." (Amos 5: 11 – 13)

The Old Testament prophets who would cry out regularly on behalf of the poor! They cried out against corruption, injustice, the court system, and businesses and against the wealthy and powerful who would manipulate the system and place the poor in more debt, distress and discontent!

Those prophets would speak to the queens, rulers, judges as well as business owners and various categories of society on behalf of the poor.

Sadly, many prophets today, who function under the New Testament, are not speaking on behalf of the poor. Most of them are caught up trying not to be poor! Meanwhile, others get caught up trying to display their level of accuracy in determining who next is going to be 'blessed'!

Today's prophets need to realize that the Prophetic goes beyond prophesying houses, cars, and land, and that there is a responsibility to speak on behalf of the poor, the fatherless and the widow, and they better study who a prophet is if they are going to deem themselves or answer their calling as Prophet!

Don't tell me that God has nothing to say about the injustices meted out to the poor? Don't tell me that you are afraid of persecution? Don't tell me that you don't want to offend your favorite Party or biggest Tither?

It is the duty of government – whether Monarchy or Democracy – to be the public servant and help the poor. (Psalm 72: 1 – 4)

The treatment of the poor globally has come up before God! Millions are dying of hunger, while millions more are wasting precious resources!

Most political leaders globally, promise to improve the lives of the poor – but how many of them deliver? In different countries systems are set up to prosecute those who are assisting the poor instead of encouraging and facilitating the action! When the poor get poorer, they get more desperate! It means that whatever they have to do to survive they will do it in order to live! Have you ever been desperately hungry to the point that you even contemplate taking something to eat even, if it does not belong to you – just so that you won't get sick or even die of hunger?

When the poor get poorer, many of them are denied good health and proper education, hence they are denied of certain jobs within the society. In other words, some do not have a certain level of access! Even institutions that were created to help the poor no longer listen to the poor. They listen to some retired consultants who are collecting a lot of money for speaking nonsense and have never been or do not remember being poor!

Even those in top positions in institutions that are set up to monitor and regulate oppression of the poor, tend to focus mainly on ensuring that their resumes are up-to-date so that if they lose their current jobs, they can be hired next door.

It has been said many times, that if we truly care for the poor, then we need to put the poor in positions of authority on Boards and Committees to watch over their own hard-earned money. Why is it that only a certain category of persons have been put on the various Boards and Committees? There are many brilliant men and women who are poor, but are more than capable of functioning and managing within such groups on a leadership level.

There are many who are still doing their best to assist the poor and needy. We commend the Catholic Church and other Denominations and Ministries that are doing their best with the small resources they receive from time to time. (Acts 2, Isaiah 58, Malachi 3: 8 – 13)

We encourage all the poor to give their 10% - the Tithe - so that the Divine Principle can function in your lives, and so that the Church can do more for you! Regardless of your station in life, nothing beats giving – especially unto God Who is your Ultimate Source!

Every nation is encouraged to reduce the interest rate for housing to the poor who are paying back their mortgage; and governments must ensure that pensioners can collect their pension every month – not a part or none at all! They have worked for it already!

From Poverty to Prosperity

*"Beloved, I pray that you may **prosper** in all things and be in health, just as your soul **prospers**."* (3 John 1: 2)

This Scripture alone shows that God wants both nations and individuals to prosper. But in order to move from poverty to prosperity, it is not about the natural/physical way you would try to achieve that. We can only achieve it God's way! So regardless of the political tug-of-war over who owns the slogan, both parties are encouraged to read the Bible again and see what it takes to achieve either. True Prosperity cannot come unless Psalm 127: 1 - 2 is in place.

In order to move from poverty to prosperity, we will need to look at the spiritual first before we even look at the physical. In every Scripture on the topic, God sees poverty, oppression and greed as evil! In order to deal with evil, the spiritual route has to be taken first!

Blessing and prosperity are first corporate before they become individual; thus, if God does not bless the nation or the city, then the individuals within it will struggle.

In Judges 6, when Israel was struggling, there was one called Gideon, who prospered while nation became impoverished, and God clearly outlined to him the root cause and what they should do to move from poverty to prosperity.

Likewise, when Egypt disobeyed God and refused to serve Him, God allowed Pharaoh's house to prosper while the nation delved into poverty. It was the greatest wealth transfer that took place – from the people to the leader. The only thing the people were left with were land and labor; and they voluntarily had to give up both for survival! Pharaoh relocated them and then charged them 20% tax on production. So, if the people want to move from poverty to prosperity, they will need to repent and return to God instead of placing total dependency on politicians.

Prosperity comes to those who seek God! (Matthew 6: 33) Many global leaders no longer seek God for wisdom and power to get wealth; they instead seek the modern-day

Midianites, Babylonians and Egyptians for advice, which only brings more poverty.

If prosperity is the physical manifestation of God's blessings, then the environment must first be created spiritually. Then God will give dreams and visions, ideas and inventions for Job Creation.

True prosperity comes to those who trust in God and those who obey God's Word! (Joshua 1: 8) Prosperity is not a right, but a privilege and a responsibility. While leaders in a nation have the responsibility to create the environment for prosperity physically - the choices and covenants they make with other countries – those choices will affect us whether negatively or positively.

A country can only truly become great when it becomes industrious from within, its greatest investments are in the assets within (including the people), the profit remains within the nation and nation's currency remains stable.

Other factors affect prosperity and can cause poverty – unfair distribution of resources, social injustice, bad management, lack of vision, sin, greed, un-forgiveness and the education system. Develop the people to create wealth!
Tithing also brings prosperity, and if nations begin to tithe to poorer countries, or give 10% of tax collected to not-for-profit or religious organizations and create sustainable development, then you would see the reduction of crime and many other issues affecting the nations - there would not be the need to build more prisons.

There cannot be prosperity within a nation where the focus is on large contracts, big businesses and impressing first world nations, while ignoring Family – the first line of government.

Prosperity will also come when you have the right persons in the right positions! Not everyone is a builder! The ability to build is a gift of God.

There are many wrong/bad things that have been done to people by other people that were never rectified. If things of the past are not resolved then that will also hinder prosperity! Therefore, the negative things done by past Administrations that have not been resolved/fixed will have negative repercussions on present Administrations and the prosperity of a nation.

We absolutely need to move out of poverty and into prosperity, but it can only be achieved when Godly principles are applied!

There is no way a nation with so many natural resources and so many empty buildings for it to be poor!

Value Within What You Call Garbage

Many times, when plans, ideas or suggestions are made by some within the society, many quickly label what they do not understand as garbage. The greatest value is often found in the garbage, the dump, the reject pile. In some countries, it is almost impossible to get a job on a garbage truck as a collector. The greatest problem we have in society is that we are quick to discard some valuable things into the dump heap! Society needs to have more recycling hubs than they do garbage heaps! This is a two-fold situation: There is the literal garbage and the human beings who some regard as garbage that are pushed aside and ignored. It is said that "One man's trash is another man's treasure." If society is going to change, then we are going to need to get our hands dirty by sorting through the 'garbage'.

There are some expensive and antique furniture, valuable equipment and useful scrap items that can be found in the garbage and scrap yards. There are even some machines that are in use today that companies have stopped manufacturing but are still useful; and the parts can often only be found in the scrap yards!

Jesus showed us the importance of what we consider as waste, fragments or crumbs in the Parable of the Five (5) loaves and Two (2) fish, that for proper management of your economy with the small resources, there is greater value within the crumbs even after distribution takes place. After distributing the loaves and fish, the team collected twelve (12) baskets of crumbs. The number 12 signifies **Government**.

A nation will never realize its full potential unless we start to pick up the crumbs instead of trampling on them! Focusing on the large investors to restore an economy will only bring the nation further into problems and greater debt. Focusing on what we call "crumbs" will bring greater benefit within a nation.

Very shortly, the greatest place for investment in the garbage dump; and the greatest revival in terms of bringing solutions and change to a nation will come out of people who are labeled as such by society. In many countries, the garbage dump provides employment for some. Surprisingly, in what is called the inner city or ghetto, even in the homeless bring the greatest glory or fame within a nation.

Pricelessness in The Trash

Every area of society is important. Many times, governments fail because they try to associate themselves only with like-minded people or people they consider specialists in a particular area who are failing! Unless, as in the book of Nehemiah, we rebuild the Dung Gate – a place to where we carry our filth. Many investors even tend to look only within the upper echelon of the community. But those within the communities which are run down and are falling apart will bring greater return on investment. There are artefacts, ancient relics and discarded but valuable items within the dump.

When God is going to restore a society, he raises up/deals with the dump first. If the dump was not a place of value, why would scrap metal be so expensive? Scrap brings new business! Even solutions that people have received to bring change - that may not fit within society's textbook formats and diagrams - have been rejected and the problems continue. If leaders would revisit their dumps, archives and File Thirteens, they would be surprised at what they find.

Search the Dump

Every household, organization or nation must have a proper storage or 'dump' site to place what they consider to be junk or trash. Then take time out to carefully search that site from time to time, you would be surprised to see what you find. You might find gold, antiques, paintings, silver, letters, articles and other items of great value that you never realized you had. Maybe some of the things you will find will stop you from spending/wasting money trying to find something new or from re-inventing the wheel because what you needed was already there in the 'dump'!

Even visions and policies that have never been executed or implemented could be found and will result in less stress if implemented! You may also find other items that can be given to a humanitarian effort.

If each person starts from within their household, to see what items of value they possess, they would be surprised. Nations can only go forward if they begin to search the 'dump' and see what value they can find in the 'garbage' that can help to move the nation forward.

There is a famine coming and only those who are willing to search and embrace the 'garbage' and see the value within it will be able to bring change.

Jobs Decrease, Prostitution Increases

A 2001 Study funded by the International Labor Organization – International Programme on the Elimination of Child Labour (ILO-IPEC), found that children as young as 10 years old were actively engaged in prostitution, catering to tourists, strip clubs and massage parlors.

The economic difficulties and social pressure contribute to the prevalence of Child Prostitution. Many hotels are developing new packages that facilitate the child sex trade, under the guise of professional or business class services. Some offer this VIP service on the basis of helping them de-stress from the current economic situation, or offering entertainment.

While the law of the land must be obeyed, it is absolutely ironic that in some nations, there are costly efforts to remove the "little man" from the sidewalk, (who doesn't have a proper permit) stopping him from selling his biscuits and juice to support his family. When they are removed, they migrate to the areas of the nation where they can access the money they need and sadly, prostitution is their solution.

Looking at Jamaica, for example, while they are attempting to fix one problem and cut down crime and make Jamaica more palatable for tourists, we have in fact shifted the problem to another section on the society and creating an even greater problem for ourselves.

Check the classified section of the national publications and you will see the extent to which prostitution has saturated the nation. It is even more ticklish because most of those involved are the 'elite' of the society.

The Positives and Negatives of Prostitution

The only seemingly positive aspect of prostitution is increased revenue for those engaged in or supporting it.
The negatives include but not limited to:

1. Increase in the spread of HIV and other STDs
2. Increase in Divorces and Family Breakups
3. Increase in Abortion
4. Increase in Absentee Fathers
5. Reduction of Life Expectancy
6. Increased number of Missing Children
7. Increase in Sexual Immorality
8. Increase in the number of Pedophiles and other Undesirables entering the country

Economic Reform and Job Creation

What more will it take for the politicians, the Business sector and the Church to see that we are going in the wrong direction? It is causing great humiliation on the nation! Do we want more countries to impose visas on Jamaica due to our economic situation and wrong policies before we wake up? They ignore helping the small businesses in employing more people. They are more interested in helping the foreigners who are not keeping the money in the country anyway! We are going after the foreign exchange and this increases its demand! When this happens, demand for foreign exchange increases which makes them increase the cost of the foreign exchange and put us in a deeper economic rut.

Potential Strategies for The Caribbean

Many countries particularly in Europe and North America, want to influence other countries to accept the new norms that they are putting forward. Jamaica is special because of the strong Christian background of its people, and influences many actions and decision of other Caribbean islands. Many world-renowned people have come out of Jamaica, who are influencers that have impacted many other nations - Marcus Garvey, Bob Marley and Jimmy Cliff to name a few.

The Jamaica Gleaner and The Jamaica Observer, Jamaica's two (2) main newsprint media houses, should look at implementing several things to boost sales and help the community. They should advertise by throwing it out to the schools advertising summer programs to encourage the students to become young writers. This would also help them to understand the English Language better and help them improve in English Literature thereby allow for greater passes in these subjects.

1. Should other media houses adopt that model, it will help those in the Universities majoring in Journalism and Communication to find jobs and get the necessary experience.

2. Such a move can also provide special rates to companies, whether large or small, such as discounts and for longer contracts that will attract an even bigger discount.

In addition to that, they can:

1. Visit homes within the inner city and rural areas to deliver newspapers free for a month and sponsor children within these homes whether they are in school or not.

2. Have fund-raising events for children in inner city and rural areas.

Furthermore:

1. The government should develop free, public Training Seminars to help jobless, inner city residents. To cut costs and to show that they care, the government officials and members of the opposition should employ their own skills and teach these seminars.

2. All inner-city residents and 'uptown' business persons should make an effort to renew their minds, so that uptown employers can be more confident in employing inner city job seekers.

CHAPTER 8

CRIME AND DEVELOPMENT IN
THE CARIBBEAN: JAMAICA

If the nation is truly serious about effectively addressing and dealing with the problem of crime, the nation will need to face serious truths and hard facts on the issue. It is not about implementing new laws, or allocating more financial resources to law enforcement or building more prisons. The fact of the matter is that every member of the society must take responsibility for the role they each play in the development of their community and nation.

Poverty and rebellion are the basic instruments of crime and lack of jobs, lack of training, broken families and a general lack of opportunities all contribute. In order to deal with the problem, we must proactively achieve the first four (4) Sustainable Development Goals as agreed by the member states of the United Nations, of which Jamaica is a member. Those first four (4) goals, when achieved, can make a profound contribution to the elimination of crime. When that is accomplished, there will be significant reduction in blue and white-collar crime.

Those first four (4) goals are:

1. **No Poverty**
2. **Zero Hunger**
3. **Good Health and Well-being**
4. **Quality Education**

Goal 1: No Poverty

When this is achieved in all forms, for example through raising the minimum wage and reducing land tax, it will have positive impact on their emotional and spiritual well-being, which will help to decrease crime and violence. Poverty affects even the mental health of a person and minimizes their participation in crime and violence.

Goal 2: Zero Hunger

We need to begin focusing our efforts on our Agricultural Industry and begin to reduce the price of food, cut down on waste, and lease land to the people that they can farm, and remove the bureaucracy that they can be allowed to get their products in the marketplace. They can also issue fertilizer at low or no cost, and cease divesting the land so that it can be utilized for rearing livestock as well as farming. Furthermore, giving free basic items such as skimmed milk powder for the babies can go a far way in ensuring that they do not go hungry. Remember, a hungry man is an angry man – at any stage.

Goal 3: Good Health and Well-being

Establish more clinics, begin training more community nurses and nurses' assistants and make available good medication at low or no cost – no generic medicines. Engage in home visitation of the elderly and physically challenged to give vaccines and other medication as needed. Have properly trained Family Planning Counselors go into the communities to counsel the Youth on getting an education first before positioning themselves for family.

Goal 4: Quality Education

We must have more technical schools for those who have skills. Literacy programs must be brought back – that similar to J.A.M.A.L. (Jamaican Movement for the Advancement of Literacy). Change the approach to Basic School (Kindergarten Level) Teaching and employ the Montessori model. Have empowerment sessions to broaden the mental scope of the young people and give financial assistance to High School and University graduates until opportunities for employment present themselves.

Focus for Achieving

The focus must now be on four (4) Ministries – Finance, Health, Agriculture and Labor and Social Security.

The number four (4) is significant and symbolically represents Creation, Seasons, Direction, Rule/Reign and the Planetary Bodies. Nations have to be aligned with God's design of the Universe and how He ordained business to function.

Solving crime will require these four (4) sectors. Private and Public Sectors, the Church and Civil Society must work together. The Church can maximize its building use by offering them as Counseling and Training Centers. Meanwhile, the Private and Public Sectors in conjunction with Civil Society can engage in Job Creation, Training and Giving.

God's Will for Jamaica

As the nation goes through the motions of Labor Day, and what it currently represents, there are many Jamaicans who are unaware of how it came to be and somewhat disconnected from its true meaning and purpose.

Before 1961, May 24 was celebrated in Jamaica as Empire Day in honor of the birthday of Queen Victoria and her emancipation of slaves in Jamaica. In 1961, Jamaican Chief Minister, Norman Washington Manley proposed the replacement of Empire Day with Labour Day, a celebration in commemoration of May 23, 1938, when Alexander Bustamante led a labor rebellion leading to Jamaican independence. The 'labour' here has nothing to do with a political party, instead it speaks of the hard work and those who worked very hard to the point of personal sacrifices to see the nation achieve independence, growth and development.

Until May 23, 1971, Jamaican Prime Minister, Michael Manley promoted Labour Day as a showcase for the importance of labor to the development of Jamaica, and a day of voluntary community participation to beneficial projects. Since then, Labour Day has been not only a public holiday but also a day of mass community involvement around the country.

Many may not be aware of this background because Civics and Jamaican History has been kicked out of the Jamaican school system and if our youth do not know where we are coming from then they will not know where they are headed.

Labour Day is more than a weekend celebration. We should use this Labour Day as a time of reflection to recognize and evaluate where we are coming from as a nation, where we are now in terms of true national growth and where we are headed as a nation.

How can we talk about Focus on Children when Abortion is being presented as an alternative? How can we Focus on Children when the nation's leaders cannot even make a decision on its own – following the policies that others are pushing? How can we Focus on Children when we are not even leaving an inheritance for them – divesting everything in sight? How can we Focus on Children when the family values have been eroded so significantly – particularly through anti-family economic policies? The family, which is the first line of government has been sorely neglected by both parties!

There is nothing against children and the development of our children and youth. Quite the opposite! There is unwavering support of anything we can do to develop our children and youth. But we cannot effectively develop them without a proper foundation being put in place to support what we need to do for them.

Jamaica's Ministry of Education, Youth and Information can make an invaluable contribution to the development of our children and young people, for example, by having the schools throughout the island, engage in Labour Day projects for public display, that showed the history of Labour Day, the importance of the work of those before who contributed to Jamaica's History and the positive changes, and also get their ideas on how they think the nation can move forward.

Moving Forward

God is looking for leaders – both political and otherwise – who are willing to enquire of His will for the nation! It is God's will for a third political party that is vibrant, willing to unite people beyond tribalism. The nation has been kept in tribal politics for so long that it has become almost cultural. Meanwhile, other nations laugh at Jamaica and dictate to Jamaica that it is their way or no way at all – and

Jamaica has to simply accept that! That is unacceptable! It is not God's will for Jamaica to depend on any other country as a way out, but to instead, develop a blueprint from among the people to be the next financial hub or place for family!

It is not God's will for the children to be slaughtered. But because of the decisions of the leaders in every category, while they use it to score political points. It is not God's will for the nation to join the Caribbean Court of Justice (CCJ) as the highest court of appeal, when we do not even have justice within the local justice system. Stay with England and fix our justice system.

It is God's will to have a constitution for the people with checks and balances and separation of powers.

It is not God's will for the nation to divest everything including our beaches, but instead to create opportunities through health, educational, and agricultural infrastructure, as well as Tourism.

God has given the nation of Jamaica everything to create jobs locally, so that the nation is not completely dependent on any country to be its savior.

Spiritual Reform

Our nation cannot and should not continue to look to other countries for their blueprint to fix our nation's problems. There have been many advisors over the years from different countries and we have divested practically everything, leaving the next generation with next to nothing. We need leaders who will not focus on personal legacies, but instead make decisions in the interest of the nation. We need leaders to rise up who will empower locals and utilize their gifts and talents for the benefit of the nation's development. We do not need Singapore's blueprint to change our nation when we have good people with good solutions at home. Jamaica is certainly not short on talents, solutions and ideas. However, what we are lacking is the will to empower and utilize our own. We are still of the belief that anything that comes from overseas is better and this has been bleeding the country over the years. There cannot be economic, judicial or security reforms unless we first have Spiritual reform. Where the foundation is cracked and polluted, we need everyone - from every category and strata of society to engage in spiritual repentance for spiritual renewal to take place. Then we will see the pouring out of God's Spirit upon the nation – particularly among the youth who will rise with new visions and dreams and build. It will be one that will fit the culture of our people, and one that is for Jamaica, not for a political party. Unless the feet and the fragments of the nation (that is, the common man and the broken who are being overlooked in society) begin to rise, we will continue to lose out on golden opportunities in favor of our nation.

We need leaders with the spirits of Hezekiah and Josiah who will rise and enquire of the Lord themselves, Who will then reveal to them His plans and purpose for the nation. It is not about a leader's plan, it is about God's plan. Only when a leader or Administration seeks the Lord (2 Chronicles 26: 5) then will we truly see prosperity within a nation – because both come from God. Prosperity does not come from natural reform without the Spiritual reform. (That only increases other problems.) Spiritual reform allows other nations to come to us and give to us not to take from us or infiltrate us.

Prosperity does not come from outside it comes from within.

Spiritual reform brings unity, effectiveness and the synergizing of the Government of God, the Civil Government and the Family – which is the first line of government.

When will we see a leader who is bold enough – not afraid – to call the nation into atonement for change who will challenge the priests as in 2 Chronicles 29: 3 – 5, to remove the rubbish from the Holy Place and sanctify themselves?

Call a regular, Spiritual Cabinet retreat, praying and seeking God for His intervention, and that He will break the political instability that plagues the nation.

When will we see a government who will begin to Tithe from the taxes they collect and use it to help the poor? (2 Chronicles 29: 24 – 27)

When will we see politicians who will deal with the social ills of our nation, and begin to go into the communities and create opportunities to prevent our people from looking into prostitution or other un-Godly activities as a solution?

Our leaders need to be like Hezekiah who taught the people, and like Jehoshaphat "... *he sent his leaders ... to teach in the cities of Judah. And with them he sent Levites...and with them ...the priests. So they taught in Judah, and had the Book of the Law of the Lord with them; they went throughout all the cities of Judah and taught the people.*" (2 Chronicles 17: 7-9)

Fidelity to the Word of God brings blessings. It is time to prepare an inheritance for our people.

Looking at Jamaica

Many people have been turned off or have become bitter about the direction in which our country is going. We see the various comments being made in the social media about this little rock! Some are embittered about the fact that countries which we surpassed in years gone by have surpassed us in practically every area!

People have even cursed the country! But let it be known that there is nothing wrong with Jamaica, it is the people!

The land is not what makes the nation – the people are the nation!

Let us examine the negative and the positives of our nation:

Negatives

The mindset of our people generally holds the nation back. The issue is not about gender, age or the existence or not of 'dinosaurs'. You may be young and still be a dinosaur in your mindset! Furthermore, the amalgamation of logic and arrogance are rife and have become the biggest obstacle to the growth of the nation.

1. The Dependency Syndrome has to go. We feel an entitlement as if somebody always owes us something!

2. The Pirate Syndrome has to go!

3. We are too quick to embrace anything or anyone foreign and we negate the value and capabilities of our own people.

4. We are too quick to embrace gifts and deals, not realizing that these are oftentimes Trojan Horses that are deployed to bring defeat to our nation.

5. We need to check motives so that we will not be plundered in the long run. We have allowed foreigners to know more about us than we endeavor to know about them. Some even know places in our own country better than we do!

6. Many still have the mentality that one's capacity to speak the 'Queen's English' is a sign of common sense and intelligence, and also that the opposite is true. Some, because of their capacity to retain 'big

words', speak over the people's heads and think this to be a sign that they are intelligent and the general public is stupid. Take note, the churches within the nation are also a part of the syndrome and the culture.

7. The worst of Jamaica is found in those who think they have arrived. The old Jamaican saying goes "Dish towil tun tableclaat". (In English: "The dish towel has become the table cloth") It means that someone has received a promotion that they did not deserve or do not have the skill to perform.

8. We are a religious nation, but we are not Spiritual. There is no depth to our beliefs. Many say they know God, but many don't study His Word and many others do not believe He even speaks to us. There are those who even believe the devil is more powerful than God!

9. We are not a reading nation and we have short memories!

10. Generally, our very education system does not encourage us to think outside the box, but instead conform.

11. Lack of confidentiality.

12. The Political Arena is in need of revamping! There is need for a New Political System because the present is outdated and has done its time. When new, young people enter the playing field, there is very little flexibility or scope for change for the nation. In the same way that our country fails to engage new entrepreneurs and inventors, likewise our politics is not ready for radical positive changes as things stand.

13. There is the need for Managers with the skills to implement strategies and do so fearlessly, rather than simply pushing paper.

14. There is no accountability in any facet of the nation, there is only the passing of excuses and treating the public as if it is blind or stupid.

15. Many want to lead and nobody wants to follow; they always feel they can do a better job than the person in the job.

Positives

1. Jamaicans always excel when they are put into new or different environments!

2. We are very resilient, and we bounce back from hardships quickly.

3. Our people are generally warm and loving.

4. Those who would be considered simple, and those who have not had the full benefit of the education system remain those who are most humble and still reveal the better qualities of the nation.

5. Some within the Private Sector still have the potential to bring positive changes to the nation.

6. The Jamaican Army have a great deal to offer in terms of rebuilding the nation.

7. Grace Kennedy's performance and expansion globally show us that Jamaica can do it!

8. Many in the Jamaican Diaspora have been flying the flag globally, while many of them have been ignored because of politics.

9. Our Sports and Music Personalities, as well as internationally-based Jamaican entrepreneurs, have certainly represented the nation well.

10. Jamaicans are visionaries! Some have exceptional ideas to be realized.

11. If Jamaica can do so much on the World scene – Medicine, Law, Music, Sports – why can't we achieve even more locally?

Let us think on these things!

Divestment: Jamaica's New Threat

"And Hezekiah was attentive to them, and showed them all the house of his treasures. . . Then Isaiah the prophet went to King Hezekiah, and said to him, "What did these men say, and from where did they come to you?" So Hezekiah said, "They came from a far country, from Babylon." And he said, "What have they seen in your house?" So Hezekiah answered, "They have seen all that is in my house; there is nothing among my treasures that I have not shown them." Then Isaiah said to Hezekiah, "Hear the word of the LORD: 'Behold, the days are coming when all that is in your house, and what your fathers have accumulated until this day, shall be carried to Babylon; nothing shall be left,' says the LORD." (2 Kings 20: 13 – 16)

There is nothing wrong with divestment, but it is critical for us to seek God and know with whom we must enter into any agreements, covenants or investments. When going into agreements with any other nation, a country must look into that country's system of government, beliefs, religion and policies, including their human rights records.

How do we prevent our country from being infiltrated? Divestment for investment purposes is not about creating jobs, or addressing environmental concerns. A nation has to do serious research and look at the various consequences for the nation should the covenant or agreement be made.

The problem that Jamaica is faced with now is the advice that has been heeded by leaders of the nation – past and present. The economy is now suffering the way it is because they have divested all our core assets and the nation has become worse, and more devastating to our people. The electricity/energy industry, the national airline, the airline routes and many other things – divesting all these have put the people in a difficult place. Which of the divestment activities have benefitted the nation? Not one!

Furthermore, it sends the signal to the world that Jamaica cannot manage and is making Jamaica a laughing stock. But it is not a management problem that is affecting Jamaica; the problem is political! There is politics in everything – even in areas where politics ought not to be. Everybody has to 'eat ah food' (get a piece of the pie); and the nation's spiritual inheritance has been sold for the proverbial 'plate of stew'! Even the religious men have to remain silent because many of them have 'eaten a plate of food too'! The perception of religious men that is held by the politicians is that they are money changers so they (the politicians) don't need to listen to them.

Logistics Hub at Goat Island

(There was once talk - in fact – contention about) The main fact that there is contention about the development of a logistics hub in Goat Island, is an indication that there must be something deeper happening. In the same way that Jamaica can borrow money to build roads and other infrastructure, why not borrow the money to build its own Logistics Hub, so that there can be a future for the next generation? Get all the trained Diaspora to contribute their talent and other resources. We can do it ourselves! When other nations invest at this level, Jamaicans get the scraps of labor positions, but they do not want to have Jamaicans in positions of authority. Furthermore, the money they make from the deals do not stay in the country. So the country is being raped of its valuables.

Is there gold, oil and other valuables which the nation is not being made aware of? Items which can take us out of debt?

Do foreigners know more about what is in the nation than its own people do?

Are we being penny wise and pound foolish?

At the end of the day, whoever puts up the cash calls the shots. Will we see our laws begin to change to appease investors? Will it be, for example, Birth Control laws and the Reduction of the Birthrate by any means necessary? The takeover of all crown lands? What new monuments and street names will we be seeing in the near future? Who will be setting up offices in the nation next? Will there be security concerns with regard to our North American neighbors?

A nation that refuses to seek God for direction is much like someone driving a vehicle without any sense of where they are headed, and not knowing where to turn, where the dead ends and detours are and which paths have potholes. Many say, "We don't need God, we have a GPS system" and they depend on that manmade system. But remember that the GPS system can also lead you to a precipice!

Jamaica Can Have Its Own Logistics Hub

I love Jamaica and I desire to see its people reach their full potential individually and nationally. Jamaica possesses all the resources to take our nation out of its current economic situation.

I have always felt that the nation possesses tremendous resources and that there are some who want to rob the nation of its land, resources and wealth. Many of them already know the valuable resources that exist within our nation. The leaders over the years do not discern, but they also refuse to listen!

1. The Goat Island Logistics Hub situation goes beyond environmental issues. If the Chinese are successful in acquiring the lands, it can be a gateway for serious problems ahead for the nation. There is nothing wrong with a logistics hub, but it must be owned and managed by Jamaicans and we do have the capacity to do it.

2. How will the ownership of the Goat Islands by the Chinese affect the Sovereignty, Culture, Religion and Political system of our nation? Will their acquisition be the last straw that breaks the camel's back?

3. With the track record of the Chinese concerning public health issues, and in particular, Air Pollution, their treatment of the Aquatic Environment, in addition to their death tolls and treatment of the environment, won't that put our island and its people at risk?

4. For every major investment there must be clear business and strategic plans for the properties, and none have been put to the fore. Will we see more gambling, immorality and possibly a military base as a strategic place .in the Caribbean? Will we see the imposition of visas for John Q. Public?

5. While we may not know the magnitude or nature of the agreement with Jamaica, considering the present economic situation we are in currently, as well as

the environmental aspects, what will the monitoring mechanism be?

6. Isn't 'giving away' the Goat Islands also a matter of giving away our territorial rights? Jamaica is made up of several island masses. Will we see Negril, Lime Cay, the Pedro Cays and the Blue Mountains go? What is nothing sacred in Jamaica (anymore)? Shouldn't divestment of this magnitude be decided by the people of the nation by a Referendum?

Important Points to Note

This is not the first time that a foreign entity has sought the rights to utilize one of the many Cays that are part of the archipelagic boundaries of our maritime State. We should recall the illegal drilling for oil several years ago; clandestine attempts to scout for other precious minerals; and legitimate proposals for underwater exploration off the coast of Jamaica. Both legal and illegal attempts to gain access to potential resources within Jamaica's maritime borders indicate that this is a tremendous asset that ought to be carefully managed.

The current plans are part of a long spate of divestment, privatization, rationalization, fire sales, and other sales of important Jamaican assets with little, if any, benefits accruing to the people of our beloved country.

If we should take stock of some of the sales/divestment/privatization we can see the significant changes that have taken place in our land over the years.

In the 1970s

1. Bauxite/alumina resources were mismanaged and there was no proper planning. As a result, that

industry is now dormant and the market has shifted to working with other countries.

In the 1980s

2. Under a deal with the IMF, through bad advice, the then government sold all overseas assets belonging to Jamaica, including prime real estate held in New York, Toronto, and London to foreign entities.

In the 1990s

3. Jamaica Mutual Life Assurance Company, Jamaica's premiere insurance company, was divested to foreign entities and no longer exists in Jamaica.

4. Air Jamaica, Jamaica's only national airline became privatized – private investors funded it.

In the 2000s

1. Jamaica Public Service, Jamaica's only energy company, was divested to foreign entities.

2. Air Jamaica, changed hands several times, was divested to foreign entities and no longer exists.

3. National Commercial Bank (Jamaica) Ltd, Jamaica's only local bank was divested to foreign entities.

4. The Cement Company, Jamaica's largest producer of high-quality cement and other building materials was divested to foreign entities.

This is by no means an exhaustive list of assets that the country has lost. What it shows is that in general, every industry has been affected by divestment, and divestment to foreign entities has impacted both private and public sectors. Ultimately, the people of the nation pay the price, while many of its economists boast about their deal-making prowess, and after their failures, many of them were rewarded with more lucrative jobs/positions. Jamaica has sold off several state-owned businesses. These include entities such as sugar factories and not only the national airline - Air Jamaica, but also the accompanying routes and the much sought-after terminal access to London's Heathrow airport. Many of these assets the country will NEVER be able to re-purchase. Today, all our treasured national symbols including our money, passports and our flags are manufactured outside Jamaica.

The key to Biblical Economics is to repent and make atonement for Mismanagement. It teaches about atonement for mistakes and standing up to responsibilities. It teaches us to strive to be an owner not a renter.

There were good visions in those times that should have been fought for. It is important to listen to God. The advice they were taking at that time was not Godly, yet those failed advisors were rewarded. When God is going to bless a nation, He gives us land and business. But when the nation fails, we begin to lose. Jamaica should be used as an example to other Caribbean countries and Third World nations. The same thing that happened to Jamaica, happened to them also.

The most recent proposal to lease or sell Goat Islands is one that can only be described as ludicrous. We do not know what mineral resources exist there but we do know there is a great potential. Therefore, the only deal that could be acceptable is one that ensures a majority of funds or other proceeds from exploration would be retained in Jamaica; and funds that are removed should be sufficiently taxed to benefit the nation; and employment opportunities for both skilled and unskilled persons should weigh heavily in our favor – since we know the Chinese penchant for using their own mass workers in foreign projects.

What do we own? What will drive industry for the future? What sectors of production can we say we are proficient in? How will our people obtain gainful employment? What will sustain us as a country? If we continually rid ourselves of our most valuable resources and assets, we can only succeed in destroying the country. And when the camel's back is broken, our people shall surely perish.

Yes! Jamaica needs its own Logistics Hub! However, Jamaicans must also recognize that they can do it!

Reconstructing Jamaica For Growth

Our nation is now in a critical position, and moving forward for the purpose of growth. There has to be innovative ideas –we have to now think outside the box! The nation is very good at talking but poor at implementing. The nation's focus in the wrong areas and money has been wasted in the wrong areas and on the wrong things.

Budget Presentations have been heard every year, of how many millions/billions are going toward development, but we are not seeing it in the end results! If the country is serious about change and accountability, then the time has come to create a new Agency to monitor all government spending, contracts and infrastructural development.

For this Agency pull people from the various sectors of society – in particular from the Private Sector – Lawyers, Bankers, Accountants and different ones drawn from the various facets in our communities. All this Agency would do is scrutinize and investigate all the relevant documents and systems of operations and publish in the Newspapers, their findings and receipts for all the things on which the government spent the taxpayers' funds for the purpose of accountability and so that John Q. Public (great and small) will have a clear picture and understanding of what is going on in the area of government spending. Many times, we hear of how much money is being spent to improve the lives of the poor in our country but there is no evidence of that.

Another area of change needed is that more homes – state of the art homes too - must be built in each parish for housing children, particularly those who are being abused. What is so difficult about investing in re-opening the factories that have been closed down and start again to make the clothing and furniture, and engaging in a huge marketing campaign to bring awareness and quite possibly and the interest of foreign buyers for our products!

Before the nation's Health Industry crashes, we need to invest heavily in state-of-the-art equipment – not just focusing on the Kingston Public Hospital (KPH) or the University Hospital, but focus also on May Pen, Montego Bay, St. Elizabeth, St. Thomas, Portland, Mandeville, St. Mary and Nuttall Hospitals. Revive and invest in the Clinics within the communities and that will create jobs for many and help to alleviate the traffic into the hospitals.

The time has come to help small hotels and create major facelift and beautification, if we want to be and remain competitive globally.

How about building a bridge from Kingston Harbor to Port Royal – right across the sea?

Why not re-locate the Jamaica Defense Force's Coast Guard to St. Thomas and turn the current building in Port Royal into a Hospital – especially since a Hospital is needed in that area?

Why not:

1. Upgrade and equip the Port Royal Fire Station?

2. Expand the Police Station in Port Royal; and instead of being Marine Police – relocate the Marine Police to St. Thomas and have Foot Patrol and Tourist Police who dress in bandana and not the regular Red Seam?

3. Re-institute the Ferry Service?

4. Set up a Wi-Fi Internet Café with multifunctional copying equipment that the children can utilize it?

5. Build an Entertainment Center with Basketball Court, Lawn Tennis Court, and Food Court that can host culinary competitions, and/or have a place set up specifically for water sports particularly for children?

6. Set up Conference Halls and Rooms for large and small Conferences – whether Faith-Based or otherwise?

So, Port Royal would be a 24-hour tourist area.

In addition to this:

1. The entire Harbor View area needs a facelift

2. Construct/Rebuild a Cinema for the Harbor View area.

3. Transform the old Versair building into a 24-hour Museum with food stalls along that strip with a greater variety of our culinary creations – gourmet and international foods.

4. Use J. F. Mills, The Jamaica Cement Company and the General Penitentiary for field trips and charge a fee which will go towards helping to maintain and sustain our Children's Homes.

5. Why not re-vamp and expand the JAMAL Program through the joint efforts of the Churches in the nation and the Government, and include subjects like Proper Parenting, Grooming and Etiquette?

6. Agriculture, Civics, Information Technology and having a Uniformed Group (Scouts, Girl Guides, 4-H Clubs, etc.) should be mandatory in all Secondary Level Schools.

There are so many things that can be done to make changes in and for the nation at low costs. Furthermore, we cannot afford to divest anymore of our nation, particularly our historical sites! Divestment is an act of laziness and it sends the message that we are incapable of managing our own resources.

G.A.S. For Crime Reduction

The rise in a nation's crime rate calls for drastic measures to be taken. We must recognize that nothing will be accomplished until we find the root cause of these actions. We need to look at economic, political and most importantly – spiritual issues; the same spiritual issues some pretend are irrelevant and are of no consequence.
We need to ask some serious questions:

1. Who are the winners and losers when Crime is reduced?

2. Are monies being paid to increase crime? If so, by whom?

3. From where are such monies coming?

4. Is the crime tied to maintain wealth or to getting rich or getting power?

5. Why is that over the years there is a trade off because where violent crimes decrease, road fatalities increase?

6. Is there sabotage or undermining within the government that influence the increase in crime?

Spiritual Views

Why are certain geographical areas problematic? We need to take a closer look at the parishes/states/provinces and their activities. It is always said that where problems and fights exist, great blessings exist also; and that is a spiritual fact. We call those fights and problems distractions.

In those areas the secrets and the resources lie that can potentially turn around the nation's economy – oil, gas, gold and other resources within the earth. It could also mean that it is also the place to establish global economic centers.

When crime rises within a nation, there are strongholds and for every stronghold there is a strongman. For every strongman to operate there are portals that open. For a portal to be open and negatively affect a nation they must be given authority – which we call Legal Right!

To stop that, we would need to have the highest authority within the nation to make a decree against it and asked God to intervene. We probably need to call upon the Governor General, the past and present Prime Ministers along with the Church to shut the door.

G.A.S.

It is not a lack of academic qualifications that causes us not to have this issue of crime resolved. We have the Security Forces, numerous Ministers and various experts that have brought different solutions to the table, so we must now move away from the normal way of learning to reduce crime! We must begin to look at **G.A.S.** for reducing Crime!

G.A.S. carries with it a threefold focus:

Guidance
Assistance
Substance

This is what is needed to truly address the issue of Crime and to take on the challenge of Crime Reduction. This was the focus of Ezra's Fast in Ezra 8: 21 – 23 called the "Guidance and Focus Fast". It deals with issues of Security and brings protection, as well as direction, tactics and strategies and exposes the plans of the enemy.

Fasting brings Spiritual Breakthrough. The nation needs spiritual breakthrough! We need healing and restoration!

A spiritual problem needs to be addressed spiritually; and we are not speaking about a Prayer Breakfast where rituals and formalities are carried out! We are talking about genuine atonement for things people have been doing wrong!

We cannot fight crime and win unless we divorce ourselves from any unclean thing – law makers, security personnel, politicians, business men all have to be free from the occult. (Read the account of Achan in the Book of Joshua.)

We must fix the Justice system! We also need more judges who understand spiritual warfare!

Every institution needs to engage in Daily Devotions if genuine change is going to come!

As in 1 Corinthians 1: 25, we need to look at these following four (4) potential points of solution:

1. The Foolish Things
2. The Weak Things
3. The Base Things
4. The Despised Things

Incentives for security forces.

We need to give a fair performance incentive to reduce crime that is not based on how many people are killed or how many persons are arrested! It must instead be based on how they transform the community.

There must also be a reward system to reward the true crime fighters. Oftentimes in some organizations, only the commander or the manager gets the praise.

We also need to look into bringing the army on the frontline. They are based in several parishes; and they must mobilize accordingly. We may even have to consider a 6-month power of arrest to be given to military!

The nation also needs to have tighter controls around our sea coast.

Idle Hands and Minds: The Root of Crime

If we are serious about dealing with the crime that is plaguing our nation, then it is the responsibility of everyone within the nation to get on board. The number one problem influencing the issue of crime is lack of opportunity for idle hands and minds.

Many times, we have heard that Jamaica's workforce is unqualified so we should open up to expatriates. **That is not true!** It is, however, the responsibility of both private and public sector to train our local workforce. Most workers are only given the opportunity for training when they will soon be retired. Jamaica has first class workers but they are not being given the opportunities nor the respect – an offshoot of colonialism that anything (or anyone) that comes from overseas (foreign) is better.

There are so many empty lands and lots in Jamaica where nothing but bush grows there; and the government needs to start cleaning it up and build malls, houses, additional roads, more hospitals. They need to go around with the Solid Waste Management team and check the lands they have deemed unfit and see what can be done to utilize these properties effectively. They need to get the infrastructure going again thus creating jobs and get the real estate going. More factories need to be built - the Garment Factory needs to be revamped and made productive once more so that we can revive the garment industry in Jamaica and begin to export.

The Opportunities

We need to put the idle hands and minds to work, create hope again and you will literally see the crime diminish. When we fail to create opportunities, then the gunmen will create their own jobs and opportunities – contract killings, guns for hire – we all know the deal.

How about a collaboration between the Ministry of Agriculture, and the Ministry of Health? Get them to plant lemons, herbs, fruit trees, peanuts, corn, even wheat, and make tonics from roots. These are billion-dollar businesses that can also create opportunities for the idle hands. We have the potential to be the Health Capital of the world.

We have natural talents – musicians, actors, dancers and other wonderful talents in the nation. The Nigerian film industry – also known as Nollywood – make over US$590 million annually in an industry that is not even properly managed. Over a million people are employed in that industry. They are even getting support from the World Bank. We, on the other hand, have a grand and historical theatre rotting daily. Every year, we put on a few festivals for the year and that's it. It's time to move past that now. We need to stop riding on the wings of Bob Marley and Usain Bolt's fame and do more than we are now because the nation's potential is immensely greater than that. Nobody has to leave their country to come to Jamaica for Jerk anything, because they can download the recipe from the internet!

Gunmen, Put Down Your Guns!

Every gunman must know that his life is not in his own hands, it is in God's hands! Every one of them is on borrowed time. Witchcraft and guards cannot protect them! Every gunman must value life. If somebody else pays you to kill whether a businessman or politician, don't you think they have someone lined up to kill you too? The man who pays you to do the work is a gunman too.

Every gunman needs to answer this question. What lesson are you teaching your children when you live a life of crime? Think on that and write down ten (10) things and think about it for the next ten (10) days.

Nations need to start a project for children who are sick with terminal illnesses and get those who remain idle to be a part of the project.

Ask those owners of these idle hands and minds what they would do to bring joy to the lives of these children.

Ask them if one of their children was sick with a deadly disease, would they allow the circumstances to change their lives permanently.

How many rich men or politicians do you see in prison? Gunman, before you kill another person, think about your own children or family members, because even if you should get away from man, you cannot get away from God.

There was once a project done in Jamaica by a distribution company who employed for the month, most of the idle hands from the inner-city as casual workers/laborers. Literally, not one gunshot was fired in the area and it was discovered that some had never even set foot in a bank nor did they have a bank account. They were so thankful and appreciative that they became the security and no one could steal from the company.

Toxic Environment! Take A Stand!

With all the happenings in the nation these days, the nation has become a toxic environment as a result of happenings over the years. This is not just limited to politics, it is a culmination of activities of every person in the nation and each individual now needs to examine his or her contribution to the current state of the nation. We cannot allow partisan politics to blind us from seeing what is really happening within the nation.

Our focus must be for the benefit of all and as it stands for the rebuilding of our beloved nation. I am surprised that the churches of Jamaica who have the power to bless and speak life have allowed poison, venom and greed to overrun their hallways. Unless something drastic takes place, very shortly the evil will go directly after the pastors and politicians!

With all the good intentions of any government or business in order to experience growth (such as that needed by the present government) and with the appointment of economic ambassadors (which is a good move) we cannot have growth unless the toxic environment is first dealt with.

Any farmer will tell you that when the ground is not prepared, farming cannot take place. The soil needs to be tilled and the debris removed. By principle, this is what will need to take place in Jamaica before any growth can take place. When spiritual laws are broken, we have to make atonement!

The past and present administrations were wrongly advised and they have made covenants and policies for economic reasons, but now the nation is now suffering for those decisions! Gambling, Flexi-Week, and even the anti-Israel stand taken by the nation, have contributed to the current state of affairs in the nation.

It would be unwise for the present government to engage in economic agreement without any ethical or moral guidelines. It will cost us dearly! Everyone who comes says that they will provide jobs and grow the economy. But when there is no ethical stand or guideline, we cannot even vote the way we should. Instead we would have to compromise and do the bidding of other countries. We will even compromise on our foreign policies.

The current administrations inherit all the ghosts and demons of the past decisions from the different administrations before them. Some have come through business and we label it culture. The nation imports a great deal of goods and services and everything that comes with that!

The past and present administrations do not need to waste time and money to find out why they lost! But instead, should try to make atonement for the path and direction that they were going and be true to themselves. When God allows them to be out of office so that they may re-evaluate the path they were on.

The present governments need to understand that it was not their intellect or campaign strategy why they are now in power; but God has given them a second chance to make it right for and with Jamaica! They cannot depend on man to make change, but they must look to God! (Jeremiah 17; Psalms 121)

The past Administration was looking to man, money and fame to give them the victory – but they suffered defeat! The present Prime Minister needs to look and see the mistakes of all the past Prime Ministers. Any Prime Minister who is willing to look to God to bring change to the nation, God will bring that change through their Administration. (2 Chronicles 15)

Economic growth in a nation can only come about by God's tactics, strategies and intervention. Only God can bring power to get wealth. Oftentimes we hear the economists talk about how well the economy is growing, but it is only words put together to deceive the masses. Growth begins with a new heart and a new mind.

Create A New Environment

We need to create a new environment for growth! The Administration needs to call a spiritual retreat to move forward. There are many vipers who do not have the country's best interest at heart; neither do they genuinely care about the Youth! The government, in trying to find solutions, must be careful that they do not make wrong covenants and sink the nation lower.

There are many out there who want to see Jamaica's demise, and even the media must not be fooled! We are not fighting a political war, but ideologies, greed, manipulation and even witchcraft! Little did we know that there would come a time in Jamaica when we would be importing witchcraft, but alas, it is so.

We have even allowed a 'free-for-all' in our Business sector; particularly in the area of Tourism! Anything goes in the island!

Here are a few ideas that could bring the nation back.

1. Call the nation into three (3) days of Fasting

2. Reduce Sales Tax

3. Re-open the Factories and focus on Garment Production

4. Target Spanish, European and African countries

5. Seek the Diaspora who are involved in Auto Mechanics; it is time to manufacture cars locally – we can do it!

6. Build new houses and move the people away from the dump!

The model for solutions regarding the nation of Jamaica can be tweaked and applied to other Caribbean, African and Latin American nations. However, it can also be applied to many First World nations around the globe.

CHAPTER 9

THE GOVERNMENT OF GOD

There are many genuinely righteous people today walking away from the secular industries because they believe that it causes them to compromise their beliefs, and they take with them invaluable contributions to their organizations, groups and the nation. But that is not always the right choice. There is need for light, particularly in the secular world, in order to allow change to come. The absence of light is darkness. There is no such thing as a separation of church and state. There ought not to be a separation of secular and religious. God did not make secular and religious people; he made **man**, in **His** own image. It was man who *chose* separation!

The global failure at this point is the lack of light within strategic positions. Those that are light will operate under the government of God.

In order for us to see and experience change, God's government must be seen in all areas – Media, Politics and Finance. It was God's government, in time of recession and famine, which rescued Pharaoh's government.

Pharaoh was a secular king, but Joseph was operating under God's government. In Politics, if the Administration is operating under God's government, there will be a rebuilding of the wall within the nation. Politicians would walk in integrity and principle and would deal with excessive spending, oppression and engage in self-sacrifice for others to follow, as they lead by example. They would also champion the cause of the poor. They would help those who fell on hard times because of their economic circumstances; as well as those who are victims of Human Trafficking, Prostitution and the Sex Trade.

The Government of God creates an environment for investment and gives the poor an equal opportunity to function in a competitive market, remove exclusivity and criteria that only the rich can meet and provides a fair tax policy.

Foreign Policy/Tourism

The Government of God does nothing – that includes making major decision, developing foreign policies or implementing tourism-based plans – without seeking God's guidance and using His Word as a guideline.

Recently, most of the Caribbean countries, including Jamaica, made a decision which is violation of God's Word. It is going to negatively affect all involved at some point in the future. As an example, in order to boost Tourism, Jamaica is recommending the removal of all visa restrictions to allow other countries to come into the nation.

Given the fact that Jamaica does not have the necessary resources to protect its borders, and considering the moral, security and labor issues that exist, they should have addressed the logistics issues overseas, by setting up more embassies in the other nations. But opening our borders, especially for the sake of increasing tourism, will create major problems on the nation; problems which we are not equipped to handle. Furthermore, there will be a loss of revenue. The only beneficiaries of such a situation are the various All-Inclusive Hotels. The poor do not benefit in any way. The country needs to fix the crime problem; one way to do this is to do screening and collect Visa Fees at the port of entry.

The Government of God is built on the principles of God. We cannot depend on loans and other governments to help us come out of our circumstances; neither can we trust man. (Jeremiah 17: 5–8). We have to trust God to help us turn things around. There is a Jamaican adage which says '*Short-cut draw blood*'; embargos do that too! Some of the decisions made concerning the nation will bring serious embargos in the future.

Learn from Nehemiah

In order for Law-makers and Politicians to create a new environment, we must rebuild the walls that are broken down. We have to encourage all sectors to unite; rebuilding family values and put laws in place that encourage the building of families.

There needs to be reform to National Security and to the Justice System.

There needs to be a strengthening of the Curriculum to inculcate discipline within our children's studies while they learn the traditional subjects. They need to be taught the implications and repercussions of negative actions – including tattooing, gambling, sex before marriage and the facts about HIV and other Sexually Transmitted Diseases. They need to be made to understand that going after gifts from men and women who are not their close family members has the potential to make them victims of human trafficking and the global sex trade.

We need God's Government for things to change.

God Governs in the Affairs of Men

When will mankind understand, that regardless of their plans, God has the final say! He rules in the earth!

The more we try to remove God's presence and principles from the governing of a nation, the more chaos, crime and confusion will increase. Every leader and government are accountable to God. God ordained the institution of government for the regulation of human affairs; and one of the rights of any government is to protect the rights of its citizens. Government is a respected institution extended to all. No government is independent of God's rule!

Governments must seek God for wisdom on:

1. God's number one priority for a nation or for his people in a season
2. The laws should they institute or remove in a season
3. How to please Him (God)

Any government that tries to please the people and the investors at the expense of displeasing God, will have a short tenure! There are leaders – locally and globally – who are listening to everyone else except God and what He has to say. We cannot build a nation without seeking God and applying His principles.

Benjamin Franklin – Past President of the USA – quoted from Psalms 127, Daniel 4 and Genesis 11 as he spoke to Congress, *"Sir, a long time, and the longer I live, the more convincing proofs I see of this truth—that God governs in the affairs of men. And if a sparrow cannot fall to the ground without his notice, is it probable that an empire can rise without his aid? We have been assured, Sir, in the sacred writings, that "except the Lord build the house they labor in vain that build it." I firmly believe this;*

and I also believe that without his concurring aid we shall succeed in this political building no better than the builders of Babel. . . I therefore beg leave to move—that henceforth prayers imploring the assistance of Heaven, and its blessings on our deliberations, be held in this Assembly every morning before we proceed to business"

How many leaders, government offices, security forces or private businesses and institutions know this, and how many take time out to even take time out of have a retreat or daily devotions in their organizations to seek God on how to run the affairs of the organization or nation?

It is better to be ridiculed and laughed at by men as you seek God's direction and succeed as a result of, than to be accepted by men and fail God!

Local and International Focus

Everyone had their eyes and ears tuned to the USA's upcoming election and the rivalry between Donald Trump and Hilary Clinton. One slogan was '*Make America Great Again!*' The other was '*Stronger Together*'. However, without God, His principles, presence and blessings, can that really happen? Although God allowed America to be great, greatness can only continue and be maintained with God's grace, favor and blessing! This is why God wants America to turn back to Him!

Ezekiel 22: 30 reminds us that God is looking for people to stand in the gap that the repairs and restoration can take place. When there is a breach, anything can and will take place. America needs to focus on rebuilding the Spiritual walls that have been torn down, not on the physical walls! Likewise, the same problem exists in Jamaica. Jamaica is trying to build on a foundation that is already broken down! There are no walls or gates, and implementing laws and harsh measures on the poor will not bring change. In fact, that will continue to keep the nation in political instability, and cause the people to be rejected by other nations; furthermore, the nation's sovereignty will weaken.

When a nation continually disobeys God, then foreigners will rule over the nation. Deuteronomy 28: 43 – 44 says, *"The alien who is among you shall rise higher and higher above you, and you shall come down lower and lower. He shall lend to you, but you shall not lend to him; he shall be the head, and you shall be the tail."*

Prioritize

Because leaders fail to obey God and seek Him, the priorities of many are skewed. Meanwhile, they look to man to solve the problems that arise. We should never take our eyes from Jeremiah 17: 5 – 8. The priority locally and globally should be

1. To focus on the poor
2. Restore the family
3. Rebuild a fair justice system
4. Have universal health care
5. Have a fair immigration system (to include calling an Amnesty)
6. Have a fair business and political environment where small businesses can compete and,
7. Put merciful and compassionate leaders in strategic positions

God, Government and Legislation

The continued disregard for Biblical Principles in governing the nation, and the fight to totally secularize it, is causing grave problems for and within the nation, and is affecting every sector. This is so because the Bible was the original foundation for politics, government and the formulation of legislation.

Let us look at Isaiah 32: 22 which says, *"(For the Lord is our Judge, The Lord is our Lawgiver, The Lord is our King; He will save us);"*

This speaks of Judicial, Legislative and Executive systems of Government. It also shows that Jesus Christ is in everything; so there is really no separation of Church and State. The Bible governs both the Church and the Civil Society. It should be the primary source of instruction and of establishing all institutions. No nation can be blessed if God is not their Lord; and the true measure of success or blessings is not financial abundance!

Daniel 2: 21 says lets us know that God has the final say in all things, including the governing of a nation at any level. The electing of a leader for a nation is not just about formulating political strategies. God allows things to happen for the fulfillment of His purpose – whether we see what that purpose is or not.

Romans 13: 1 – 3, but especially verse 1 says, *"Let every soul be subject to the governing authorities. For there is no authority except from God, and the authorities that exist are appointed by God."* Thus, God ordained Civil power, hence the civil power is accountable and subject to God! God instituted Civil government to manage human affairs, and the Bible is a guide to Civil Government on how to carry out their tasks with fairness, justice and integrity. In the same way, the law of the land must be obeyed by its citizens once it does not go against the Word of God. Governments must also protect its citizens. Governments are God's ministers and must therefore be just, fair and must do what is good.

Legislation

All legislation was designed on Biblical Principles for justice and blessings to flow upon mankind, not for the destruction

204

of mankind. Exodus 21 shows the original guide God instituted for mankind on how to deal with Labour Laws, Murder, Parental Dishonor, Kidnapping, Small Offenses/Petty Sessions, Abortion and Theft.

Clearly, there can be no separation between Church and State. Today, every law that God condemned is what mankind is attempting to re-institute. Instead of reaping blessings, we are embracing the opposite. If nations do not use the Bible as a guide, Iniquity, Debt, Disease and Crime will have dominion over them. (Psalm 119: 33; Ecclesiastes 12: 13)

Politics and Self Rule

This arises as a result of man's attempt to be independent of God's rule and principles. (Genesis 4). Self-rule begins when man wants free choice to do whatever he wants to do, and this always leads to one losing one's original status or domain. This concept of 'free choice' always leads us into slavery and bondage, because if we walk away from God's rule, then we will run head on into another ruler. We must remember that we are God's creation and the earth is His and everything in it – whether we believe it or not. Thus if He gives His instructions on how to function on this basis, coupled with the fact that He desires what is good for us, then when we attempt to disobey and distance ourselves from Him and His principles and rule, - this always results in trouble. 'Self-rule' in itself is a kind of deception because it indicates that we know all everything and we are capable of ruling ourselves independent of the One who created us and know us inside out; and that is not so.

When people want 'free choice', thereby rejecting God and His principles, He always raises up leaders to put the people back in line through the implementation of harsh measures. When the people cry out, He changes the times and seasons in order to bless them. If the people continue to rebel against

His rule, He raises up 'Chaldeans' (Habakkuk 1: 5 – 6) The Chaldeans of today include scammers, international lenders, Ponzi schemes, money launderers, dons and hackers.

Secular Government Needs the Government of God

The success of every secular government or leader depends on how they deal with the government of God. Many believe that their success is dependent on how they relate with other Administrations.

No earthly king wants infertility. Every leader has to lead by example, so in order to be fruitful, they must support the government of God. It is the government of God that stands between the secular government and God to avert judgement on a nation. They are the ones providing atoning covering for the civil state. Many times, the people try to criticize the government of God, and ask what they are doing. But if the government of God ceases to stand in the gap for the secular government and civil society for one day, there would be more chaos than you could imagine. (Genesis 20: 14 – 18; Joel 1; Joel 2: 17)

The local and global crises we see happening – unemployment, economic problems, crime and other issues – is the absence of the secular government's/civil society's support of the government of God. Many have diverted to supporting Paganism. Only the government of God has the authority to bless and make atonement for the people. Nehemiah, Ezra, Hezekiah, Pharaoh, Joseph and Daniel – they all collaborated the government of God and the secular/civil society.

In the same way that we must pay secular taxes to the civil government, the Tithes and Offerings of a nation are God's taxes to His government to carry out its function – to facilitate basic healthcare, education, care for the poor and carry out their prophetic mandate to the nation.

There are three (3) types of government that must come together for growth, prosperity and blessing of a nation. The Family – which is the first line of government, the Secular/Civil government, and the government of God, which is the Church. (Ephesians 4: 11)

Matthew 13: 11, *"He answered and said to them, "Because it has been given to you to know the mysteries of the kingdom of heaven, but to them it has not been given."*

This Scripture shows that there are many mysteries globally to be unfolded. Only the government of God qualifies to explain to and to guide the secular government concerning apocalyptic events, the activities in the cosmos, economics, migration and even solutions to deal with sustainable development. Diseases are breaking out like never before. Certain bilateral agreements with other nations that should not take place are rife globally.

The eye of the secular government is the government of God. The secular government cannot continue to operate blindly. There are many, even those who deem themselves part of the Government of God, who promote a secular society excluding the Government of God! Their concept of society instead ought to be ignored!

Regardless of how brilliant those within the secular government are and what plans they will come up with, unless it is blessed by the government of God, then billions will either continue to go to waste, or be distributed among those in secular government. Those who truly represent the government of God are not getting the physical and spiritual support to deal with the needs within the communities. Understand that if the government of God is not allowed to prosper then the Secular government will not prosper at all, and will continue to go around in circles.

The government of God is not about knocking shoulders with VIPs or being invited to a few dinners and functions like tokens. They are in charge of the Spiritual aspect of the nation. They are the Gatekeepers. They are the first line to the community, the widowed, the poor and the needy. They are God's representatives in the earth! They are the ones who should show the secular government why we are facing what we are facing and which spiritual laws have been broken as well as what we need to do to bring change and reformation.

Those who are a part of the government of God are not exceptions from society. They have voting rights, pay taxes, they have the power to decree and declare. They have the right to representation if they feel they have been called to serve in secular government.

They also have the right to pray concerning the governance within a nation as well as peace and prosperity, and for unity among the three (3) governments within a nation.

CHAPTER 10

MONEY MUST DO GOOD THINGS

1 Timothy 6: 10 says,

"For the love of money is a root of all kinds of evil, for which some have strayed from the faith in their greediness, and pierced themselves through with many sorrows."

There is nothing wrong with money itself, however, it is the love of money – the heart condition and motives behind the money that is the problem. Money is a defense, it is supposed to do good things and it is also to be used to create more money to win wars and transform lives for the better. When you have money, you have power and access. Money is even mentioned more than faith and prayer in the Bible – over 2000 times. When you have money, you can sit on Boards in various organizations, run for political office and when you speak nonsense it will make headlines. People outwardly show you respect and treat you a certain way when you have money.

Christians should by no means be afraid to get money as long as they are getting it legally. If the kingdom of God is going to be effective in the end-time to transform nations, then we need money to impact lives.

Oftentimes we hear people criticize Christians who have money or those Christians who talk about money. But contrary to popular belief, there is no vow of poverty in the Scriptures. Many have no problem when politicians or drug dons get money –whether legally or illegally, but as soon as a man of God begins to prosper, they have a problem – even when they get it legally.

Money allows us to sit at the tables of influence feeding the poor, help by giving people scholarships, help University students who are struggling and cannot pay their tuition fees – most of them get locked out of the system.

Money Should Not Sponsor Evil

God allows people to have money, not to sponsor evil. Money is for the purpose of doing good things. (Isaiah 49: 50; Deuteronomy 8: 19; Proverbs 22: 16). That is why He allows organizations to make profit. We should not use our money to oppress the poor or give only to our rich friends, or use it to fund murders, rapes and sexual immorality.

Some would prefer to pay a witchdoctor to hurt someone, rather than pay for someone's doctor bill or buy them groceries or give a child lunch money for school. Do not allow money to become your master or your addiction – you should master money!

When man loves money more than God, then it becomes an idol to him. and they would also try to come against someone who is trying to make a living. Everybody must have an equal opportunity and an equal right to make money. Do not use money to put regulations in place to stop someone else from making money. Do not rob anyone of their wages and livelihood. (James 5: 4; Jeremiah 22: 13)

Money Should Not Separate

Never allow money to separate you from God or from good friends. Money comes and goes, you never know which way the wind will blow. You may be a billionaire today and a pauper tomorrow.

Always pursue true riches, which are spiritual in nature – Righteousness, Godliness, Faith, Love, Patience. Do not allow money to cause you to betray those who trust you, including your leaders. Riches are so transient and the value changes. Earthly riches are only as good as the present value.

Wealthy people should be good stewards. The good we do today will bring eternal dividends. Find someone and begin to help them.

We must stop making decisions based on money only. For example, choosing political candidates either on how wealthy they are or how hungry they are for money.

Greed stops the flow of more money. Giving means we have conquered greed. The moment our motives are/become right individually/globally, then we will see change individually/globally. There will also be a reduction of crime, violence and corruption, and people will start seeking to be in political offices – not for the love of money, but for the opportunity to serve their fellow man.

Money Within the Fragments

"So when they were filled, He said to His disciples, 'Gather up the fragments that remain, so that nothing is lost.' Therefore they gathered them up, and filled twelve baskets with the fragments of the five barley loaves which were left over by those who had eaten."
John 6: 12 - 13

Within this quote is the key to achieving local and global change – the key to turning an economy around and restoring hope to the masses.

Each person has to see God as his/her provider, not the politicians. The majority of all successful leaders will tell you that they never received a handout. Those who see politicians as their way out, will always be in bondage and be open to manipulation and deceit. Even intellects looking for change without a changed mindset is simply wasting time.

Regardless of the size of our resources, great or miniscule, if we allow God to be our Guide, we can transform a nation, even nations. Any effort to establish order within the nation will require the transformation to begin at home first!

Before distribution can take place, we first have to give God thanks for directing us and showing how to distribute. Distribution must be carried out by those who were placed in authority. They must serve the people in an orderly fashion so that no undermining takes place!

Gathering the Fragments

Within a nation, no resources should be wasted – human or otherwise! The fragments are among the most important resources within a nation. They are the parts and pieces broken off, the incomplete pieces and scraps – that are generally neglected, forgotten or ignored. Change cannot come unless everything is fitted together and accounted for. The questions then are:

1. Who are the fragments of the society?'
2. How important are they for growth and development?
3. Are there remaining resources that can turn the nation?

4. Of what value are the fragments to us and the nation?
5. Is there anything we have put away that we have considered as having no value?

The fragments of the nation decide its stability. It can also decide what political direction the nation will go. Those who gather the fragments will have spiritual, economic and political dominion.

Picking up the fragments teaches us a lot. We can see a lot more when we begin to pick up the fragments. You learn more about the people and you see things you would not ordinarily see if this was not being done. Picking up the fragments will teach us to see the value in all things and how to manage resources. Nothing should be wasted!

The fact that in this era we can turn garbage into fuel says something. There is garbage everywhere in the nation. There are brilliant students in the universities and also in the inner-city areas, who, if given the opportunities can come up with solutions on how to turn our garbage into fuel for the nation.

Have you ever seen (or heard of) a dressmaker or even a grandmother, who would take the scraps of material left behind, and sew them together to make pillows, blankets, pin cushions, even curtains and other craft items? The fragment is of no real value on its own, but adds value when they are put together.

Nobody cares much about gathering and putting to use the 'crumbs' of the society, especially these days. Interestingly, there are more crumbs in the society than whole ones. Oftentimes, the fragments are seen as unusable and unimportant – something we would walk upon. But when they are put together, they are of great value. It is equally important to note that the fragments of broken glass, if left unattended and splintered, can be dangerous to those around. But when they are gathered together, those around are protected and safe from harm. So, it is important to gather the fragments. Furthermore, the broken glass can be further crushed to make another drinking glass or work of art.

As such, when a political party is divided and fragmented, it can become dangerous to those around – to the people of the nation! But if they are gathered together, they would prove more beneficial to the health and well-being of the nation. Biblical Economics outlines the principle of the five (5) loaves and two (2) fish which tells us that God can take tiny and insignificant resources and cause it to feed a multitude. But the greater part of that experience is the gathering of the fragments. In this case it resulted in twelve (12) baskets of fragments being collected which, as stated previously, signifies the government of God.

Employment and Wealth Transfer Through Volunteering

Job Creation is one of the areas of greatest struggle for many nations. Many graduates today are less than hopeful, because they do not see a future in the job market. It has been highlighted before that the government should create a better environment for employment, foster greater zeal among the unemployed. There is no way the Security Budget should be the highest expenditure of any government – and it should certainly not be more than what is expended on Job Creation.

There are many within the society that have great ideas and simply only need a start. Some countries are now more focused on the Gender Agenda than they are about creating a stable environment for the upcoming generation of the Workforce.

It is very critical now for those who have no job experience to gain employment. They can begin to volunteer. There are organizations that would be willing to have them work for free. There are NGOs, Churches, Small Businesses who cannot write a business/marketing plan and cannot afford it either. You can go into these organizations and ask to work for free for a period and by doing so, you are getting both experience and wealth transfer.

Students need to begin going into the inner-city areas and begin to empower the people in different areas. Empowering can also be owning a business. There are many people who are brilliant and have the skills in areas such as: hairdressing, music production, entrepreneurship, and other raw talent – they have talent but need guidance on how to get their stuff out there.

When a person volunteers, they are learning the art of honoring and serving and those are the keys to wealth transfer.

There are a number of outstanding men and women who have a wealth of knowledge that needs to be imparted to the next generation and we have the potential to make it happen. Some of these persons are struggling and they have needs such as bookwork, accounting, record-keeping and other things that need to be done for them but they have no one to do it. This is an opportunity to gain experience and also to be the beneficiaries of their experience, wisdom and wealth.

Trade Unions and Student Unions

Both Trade Unions and Student Unions need to set up programs specifically designed with the private sector in mind – for volunteers to get the credit. By volunteering they would get first preference after graduation. Both sets of Unions would need to have full time personnel to co-ordinate these activities; and they would target places such as Airports, Manufacturing and Distribution companies.

Our people also, in gaining employment opportunities, need to start looking into Latin Countries. Hence, it needs to be mandatory that our people learn another language – preferably, but not only Spanish.

Every person in the nations needs now to think multi-functionally, not single-mindedly. Recognize that not because you studied a particular area does it mean that you will only be required to focus on that area where you work. Likewise, not everything you do will mean you must get a paycheck. A recommendation from a retired person can go a far way in opening a door for any individual. They are living in every community, and instead of people killing them, they need to go and serve them. My first job came through volunteering. I was volunteering in the community with some other boys in Boy Scouts, and I was recommended for my first job in one of the former top insurance companies – Mutual Life Jamaica.

The key to a strong economy is to ensure that the base (Small Businesses) is functioning well. Many are just focusing on the larger companies who are not keeping the funds within the nation. You can volunteer by creating websites, making marketing presentations and business plans, and bringing solutions to these companies for free. You would be surprised to see what these companies would do. Some may even hire you on the spot! It is also for the companies to make such opportunities available for such individuals to come in and present to them.

There is no way that Lawyers, Doctors, Teachers or any other profession should be struggling and be out of a job when they can volunteer. Volunteering makes a difference and opens up the opportunity for wealth transfer and the creation of new jobs, thus giving experience and can change the culture in an organization. Those employees at ease could very well be stirred into action!

Many small businesses want to grow, but they cannot afford it because of the overhead expenses. You can volunteer by assisting these companies to grow. You never know - you may be their next manager.

The $97 Billion Industry Destroying Lives

Job 31: 1 says, *"I have made a covenant with my eyes; why then should I look upon a young woman?"*

The eyes are the windows/gates to the soul and when the eyes are open everything that goes through affects the entire body. Many of the problems we encounter come through the eyes. What we hear, see or speak are critical to our health spiritually and naturally. This should cause us to realize why we have so many problems within the society. If we are going to talk about the music, then we must also willingly address the matter of Pornography. Even the way in which influential ones in the society attire themselves makes an impact on the society. For example, there was a period where influential ones in the society had a certain focus. They were dressed in their business suits and had a general focus toward presenting themselves in a manner that commanded not only attention but respect as well. Today, many of the influential are barely clothed and many look up to and emulate them.

Pornography is defined as 'sexually explicit videos, photographs, writings, or the like, whose purpose is to elicit sexual arousal.' That being stated, it also means that there are people whose influence could, or quite possibly, already does fall in this category. Furthermore, we need to realize that:

1. The Pornography Industry is a US$97 Billion Dollar industry with US$12 Billion – *NBC News.*

2. Porn sites receive more regular traffic than Netflix, Amazon, and Twitter combined – *Huffington Post*

3. 34% of internet users have been exposed to unwanted porn via Ads, Pop-Ups and other methods

4. 30% of all data transferred across the internet are porn-related

5. 1 in every 3 women visit porn sites and 66% of women watch it.

6. There are even honors and awards being given to porn stars in their Industry's Awards show.

7. Child Pornography is a US Billion-dollar business and one of the fastest growing businesses as well.

8. When we look at Hollywood, the Music Industry, local and global media – even the cartoon channels, books, magazines, video games, swing/gentlemen's clubs – GOD HELP US!

Scientists have been ~~are~~ stating that pornography negatively affects the brain. 79% of those involved in pornography are also involved in marijuana, alcohol and are carrying out physical and verbal abuse. There are also corresponding increases in Crime, Sexting, and are causing road accidents.

Even the gospel singers – both male and female – are dressed in a manner that is far from the modesty required of them.

The Pornographic Industry has caused the increase of marital infidelity of 300%. Action needs to be taken.

The Bible and Porn

There are over thirty (30) Scriptures that warn us of the dangers of Pornography – the Do's and Don'ts for both men and women - Proverbs 7: 21 – 27, Psalm 119: 37 and many other Scriptures.

The root of the problem we are now facing, even while many are playing the Gender card, is that our men are supposed to be the leaders and covering for our society particularly for our women and children. Because of this industry, they have left their families unprotected. Sadly, women are the ones most deeply involved in this industry. In fact, the Pornography industry would not be what it is without women. That is why we need women who are healed, to look past gender and fight for the boys and men with the same zeal and fervor that they employ to fight for the women and girls. In order to fight porn, we need to stop dividing the family into gender pockets to pick our favorite gender to defend.

God provides three (3) lines of Government to create prosperity and peace within the earth. Family/Parents (Mother and Father), Civil Government and Levi (The Priests). Sadly, they have become ineffective because of Pornography.

Those involved in Pornography also have the ability to transfer this addiction to others. For example, it is very important for you to know who does your hair, hands and feet. Even when you are passing through the hotels, cruises, massage parlors and spas; those in the airports who are checking you and patting you down at security check points may be involved in Pornography, Masturbation and Uncleanness. You may find that you are getting those urges as well that you never had before.

Pornography is even affecting legislation, simply because what you are around, what you associate with, is what you become. We need to look within our Tourism Industry. We give our children electronic technology without parental guidance and we fail to look at the consequences.

This is a call for everyone to unite to come against pornography, starting with our highest levels in the nation and their dress codes. Remember that it is righteousness that exalts a nation. (Proverbs 14: 34). There needs to be order in the House.

CHAPTER 11

FAMINE, FLOOD, FOOD AND WATER

Of significant importance to Biblical Economics is matter of Prophecy. Prophecy is the revelation of Jesus Christ. (Revelation 1) Nothing happens within the globe that would impact the economy of any nation (whether disaster or other things to come – including global water shortage, that is not first revealed prophetically.

The following are some of the things that Lord has revealed, that has already come to pass, and there are still more to come. Nation leaders cannot continue to ignore the voice of God. Further on the area of Prophecy and its relevance to national level decision-making can be found in the books *Tactics and Strategies for the Famine* (2012) Apostle Steve Lyston and *The Prophetic Word To Nations – 2009 – 2017* (2017) Apostle Steve Lyston & Bishop Dr. Doris Hutchinson.

April 7, 2010

✓ There will be more irregular patterns in the weather. There will be more hail storms, especially in countries that have never experienced it. Some places may experience snow and snow storms throughout the year, and even into the following year. Some may experience heat more than ever.

✓ Some of the meteorologist jobs are at risk as they will be totally confused.

✓ There will be another epidemic that will be worse than the Swine Flu that will have scientists having conflicts with each other.

July 28, 2009

✓ Many more persons all over the world will contract AIDS, SWINE FLU and other deadly viruses that will be worse than these mentioned. Scientists may not be able to handle what is about to come. These cases will be worse than those of the 1700s, 1800s, and the 1900s. Many schools, colleges, universities, and daycares will begin to lose lots of money because of the increase of persons with these viruses and some of these institutions will eventually close its doors. This will cause many persons, especially the Government and Church Leaders to come together to seek God's face and ask Him for forgiveness for being disobedient to Him — for not showing reverential fear to Him. These cases will be nothing in comparison to the different plagues expected in the Great Tribulation period.

July 7, 2010

✓ It is critical for world to understand Times and Seasons. According to 1 Chronicles 12: 32, God is now raising up Apostles and Prophets to understand times and seasons and what the nations ought to do. Many of the world leaders are out of sync, as they are focusing on the wrong things. Many are more focusing on the world economic climate, but no economist or business investor can truly forecast what is ahead unless they are divinely hearing from God. Many of them do not believe that God speaks; hence they continue to ignore biblical principles. God has been speaking but they continue to ignore God's voice in the earth. He wants to tell us what is to be done and how to save lives and how to avert disasters.

✓ Ecclesiastes 3 speaks about the different times and seasons, and **we** are in a season of crying out to the Lord, especially for protection of our president and for Godly wisdom for Him to do the right things. The question is, are we ready to make a new covenant with God for Him to guide and protect us? What about the happenings in our sea and underneath the sea? Are the nations ready for war? Are they ready for famine? Is there enough water, food, medical supply stock piling?

April 19, 2010

✓ The things that are happening worldwide, the Lord says are as a result of the Leaders refusing to lead the people in the right path. They have despised the poor, the fatherless and the widows, and have implemented measures for them to suffer. They have refused to listen to God's voice. The Lord says there will be more disasters to come.

- ✓ The Scientists have created something that is against earth's humanity and God is not pleased. Therefore, He is going to bring the Leaders and Scientists to their knees. Those who refused to serve the Lord will suffer badly.

- ✓ The things that are now happening will not be easily fixed or corrected. There will be signs in the Cosmos and God is about to show signs worldwide. The rich, the poor and the pauper all will be affected. God is moving country by country and family by family. The Lord says this is harvest time for the church. He wants His people to reap the harvest and be ready.

September 11, 2010

- ✓ There will be great flood rain. Many rivers will overflow their banks, and many rivers will be merging and flowing to the seas. There will be worldwide mourning but many will be saved.

October 16, 2010

- ✓ There is a fruit that scientists need to do testing on. This fruit carries a rich nutrient that can bring great healing. They need to plant a lot of this fruit. (*Upon discussion, we will give the name of this fruit.*)

- ✓ There will be a great shortage of rice, barley and flour because of the rising water problem caused from the melting of the North Pole. Marine Biologists need to do deeper study quickly before it is too late. This will cause famine and hardship worldwide if not dealt with.

✓ Nations need to plant more corn and sweet potatoes to deal with the major shortage of rice, flour and barley that is coming.

✓ There also need to be a cutting down on Alcoholic Beverages, as the Barley is what is used to make it. This change will deal with the increase in price and worldwide shortfall that is about to happen.

✓ There will be a serious excessive heat from the sun in the future. This will be beyond human knowledge. Scientist needs to do study quickly to deal with the problem to come.

✓ A watchful eye should be kept on the peanut industry by the farmers. Insects and diseases are about to attack this crop. This will bring hardship and suffering.

2011

✓ Salt will be in short supply. The great oceans and seas will be disturbed by unusual weather patterns; this will cause hardships for multitudes of people.

✓ Those who manufacture the food should be careful of the preservatives they use and the amount of chemicals that goes into them, as it can cause serious health issues, which will take a long period of time to detect. This will be the cause of recession. The World Health Organization (WHO) needs to beware.

✓ Pray to the Lord to reveal the herbs of the land which is for the healing of the nation (Rev. 22: 2). Most of the drugs we are taking for various illnesses carry serious side effects which destroy the very fiber of our bodies.

✓ Global warming - There will be major heat waves worldwide and major environmental problems.

✓ There is a substance that will hit the water, and God is calling people to purify the water they use/consume. Use water purifying tablets or water filters.

✓ There will be a lot of food contamination. Thousands will die if there is not proper screening of all food. When the truth is revealed it will be too late. Those who produce, package, manufacture, store and prepare food may try to get food out in the market before exposure. Most of the foods we are eating are not fit for consumption. Contamination of food will be in its highest form. It will be hard for the authorities to detect it. We call upon the Food and Drug Administration (FDA) to analyze and scrutinize food more properly so that lives will be saved.

✓ World pollution will be in its highest form. We are to pray to God to purify the oxygen that we breathe in. Different gases being circulated in the atmosphere can be very destructive to the human race. There will be a battle of survival of air and water in these last days of history. We should pray over everything we consume and ask God to bless and purify it.

✓ God is calling on the World Health Organization (W.H.O.) to stockpile vaccine and drugs.

✓ God is calling on all scientists to seek Him for direction. The destruction of land, crop, and animal of any kind will cause the earth to absorb dangerous substances that will be difficult to control by scientists. Many scientists do not believe in God, and because of this, it will be difficult for them to gather and find the solutions to help sustain life

October 1, 2012

Global Warming

✓ Serious problems with weather patterns will continue. Tsunamis, earthquakes, flooding, fire, and hailstones will occur. Most geographical areas and landscapes will change. Environmental problems will increase. Food and water will be contaminated because of the high level of activities within the ocean. The fish are not safe, and there needs to be major testing.

✓ Melting will continue due to a high level of heat waves. More cosmic problems and pollution problems are in store for us. There needs to be a united joint effort with nations to tackle these problems before it becomes worse.

Food and Water

✓ There will be a critical shortage of wheat and grain. Insects will attack our food supply, which in turn will affect price and lead to a price increase. From 2007, the Lord has been calling for nations to stockpile (store) food and water. We need to develop our water containment areas – e.g. springs, lakes, etc. We need to stockpile vaccine, bleach and purification tablets, as fresh water will be a problem very shortly. The Lord is calling on nation leaders to address these areas.

Humanitarian

- ✓ With poverty on the increase, there needs to be a united effort to reduce poverty in 2012. If not, poverty will increase to a new level. There are many areas we need to cut down on in order to take care of poverty such as what we spend on roads and animals while people die of hunger.

- ✓ In global recessions, organizations should increase Humanitarian Activities, such as their budgets for donations. Many have cut their budget to this area, but this is the wrong method. Cutting back on donations will only extend the global recession. (Genesis 26)

- ✓ Countries need to unite and focus on sustainable development to help the poor. We have to look on poverty through different eyes and identify what are the causes and solutions to minimize this problem. More grants needed to be given to address these problems.

- ✓ More assistance should be given to NGOs, who can make a change.

Medical Supplies

- ✓ The time is right and the time is now for nations to unite and look at finding new cures for diseases. The cure for every disease can be discovered if new approaches are tried.

- ✓ We need to store numerous medical supplies for impending disasters, particularly vaccines.

- ✓ Scientists and Doctors need to have open minds to 'unusual' methods of miracles and healing that will be taking place.

- ✓ We should also unite and find ways to provide access to the poor to the best medical assistance available. No one should die for lack of finance!

June 11, 2016

Health/Water

- ✓ There are many medications on the market that have been causing serious side effects for over four (4) decades. Doctors, Nutritionists and Lab Technicians need to explore the natural things that God Himself made for the benefit of man's continued existence. He has given us plants that can sometimes be employed to cure us. There are medications that need to be banned from off the market immediately to eliminate fraudulent business activities within this field. More tanks and wells are needed urgently. Instead of focusing on Marijuana, government needs to focus on the herbs in general and make an effort to see how they can help in healing for the nation's people. The focus should be on curing – not on treating. There should be a program where the focus is on training more Paramedics and First Response Personnel. There also needs to be a reduction in the price for drugs to the general public.

Agriculture

We need now more than ever to preserve our trees - many of their fruits are not given the chance to grow and be part of God's beautiful purpose. The trees help to preserve the environment – they provide shelter and shade. There must be more attention given to animals that are butchered for consumption to ensure it is properly done. Focus on the usefulness of local plants is just as important as many of them, such as Thyme and Sage for example, can be useful in marinating and preserving meats and fish. Begin to produce more fresh water fish. Also, rent warehouses and store food and water in the event of a disaster. Remove any taxation from food brought in by NGOs (Non-Governmental Organizations) which would not compete with local entities.

Fertile Soil and Harvest

Many times, people ask the question "Where do I sow my seed?" Many try to determine what soil is considered fertile and question why they are not seeing certain harvests manifesting, or why they cannot see the prosperity they expect when they sow.

The first thing we all need to recognize is that the key to your blessing is to obey God and sow where He says – the place He instructs you to go and plant your seed. Many have missed their harvest because of this – their local pastor prays for them to receive their blessing/miracle/breakthrough/victory and when they receive it they rejoice. However, when it comes to money, that local pastor is not good enough. Luke 10: 2 reminds us,

"Then He said to them, "The harvest truly is great, but the laborers are few; therefore pray the Lord of the harvest to send out laborers into His harvest."

We are in a great time of harvest, but many - both the Church and the World are confused about sowing and reaping. Some Pastors will labor with different people, but when the time of harvest comes for them, those people they worked with say other Pastors have told them that their local church is not fertile soil. So the question is, "Why would you take counsel, prayer and support from your local church and then take your money to other churches or external church leaders after you receive your blessing/breakthrough if it wasn't fertile?"

God never told us we should bring our seed to any or every place we feel like. By example, God told Abraham the specific mountain to go and offer the sacrifice. (Genesis 22; Genesis 26: 1 – 3). Deuteronomy 26: 2 says,

"that you shall take some of the first of all the produce of the ground, which you shall bring from your land that the Lord your God is giving you, and put it in a basket and go to the place where the Lord your God chooses to make His name abide."

The Lord says in Deuteronomy 16: 16,

"Three times a year all your males shall appear before the Lord your God in the place which He chooses: at the Feast of Unleavened Bread, at the Feast of Weeks, and at the Feast of Tabernacles; and they shall not appear before the Lord empty-handed."

Soil

Soil is very important in sowing our seed. Soil refers to the place that seed is sown. Mark 4 speaks to us about different grounds and also regarding our heart condition and what it takes to bring a harvest. In the natural realm there are five (5) different soil types; and all five are a combination of three (3) original types of soil.

1. *Sandy soil* has nothing to support the roots and nutrients cannot be kept by sandy soil.

2. *Silty soil* has poor drainage, and does not hold nutrients.

3. *Clay soil* is heavy and hard to work with when it gets dry.

4. *Peat Soil* is high in organic matter and retain a large amount of moisture

5. *Loam Soil* is a mixture of sand, silt and clay that are combined to avoid the negative effects of each type.

Loam is the best type of soil in which to plant. Some of it may be sandy, some of it clay and so on, but together it all brings balance and stability.

Every soil has to be tested, as not every soil will allow your seed to grow. Not only do you as an individual have to be tested so that you can see your potential and what is within you, but the soil that God instructs you to sow into also needs to be tested - He knows what is there and that it is the best soil for you.

Good soil in this context, is any place that the undiluted Gospel is preached and the following is taught:

1. Repentance
2. The Cross
3. The Crucifixion and Resurrection
4. Holiness
5. Healing
6. Deliverance
7. The Gifts
8. The Holy Spirit
9. Helping the Poor
10. Living according to the Word of God

Harvest

Amos 9: 11 – 15 says, *"On that day I will raise up the tabernacle of David, which has fallen down, and repair its damages; I will raise up its ruins, and rebuild it as in the days of old; that they may possess the remnant of Edom, And all the Gentiles who are called by My name," says the Lord who does this thing. "Behold, the days are coming," says the Lord, "When the plowman shall overtake the reaper, and the treader of grapes him who sows seed; the mountains shall drip with sweet wine, and all the hills shall flow with it. I will bring back the captives of My people Israel; they shall build the waste cities and inhabit them; they shall plant vineyards and drink wine from them; they shall also make gardens and eat fruit from them. I will plant them in their land, and no longer shall they be pulled up from the land I have given them," says the Lord your God."*

There are things that have been promised to us that are in God's Word which **must** manifest in our lives. There are things with our names on them, which belong to us that we must receive. Our blessings will be so great that by the time one harvest is ending, another is just beginning. Even harvests we have given up on are about to manifest in our lives. Never try to figure out where your harvest is coming from. Focus on the God that you serve – the Lord of the Harvest!

Sowing and Reaping

Never look for your harvest where you have sown, look for your harvest BECAUSE you have sown. The return on your seed - which is your harvest - always comes from God and He chooses the direction from which it comes. Just keep doing good, you never know from which direction your harvest is coming. The Word says what you sow you will reap, NOT from where you sow you will reap!

You may sow in my field, but get your harvest from Boaz's field! Jesus is the Lord of the Harvest - not man! When someone tries to deceive you about the harvest, remind them Who the Lord of the Harvest is!

Stop worrying about the ones who robbed and cheated you, God will allow you to reap a harvest from places you never expected. He Is Lord!

(Remember Joshua 24: 13 and Deuteronomy 6: 10, Psalm 105: 44, Mark 10)

Farming: The Key to Sustainable Development

Everything that to do with man's sustenance comes from the ground; and that includes man as well. This tells us that much of what we need to turn the economy around and sustain mankind can be found in the ground.

When nations are facing economic challenges, the first thing that heads of states should be looking at is to move away from international lenders and expanding the agricultural and aqua-cultural sectors.

God outlines, through Genesis 26, as He spoke to His servant, that he should not borrow from the Philistines, but instead cultivate the land. Going to international lenders gives way to significant and unexplained increase in interest rates, increase in international debt, political turmoil and the disintegration of moral values.

What heads of states worldwide, and in particular leaders of Third World nations and Latin America need to do is preserve existing properties and acquire under-utilized land and properties, build warehouses, create jobs in that particular industry, dig wells for water preservation, increase the rearing of livestock? There needs to be a decrease in spending on the infrastructure for a period of time and redirect those funds to expanding the nations' agricultural programs.

The governments of such nations also need to increase classroom space at all levels, as well as agricultural training.

This will allow them to employ more teachers. The student/teacher ratio in secondary level institutions, for example, is to be 25:1. However, as it stands, it is on average 50:1! So clearly, there is need for improvement in this area, because it means students are not receiving adequate attention. If this matter is corrected, more teachers can be employed, especially in the area of agriculture and the sciences. Furthermore, this will improve academic output from the students. Once there is a full complement of teachers with the guidelines stipulated in the Education policy, they can employ an additional 10% of that full complement as assistant teachers, it will solve many of our problems and steer us in the right direction.

Any nation that has food and water in abundance will have power. They will hold the reigns.

Further to this, farmers need to practice the principle of Giving, as outlined in the scriptures – the Law of Gleaning. (Leviticus 23). At least 10% of their produce should go to feeding the poor in the various communities and the church. This will allow new markets to open for them. It would also give them good harvests, reduction in infestation and praedial larceny.

For farmers to go to the next level in farming within the nation, they will need to employ Biblical Principles as their farming guide. They must also have a day of rest, and God will give to them, new ideas and strategies. September and October are going to be critical for our farmers; that is the real period of Jubilee!

Nations must begin to compel the people of the nation to eat what they grow. Shift some of the public sector organizations into farming. For example, give public sector employees the opportunity and good benefits for entering the agricultural sector. Also, use the prisoners once again in agriculture by training them in the different areas of agriculture, so they can leave the prison system as an entrepreneur with the potential to be a job creator as well rather than a weight on the society and the system. Additionally, taxes, duties and fees need to be removed from such items as tractors, heavy duty trucks, water pumps, solar panels, farming tools and even fruit-bearing/vegetable-bearing seeds and plants.

Unless national leaders address this area, then we are going to face crises ahead! Nations cannot depend on international lenders to take us out of our situation. There needs to be new thinking and new ideas to create jobs and to take us out of the hole.

If governments do not assess their advisors and ensure that the right persons with the right motives for nation-building are around them, then there are serious times ahead. It is time to grab our hoes and forks and build the nation!

Farming: The Key to Job Creation

With all the problems nations are facing and the stringent measures resulting from the economic policies we are pursuing, lack of job creation and the emergence and threat of various diseases, Farming is the key to Job Creation. Until the government and the opposition understand this, they will continue to face employment issues and will still be borrowers!

No Third World country can become a superpower until they have a clear vision and methods of diversity on Farming.

Surprisingly, Farming and the related Ministry, should be the most important thing in the nation and it receives the least attention and funding!

For change to come, there needs to be young, bright economists inspired by God, to drive that ministry.

The four (4) most important things to focus on within a nation are:

1. Food
2. Water
3. Health
4. Shelter

And they all have to do with LAND!

Astoundingly, the country is giving away the land – the very thing God has equipped us with to take us out of debt - we cannot be a superpower if we do not own land!

Farming and Livestock are the foundation of the economy that God created. Every tree was created to sustain man. Even Noah, after the flood, got a revelation. (Genesis 9: 26)

God wants to teach both government and farmers how to farm in a different way and how to make profit! Our minds are too narrow!

Farming is a God thing! The very Word of God contains seeds to change the economy - Isaiah 28: 23 – 29. In the same way that farmers bring forth a crop – according to the Divine wisdom that God has given them – to bring forth a harvest, God wants to teach leaders – political and otherwise - how to turn the nation around, He wants to give order, guidance, direction, principle, tactics and wisdom; everything for man's survival comes from the earth.

Man comes from the ground and man upon death will return to the ground. Solutions are in the ground, money is in the ground. Jamaica and other Third World countries have good ground/soil.

Cures for diseases often come from the ground or plants. What nations are fighting for are things that come from the ground.

It is recommended that politicians spend one month on a farm and listen to the voice of God and allow Him speak to them.

The failure of the nation is not only because of poverty, corruption, and politics – those will always be within a nation. The failure comes where leaders refuse to listen to the voice of God. Both the organization and the nation would benefit if they would just listen.

We must stop blaming the Queen! The Queen has nothing to do with our failure.

Agricultural Alternative For IMF

The healing of the nation's economy is in the ground. (Revelation 22; Ezekiel 42). Farming is the lifeblood a nation. Much of man's sustenance comes from the ground – oxygen, food, fruit, water, oil, natural gas, wood, dye, paper, coal – are some of the things generated by/from the earth. Everything needed to sustain man can be found in the ground.

In Genesis 26, when the nation was experiencing on-going famine and economic problems, God instructed Isaac not to go the path of the Philistines, but instead, till the land and sow, as an alternative. The Philistines today would be represented by the international lenders.

Many times, farming has been treated as the least important activity within the society; it is a ministry that is put on the back burner. There needs to be a shake up right now before it is too late. Farming is the first, foremost and most important profession in the Bible. With the crisis now facing the nation, agriculture should be getting a great deal more funding than it is currently. There is a great need for visionaries in that Ministry in order to bring about change.

The relationship between the government and the nation's Farmers/Farming community needs to improve. There also needs to be Basic and Advanced courses in Agriculture in the Secondary Level Schools. There should be special classes for Farmers (open also to the regular members of the community) in each parish updating on the various kinds of insecticides. For new farmers, there could be courses such as *The Role of a Farmer* and *The Times and Seasons* to plant certain crops, and *The Effects of Current Environmental Issues on Agriculture*. They should also learn the Biblical Principles in Farming. The Three Feasts must be observed, as well as the Law of Gleaning and How to Prevent Predial Larceny Through Giving.

Farming Network

If the nation is serious about Farming, then the time has come for them to have a Farming Network, to promote Local Farming. There should also be more competitions among schools and communities, as well as a Farmers' Hotline that not only answers pertinent questions, but will also educate them on the agricultural history of their nation.

The nation needs to provide valid contacts that will foster business relationships – long and short term – with banks, schools, universities and colleges - locally and internationally.
If we really respected the Agricultural Community, especially our farmers, how many of our nation's farmers would have received national honors or awards?

In order to get the Youth involved in Farming and save the nation, we need to get the local communications groups to get on board with the technology. We also need to incorporate our local athletes and encourage them to promote the noble institution of Farming; especially those athletes who are internationally successful.

There are so many opportunities concerning Farming and this is the time to put Agriculture to the forefront, especially as an alternative to the International Monetary Fund (I.M.F.).

Horticulture and Landscaping

If a country is serious about increasing its Tourism Industry, then the time has come for them to get the young, talented people with the *'Artisan Anointing'* (Exodus 35) involved in the process of beautifying the historical communities and inner-city areas of their nation once again.

There needs to be a meeting with the Private Sector and Civil Society. Have a competition and get the communities involved – get them to come up with new landscaping designs and ideas and/or even new breeds of plants and flowers. So, when the tourists come to our island, they will see its beauty, not only in the landscaping, but also in the gifts and talents of the people that live here.

Finally, as we seek to build and rebuild this nation, we must recognize that before the building, there has to be clearing and plowing of the land. After that, we will see the real builders – those who are not political – who have the nation at heart.

World Pollution – The Next Threat!

Based on past reports given by the World Health Organization (WHO), approximately three (3) million people die each year from the effects of air pollution alone. Furthermore, according to a WHO article, "*According to Global Health Risks: Mortality and burden of disease attributable to selected major risks indoor air pollution is responsible for 2.7% of the global burden of disease.*"

With gold mining, nuclear waste, and contaminated ground water; coupled with uranium mining, acid rain and growing garbage heaps around the world, what will be the result when they all connect? There have been numerous disasters in various parts of the globe - earthquakes, floods and oil spills - and they are all affecting air, land and sea. Is the world really prepared for an outbreak? In addition to all this, add the nuclear weaponry testing that is taking place in certain parts of the world. Pollution affects the entire environment!

While China is one the world's fastest growing economy, it also has the highest annual incidence of premature deaths triggered by air pollution in the world, according to a new study. The WHO report estimates that diseases triggered by indoor and outdoor air pollution kill 656,000 Chinese citizens each year, and polluted drinking water kills another 95,600.

Air Quality Advisor at the WHO Regional Office for Europe has reported that *"Air pollution is estimated to cause approximately two million premature deaths worldwide per year."*

The Sea

Is marine life safe? The millions of life forms below the sea each have their function and provide a delicate balance necessary for every one of them to exist.

Is fish safe for human consumption? Most of the smaller nations do not have the high technology equipment to test for poisonous substances in the fish they catch and some of the fishes caught go directly from the nets to the household tables!

Cancers and unknown illnesses are going to come from

consumption of contaminated sea food. Every person who enters the sea directly ingests some of its water. What about internal problems? When man tries to circumvent God's laws, especially those concerning nature, suffering increases and it manifests in our environment – trees and vegetation wither and die. Diseases that we have never seen before will arise and it is the responsibility of every leader to have a pollution-free environment.

The Land

The issues that arise concerning Land will undoubtedly affect our drinking water, ground water and the entire agricultural sector. Our livestock will be affected and human life in general because we all live on land.

If human beings consume the meat from livestock and ~~they~~ become infected because of the water they drink, human beings will contract the diseases as well.

The Air

Polluted air will cause serious respiratory diseases, skin diseases, diseases affecting the eyes and ear infections. The lungs will be most affected by these problems:

1. All the nations need to come together and invest heavily in Environment-Friendly Activities because pollution will be the greatest threat ahead. There has to be monitoring and testing done in all countries to see what each nation's greatest threat is and how to alleviate it.

2. There needs to be major national clean-ups globally. First World nations must necessarily invest in smaller countries, because all nations are connected environmentally.

242

A major storage of vaccines, respiratory masks, respiratory medications, eye-drops and medication, sanitizers, water purification tablets and machinery and garbage collection receptacles must take place.

3. Garbage dumps need to be moved from urban areas.

4. More tanks need to be built to cultivate fresh water (?) fish in order to sustain good health.

5. There needs to be more solar powered cars or vehicles that use an alternative to petrol.

6. Give more training in schools at all levels – from primary to tertiary – on dealing with environmental issues and hazards.

7. Protect and secure the water catchment areas and tanks.

8. Most leaders are ignoring environmental problems for investment, but there needs to be a balance, otherwise, it will be useless to invest and not live to enjoy it!

9. More countries need to go green!

10. More needs to be spent on the Public Health Sectors to monitor certain divisions.

11. Four main areas of concern must be addressed – the Air, the Water, the Aquatic Life and the Avian Life, before disease and death skyrockets. God gave us the world free from pollution and we need to fix and maintain it as far as possible.

Global Warming

There is the potential for many natural disasters to occur in certain countries beyond the ordinary. These countries will be declaring National Crises/States of Emergency. Disaster-prone areas should no longer be inhabited by people, and there should be underground domes built in the event of heavy rains resulting in floods. Tsunamis, earthquakes and tornadoes will increase. The Disaster Preparedness Committees throughout the world should seriously re-visit disaster-prone areas, observing closely the kind of disasters that are inevitable and determine how best to reach the general public and prepare them quickly! There should be at least an hour's training via the radio and television, as well as by phone. This should also be a common focal interest within schools and the work force.

Is the Globe Prepared for Famine?

There are different levels and kinds of famine that take place globally – a severe shortage of food or a shortage of money, for example. They can be caused by many issues such as a war, a drought, diseases, infestations, which can trigger significant increases in prices and costs of production. Recession and economic fallout can also result in famines. For example, a stock market crash can trigger a famine.

Throughout the Bible, and particularly in the book of Genesis, there are several instances of famine. Some came about as an effect of God's anger due to sin; other instances of famine came about because man failed to seek God to manage and govern nations well. Yet other instances of famine came about because some businesses refused to promote economic equality and fair distribution of resources; some came about to stir up and mobilize God's people for them to put plans in place to help others affected in other regions. (Acts 11: 28; Genesis 41: 45 – 57).

Lessons from Famine

There is good and bad that can be found in the midst of a famine. Nations and organizations that are properly prepared always have an advantage and will have dominion in times of famine. Stockpiling and logistics are key in moving forward. The question then becomes: Is there enough food, medication or water available globally to deal with a global famine?

During a famine, refugees and the issue of migration are always at the forefront because people will always be going toward food or a better life. The refugee issue is now dominating the globe and most countries no longer respect the preamble coming out of the 1951 Refugee Convention. Countries are now closing their borders. Many lives will be negatively affected and furthermore, the Sustainable Development Goals (SDGs) of the World Health Organization (WHO), the Food and Agriculture Organization of the United Nations (FAO) and the Office of the United Nations High Commissioner for Refugees (UNHCR) will not be achieved. If that becomes a reality, we are looking at a potential crash in these organizations – especially if there is not enough resources and not enough trained volunteers.

During a famine, all advisors are exposed, and those who are true will remain and those who are not will be gone with the wind. It is during times of famine that nations form new bilateral and trade agreements. The political system will finally realize that they need the government of God who has insight and knows times and seasons. Famine tests one's faith and brings one back to basics. Famine also, however, brings wealth transfer.

In preparing for a famine, it is critical for organizations to begin focusing on:

1. Job Creation

2. Migration

3. Crime and Violence

4. Humanitarian Outreach
5. Poverty Eradication

6. Low-income Housing

7. Extensive Food Program

8. Occupational Health and safety

9. Education Costs (for age 5-17)

Available warehouses and other storage spaces are going to be key during the famine, and it would be critical for countries like Latin America and the Caribbean to capitalize on this.

Transportation will also play a key role ahead. I would strongly encourage the airline industry to reduce the airfares for children ages 2 to 15. Any airline that does so will experience significant increases in sales. The same is even more so if they eliminate the charges for the second checked bag. Countries also need to reduce their customs duty on barrels.

Items to Stockpile

It is critical for people to begin stockpiling:

Water
Candles
Matches
Toilet Paper
Bathing Soap
Diapers (adult and children)

Bleach
Plastic Containers and Bags
Salt
Sugar
Powdered Milk
Honey
Vinegar
Garlic
Coal and other Non-perishable items.

One of the ways people can do this is to purchase an extra one or two of these items each time they go shopping and store them away; so you would be gathering up these items.

New Strategies

1. Government should begin to assist the farmers with seeds and upgrade the nation's irrigation system – especially for the farmers.

2. Universities should also have a special team of students whose main goal would be to experiment with new ways of farming or production of food for times of famine/shortage.

3. Oftentimes, it is after the fact that people then reactively begin to put 'plans' in place for 'the next time' something happens.

4. Every organization should have a strategic plan in place to save lives and remain viable. Companies that strategically plan ahead will remain prosperous – even in times of famine.

Preparing for Natural Disasters

Disasters have been afflicting nations worldwide and, without a doubt, have been creating a serious, negative impact on the national and world economies. As a result, growth and development have been involuntarily sidelined in order for government to maintain a grip on things while attempting to repair the damage - physically and otherwise. `According to the disaster statistics for Jamaica, it costs the country approximately US$1,000 per person affected by the disasters that have hit the nation. While national budgets are read every year, there is not adequate budgeting done for the effects of natural disasters.

While we cannot budget to cover every single area affected by a natural disaster, there are some things that can be done to minimize the cost to the nation through proper management and planning. For example, when we fail to maintain and/or repair roads, trenches, waterways, riverbeds (river training), irrigation systems, and other infrastructure, when a disaster occurs, it triples the cost of damage, destruction and death. Then the nation has to turn to other countries and global lending agencies for loans and repairs.

We should not attempt to patch roads a week before the beginning of a hurricane season. There are roads that have been neglected by both political parties for 30 years and more; during election season, it is used as a platform to win the election. Then having won, they again continue to ignore the horrific condition of the roads.

The nation wastes a great deal of money during disasters through improper management of resources. This type of action drains our economy. As it stands, the trend has been to try to address infrastructural damage during the time of actual disaster when the focus at that time should be on the human losses, and how to alleviate the problem. This is not proper management.

Everything that happens within a nation affects its economy. With the nuclear waste, oil leaks and explosions that have taken place in countries far away, the fishing industry in Jamaica and the rest of the Caribbean will be seriously affected, because all waterways are connected. Fishing is a vital part of the tourism sector, the hotel industry and restaurants - large or small. If fishing gets hit, there are at least three (3) other industries that will be affected. Recognizing this beforehand gives us the opportunity now to expand our freshwater fish production and the seafood farms in preparation for what lies ahead.

At every level within the nation, we must change our way of thinking and our methods of managing our resources, even the way how we plan for disasters. There has to be a change. Better management of resources will give us better results.

Recommendations and Contingency Plans

Store the following: water, water purification tablets and systems, medical supplies, dust and gas masks, vaccines, respiratory equipment, gloves, batteries, flashlights, candles, matches, lighters, and other such relevant items. By so doing, the nation would be even more ready to deal with the demands that occur during disasters. This diminishes the costs that arise during disasters.

Upgrade the Food Inspection Department and Food Storage and Prevention of Infestation Division to include testing for contamination at a higher level. How safe are our canned goods? Try to get assistance from the United States Agency for International Development, World Health Organization, and other such agencies to assist in this area.

During the hurricane season, remove tax from all disaster emergency-related items.

Seek funding to dig more wells and reservoirs and for the protection of our springs. The nation can capitalize on that because there are other nations that have water shortages while Jamaica and other Caribbean nations - Dominica, Guyana, and so on - have the best water in the world. This can boost our economy.

Coordinate with churches and other non-governmental organizations to provide support to deal with the spiritual needs of the people. Oftentimes, there is great focus on providing food and other physical amenities, but no attention is given to the mental and emotional toll that disasters have on individuals and as a result, that aspect is neglected.

The Disaster Preparedness Agency needs to set up a Disaster Fund. Businesses could contribute to this as all would benefit should this be put in place.

Farming - The Only Way!

Farming was the first job God created. Every part of a plant or fruit has a cure for something. For example, there are many ways to use the Aloe Vera. Study the life and career of George Washington Carver, who sought God for a solution! If we look at the statistics from the Bureau of Labor Statistics in the U.S. Department of Labor, the rate at which the prices increase on Food over the years is greater in amount and percentage and surpasses the rate at which Energy increase

Even if the nation becomes a republic, unless we have a clear vision in terms of Farming and choose to listen to the voice of God on how to govern the society, the very freedom that the nation enjoys will dissipate! Many in communist countries and places where the Sharia law exists envy our freedom!

Contrary to popular belief, Farming is the oldest profession in the Bible. It is what allowed Pharaoh to rise to power.

If our economists and leaders do not see the danger of the price increases then very shortly there will be chaos – hunger and starvation will turn into rising crime rates. It goes beyond visiting a few functions and giving a speech!

We need to ask some questions. With the land that is left,

1. What is the purpose of the land God gave to us?
2. What is on or under it?
3. What do we need to do?
4. What products do we focus on at this juncture to take us out of the problems that exist?

Brexit, The European Union (E.U.) and The Apocalyptic Shift

Revelation 18: 4 – 5 says:

"And I heard another voice from heaven saying, "Come out of her, my people, lest you share in her sins, and lest you receive of her plagues. For her sins have reached[b] to heaven, and God has remembered her iniquities."

Why is the world shocked about Britain pulling out of the European Union (EU)? When Revelation 13, 17 and the Book of Daniel is clearly manifesting right before our eyes! Based on Bible Prophecy, this could be the beginning of many shifts to come; other countries will be pulling out too! By the end of this year, the world will finally know the meaning of the term *'paradigm shift'*.

There is a prophetic mandate and a covenant God has with the United Kingdom (UK). It was from the UK that missionaries were sent throughout nations to spread the Gospel. The Church of England was in its heyday, the most

251

influential Church in the known World and today still carries a great deal of influence. With this pulling out from Britain, there are many things that will surface:

1. The Revival of the Roman Empire

2. The ten (10) main countries will be a part of the EU

3. The Anti-Christ will use the EU as a platform

4. We might see Germany rise again as the leader through the shaking of the financial market.

The Anti-Christ has three (3) main focuses;

1. One world currency
2. One world religion

3. One world rule – The New World Order

Promotion will start by having a cashless society and everything will be done electronically. We have already seen e-money and bitcoins. They will govern the globe with international laws and other things ~~they will try to~~ advance through the failures of economies and security! Britain's pull out will be a setback for the Anti-Christ. The Anti-Christ has to rise when there is a global financial crisis. But the time is not yet!

The pull out may allow the Euro dollar to strengthen and thus strengthen the EU's position for World Dominance. There will be opportunities for companies that were low performers in the stock market. They may now see changes – positive changes.

While trade may affect Britain and other countries, Britain does not have to depend on them and their positions. They have the opportunity now to strengthen the British Pound Sterling and re-establish the monarchy. It can also strengthen the arm of the Commonwealth Countries. Britain would need the Commonwealth Nations to fight the Anti-Christ in the End-Time. The Anti-Christ wants to have globalization and a genderless society. Britain has great designers and they will build again under the inspiration of God.

Other things that need to happen:

Jamaica and other countries within CARICOM need to unite. This is not the time for pulling out, Jamaica needs to strengthen their dollar, fix the politics, respect each other and capitalize on possible fallout ahead!

Jamaica needs to put a Visa system in place and the Caribbean needs to do so for the region. It will increase earnings and heighten security and protection. The Caribbean region needs to do something similar to the Schengen Visa and put that system where external nations must use a Visa to enter any nation within the CARICOM region! Contrary to popular belief, it is not that the Caribbean nations need the external nations – they need the Caribbean nations! In the shift that is coming, the nations that have been ignored and neglected, who have held on to their strong Christian beliefs are about to rise, and they must be very wise in decision-making and with their transactions at all levels.

Jamaica and other Caribbean nations must think carefully about pulling out of the Monarchy. What they need to do is negotiate to have free access – roll back Visas to travel to the UK.

What is happening now only strengthens my continued declaration that Jamaica must have its own national and economic blueprint, but not make any covenants, so that when nations fallout it does not affect Jamaica negatively!

Things We Need to Watch

In accordance with the Book of Revelation, we need to watch the rise of Russia military-wise and its dominance within the oil-rich Persian Gulf. They will join with the Russian-Arab Alliance which may lead to the battle of Gog and Magog – the Battle of Armageddon. All this is leading up to targeting Israel.

We are interesting times. Most decisions will be made based on Economics! It is critical for each person to begin to study Biblical Prophecies and understand Biblical Interpretation. Politicians also need to understand that we are in a new era and any agenda to remove God from the society can create serious global financial problems.

Every decision going forward must be preceded by genuine prayer.

CHAPTER 12

HONOR DETERMINES YOUR FUTURE

Many of the problems we are now facing in our society is the result of a lack of honor and a great deal of dishonor to replace it. Honor begins within the home and regardless of the various systems different ones want to implement – whether the legal system, the New Age Movement or anyone else, the real change for better will not take place until honor and the value of honor is restored.

The Bible commands us to honor God, honor our parents, honor government, honor elders, honor leaders and honor widows. These are critical for blessings. The Bible reminds us that honor brings blessings and dishonor brings curses. If you want to see the levels of dishonor being shown on a daily basis, you can catch a quick glimpse of it on mainstream or social media. You will even see the level of dishonor being shown by columnists, lobbyists/social activists to honorable people.   We need to recognize that even when people have fallen, you must honor them. Regardless of their political, social or educational background, where honor is due it ought to be given. We have seen politicians being shown great dishonor publicly, for example, The Honorable Portia

Simpson-Miller, The Honorable Bruce Golding – both former Prime Ministers of Jamaica; and President Donald Trump as well as former Senator, Hillary Clinton. Even young politicians on the political platform showing dishonor with their disrespectful statements about their colleagues or opponents and the crowd would laugh or shout in support without realizing that the dishonor shown could cancel their very future.

When an activist even shows dishonor to a man of God and people laugh, even if the man of God is guilty, this can bring a curse and wipe out their future.

In Jamaica, growing up in the "country," we dare not call an elder within the community a nickname. The entire community would discipline us. Today we see people dishonoring the police, teachers, each other and getting support from the society. Members of the police force also show levels of dishonor to the public and particularly to some elders in the public when they should stand up in reverence to them. The army is one of the few remaining institutions that teach people to honor. Every man has to pay compliment to each other. I pray they will never allow external factors and lobbyists to breakdown the system of honor that exists in the army.

Honor Church Leaders

Have you ever seen how people mock church leaders, or even God's Word when it is pronounced? In the Bible, everyone that brings dishonor always experiences retribution? David's wife Michal dishonored him by criticizing him – she became barren. Moses' sister dishonored him by criticizing him – she became plagued with leprosy. Elisha was dishonored by a group of youth who mocked him and called him names. They were killed – eaten by a bear.

256

The ineffectiveness of many intercessors within the Church is the result of dishonoring their leaders. Every good leader within the Church must receive double honor. (I Timothy 5: 17) Praying for the church, the leaders and the nation while tearing them down, gossiping about and undermining them at the same time brings dishonor which brings hardship and suffering on many of them.

When leaders look down on or curse the poor, the weak and those with disabilities, then a curse is released on them (Leviticus 19: 14)

"You shall not revile God, nor curse a ruler of your people." Exodus 22: 28.

Blessings for Honor

Every successful person – whether in the Bible or in life today, has at some point in their life/walk/career has extended honor where it was due and has reaped the benefits of it.

1. Honor promotes you and extends your life. It allows your borders to be extended and releases great blessings and deliverance. (1 Chronicles 4)

2. Honor brings favor and direction, particularly to political leaders. If the leaders were honoring God by listening and obeying His Word we would not be on the path of decline on which we are currently.

3. Honor bring s great financial blessing. (Proverbs 3: 8 – 9) When we honor Him with the finance then great blessings will result.

4. Honor brought a simple woman named Ruth, into becoming a billionaire by honoring her mentor

Naomi. There are many men and women who are in great organizations – whether secular, church or political; but they are unable to receive from the leader they serve because they curse them on a daily basis. Some even expose their leaders in order to receive recognition.

5. Never trust a person who does not honor their leader.

What we need to do is get back to basics if we want to see change in our society. In teaching and practicing honor because that is what decides your future.

Value, Vision and Success

In life, there are three elements that can cause you to experience true prosperity – Value, Vision and Success.

Value

I have realized that people will value their vehicle, tablets and phones more than the value their mentor, pastor, teacher or spouse. But what we need to realize is that whatever we fail to value we will lose them.

People today need to value the time and sacrifice, others make for them. When we place value on something, we guard it, honor, respect and appreciate it. Many times, when people fail to value people in their lives, and others begin to treat those people with greater honor and respect than they do, they begin to say "They are behaving as if they are gods or as if people must worship them!"

Every great person, whether secular or religious, there is always someone that they have valued and honored that opened the door to allow them to walk into greatness.

When you value something or someone, then you are willing to attach a cost to it. In addition to this, when you know your value, people cannot take advantage of you.

Many pastors counsel members of their congregation often times for hours, and beyond normal working hours. It is a service, like secular jobs, that pulls them away from their families, and requires the pastor's keen attention. However, at Pastor Appreciation time, for example, where someone chooses to buy the Pastor a "top-of-the-line" vehicle, or a whole new wardrobe, others behave as if the Pastor is not worthy of the honor. When you go to a doctor to attend to you, don't you have to produce your card first before they attend to your issue?

When we fail to value spiritual things then value diminishes in every area of society – including the currency.

Vision

Each time we ask the Lord for provision, He gives us a vision. Without a vision the people perish. Vision means we have to walk by faith, and it is a function of the heart not of the eyes. Sight limits us. Vision has to first be birthed through faith and prayer. Vision outlives our generation, so our vision must first go beyond infrastructure and target human development and growth.

Provision is always hidden until you put vision into action. (Hebrews 11). Remember, prosperity does not mean tomorrow's need is met today. On the contrary, it means today's needs are met today. (Psalm 68: 9)

Each day we must ask, seek and knock. This means searching, researching, asking for help from both God and human beings. Sometimes we literally have to knock on the doors of a business. Oftentimes it is not necessarily money that you need for the vision, it may be that you need revelation, access or other resources.

Success

There many who are uncertain about the definition of real/true success. Success occurs when you are in God's will and are accomplishing and being what He wants in the time that He wants according to His timetable. Are you where God wants you to be?
Success begins with serving God the Creator, not the creation or His universe. Remember, everything was created to worship God including the universe. (Psalm 148)

The first keys to success can be found in Joshua 1. Success does not come by your own force, strength, military power, money, intellect or education. Success comes by God's Spirit – He causes you to acquire success. (Zechariah 4: 6)

Interestingly, failure is part of the road to success, because there are benefits had and wisdom learned along the way; in the same way that we have profits and losses.

Material possession is not an indicator of success. You can have money and material possessions and are still not successful because you may lack balance. When God's right hand is with you, then you are successful.

When God allows us to have good staff and committed people who will put in consistently hard work, this will help us to experience true success. A vision that is inspired and dedicated to God Who gives us power to get wealth will allow us to experience true success

Tithing: The Path to Prosperity

"But God has chosen the foolish things of the world to put to shame the wise, and God has chosen the weak things of the world to put to shame the things which are mighty; and the base things of the world and the things which are despised God has chosen, and the things

which are not, to bring to nothing the things that are" (1 Corinthians 1: 27)

The carnal mind sees no value in Tithing. But the Spiritual mind recognizes and identifies its relevance and importance. The carnal mind would prefer to build up the economy on the foundation of gambling or immorality. Tithing affords us the capacity to receive the ideas and solution an original blueprint to build an economy.

When one tries to build a blueprint for a nation's economy on the basis of other nation's blueprints, then it shows a lack of creativity and originality and laziness. God created the economy before He created man – when He spoke all the elements into being and then placed man in it. Once man follows the precepts, laws and principles laid out by the Creator, then everything will fall into place.

Tithing speaks of one tenth and the number ten also speaks of completion, labor. We have ten fingers and we labor with them all. The number ten also represents the perfection of God's Divine order. These ten (10) words - Law, Testimony, Ways, Precepts, Statutes, Commandments, Judgement, Path, Order, Understanding are critical keys to a sound economy. They are the words the Lord used to direct man to effectively govern the earth. We must recognize and employ them daily.

Tithing opens your eyes to see the resources as well as how and where to invest them. It is not about being Christian or non-Christian. God commands everyone to Tithe. It honors God! Very shortly, regardless of the state of the economy, we are going to see the varying results in those organizations and individuals that tithe versus those that do not.

The Scriptures speak about the ten virgins - five wise and the five foolish. There is also the reference to the ten plagues and the importance of the ten days of consecration. In the Chinese numeral system, the symbol for the number ten is a

Cross. In science, the number ten represents the element Neon. It is a gas within the atmosphere which is used in Neon signs, television tubes and can freeze things three (3) times more than liquid hydrogen. Our numbering system is based on the number 10. In cricket, ten persons have to be bowled out before the other team can go in. The Bible speaks of the ten nations that will come together to rule the world. Even more interestingly, there were ten generations between Adam and Noah; and ten generations between Noah and Abraham.

According to Leviticus 27: 30 – 32, the tithe is holy and it belongs to God for establishing His kingdom. That it belongs to God means that it is to be used to establish His kingdom, feeding the poor, taking care of the priests as His earthly representatives. The reason the nation is suffering at this point is that the purpose for which the tithe is to be used is not taking place, so the priests and the poor now have to find alternative methods to sustain themselves. The attention that they would give to the spiritual and other needs of the people under their care are being neglected as they make efforts to survive financially.

In 2 Chronicles 31, King Hezekiah led by example by calling a tithe amnesty – to restore the order of things, thereby allowing the priests to re-focus and fulfill their duties according to the instruction of God. This brought major economic revival in the nation!

How many politicians are truly Tithing? Tithing is not for the Pastor to be rich, but for you to receive the blessings and wealth. Many who criticize tithing simply do not understand what this principle is about, nor do they seek to genuine understand. Certainly, they have no problems paying the dues and fees required to maintain membership in their clubs and other civic organizations. Tithing carries seven (7) benefits that you will receive once you are faithful in this area. Tithing is an expression of honor to God. Where your money goes to determines where your honor lies.　Tithing began in the Old Testament times and continues into the New Testament in Hebrews 7, and as such ought to continue today.

Many would prefer to see or have the Church powerless. They know the value of money and that to be effective within a society, one must have money – financial resources. When the Church lacks the finance to carry out its functions, then other organizations pushing immorality begin to strive. There are billions going to enhance immorality while people refuse to tithe unto God.　They prefer to tithe to immorality.

Thankfulness - The Key to Success

We are living in a society today where people are becoming more and more unthankful.　Some even say that God has not done anything for them.　But there are so many things we should be thankful for on a daily basis and so many things for which to thank God.

For example, of the thousands of sperm to race toward the egg, the one that created you was the one that made it! With the millions of abortions that have taken place worldwide, you are not among that number. Thanks be to God!

Be thankful that while many of us are not faithful to even acknowledge God by attending a place of worship (of Him), He still grants us the gift of Life!　Even our women are free to drive a vehicle of their choice as long as they are able to get it; they are free to dress in any way they choose – in some countries it is a crime or will warrant the death penalty.

In this age of social media, many of us are able to access it and flaunt all our business in full public view.　In some countries, it is death penalty to access such modern conveniences.

In the West, many rebel and walk away from a Church if they are introduced to a dress code! In some regions, women are so covered that only their eyes can be seen. If nothing else be thankful for the region in which you live here in the West!

Thank God that we can have as many children as we choose. In some regions they are barely allowed to have one.

In our region we can own land and even pass it on to our children. In other regions, none are allowed to own land.

Thankfulness to God and man are keys to prosperity and success. Un-thankfulness/ingratitude will bring shame and demotion. Be careful how you treat your Pastor, Mentor, Employer (Organization), or anyone who has done anything for your whether great or small. Never bite the hand that feeds you.

"And one of them, when he saw that he was healed, returned, and with a loud voice glorified God, and fell down on his face at His feet, giving Him thanks. And he was a Samaritan. So Jesus answered and said, "Were there not ten cleansed? But where are the nine? Were there not any found who returned to give glory to God except this foreigner?" And He said to him, "Arise, go your way. Your faith has made you well." (Luke 17: 11 – 19)

Ingratitude stops the blessings of God on a nation, individual or organization. It is contagious. Many long-standing organizations and individuals have now fallen because of ingratitude.

Some people only come to you when they need something. They often only remember you when they run into problems and need your help to get out! Some forget you completely when they are comfortable and have all the financial resources and they only remember you when everything has crashed and they are broke!

Never hang around unthankful people – it is contagious and will corrupt your environment. The mainstay of an unthankful person is to criticize, complain and divide! In fact, the favor and presence of God always leaves unthankful people.

For thankful people, increase and multiplication always comes upon them. Begin to thank God for your spouse, your children – because when you were without a spouse or child, you were the one crying out to God for both! Now you complain and criticize everything! If that is true, you have become unthankful and ungrateful and that is in fact a sin.

"For men will be lovers of themselves, lovers of money, boasters, proud, blasphemers, disobedient to parents, unthankful, unholy, unloving, unforgiving, slanderers, without self-control, brutal, despisers of good, traitors, headstrong, haughty, lovers of pleasure rather than lovers of God, having a form of godliness but denying its power. And from such people turn away!" 2 Timothy 3: 2 – 5

Note that the unthankful is in the same group as blasphemer, sexual immorality and so on.

Show thankfulness to God and those that have helped you along the way by reaching out to them and to someone to help them. Thanksgiving and gratitude bring great blessings and will take you to the top.

Shift the Focus for Progress and Prosperity

To bring change to a nation and to institute the right government can only be achieved through Divine Intervention. After the elections there is going to be pain, disappointment and the continuation of the blame-game cycle will continue! Friends and loyalists will now line up for their reward, and again the youth are poised for neglect!

The Church has been given the opportunity to shine and institute Kingdom Principles within the nation to help rescue our Youth and make significant and positive changes! However, selfishness has reared its head among the churches once again. There are many who are involved in politics, but have they made any impact or positive changes? Liberal views have been chipping away at our values and morals and the Christian churches remain silent.

From 2007 the Lord has been outlining that there will be a series of one term Administrations until His purpose is accomplished. Politicians have continually disobeyed the Lord and have been taking advice from wrong sources which have caused great suffering on the Youth and Seniors in the nation! The foundation of the nation has been broken spiritually, and only through Divine Intervention can healing take place. He wants the leaders to come together in a time of unity and repentance with past and present leaders and close the doors and break the curses and cycles that have plagued the nations and have brought instability!

New Government New Solutions

When there is a new government, it is imperative that the new administration does Due Diligence and genuinely looks at what they have inherited. They must be willing to make adjustments only where necessary in the best interest of the people of the nation rather than for their own selfish reasons. They must also be willing to break they un-Godly cycles that exist within their administration and nation.

Oftentimes, many administrations may have plans, but their plans may not be in line with God's plans. Unfortunately, many make plans and decision for the nation in order to promote themselves, show their academic and business prowess to be praised by others – much like Nebuchadnezzar. (2 Kings 24 – 36)

The First 100 Days of Administration

Speaking globally, the first 100 days of any administration are critical, generally speaking, and new administrations must ensure:

1. They seek God concerning the areas of National Finance, Health, Youth and Security. The persons assigned to those areas must be divinely chosen by God because these are critical areas! These persons must be married.

2. There are Mentorship and Apprenticeship programs for the Youth.

3. Tax Amnesty are actioned to help small businesses.

4. Doctors and Nurses who work in the rural areas must receive higher pay.

5. That in various nations where applicable, the Justice System be adjusted to ensure that first offenders carry out community service.

6. Tax cuts and benefits are available for retirees who help within the prison system in the rehabilitation of prisoners.

7. That more men are recruited from the school system.

8. That, especially within Third World Nations, there is a freeze on all divestment and engagement of the Civil Society and Diaspora personnel to come up with a plan to develop locally.

9. There is help for NGOs Churches and other charitable organizations to bring in what is necessary to develop various communities.

10. Establishment of a Management Trainee System so that all the University students – graduates and undergraduates - will be able to employ what they have learnt within the communities and nations!

11. On-time release of pension to pensioners and grant them better health benefits. Ensure that when a pensioner dies, the spouse continues to receive the pension until that deceased spouse's benefits have expired.

12. Merging of all statutory departments, for logistics purposes.

13. Engage the Diaspora in projects without partisanship being a part of the package.

CHAPTER 13

NEW WINESKINS FOR ENTREPRENEURSHIP

"And no one puts new wine into old wineskins; or else the new wine bursts the wineskins, the wine is spilled, and the wineskins are ruined. But new wine must be put into new wineskins." Mark 2: 22

For development and change to take place in a nation, there needs to be new entrepreneurial vessels prepared to take things to a higher level.   This has nothing to do with age, but it has everything to do with an individual, a group or a nation willing to embrace a new mindset and greater vision.

One cannot achieve social partnership, unless new wineskins are available to receive the new wine being poured out. For new wineskins to receive the new wine, there must be unity, one accord birthed by God (not man) through prayer and fasting and a renewed mind. Then we will see new investments, new products and global networking. Without new wineskins for Entrepreneurship, wasting of resources, ruin and ultimately great loss will result!

Teach a Man to Fish

Matthew 25: 14 – 30. Every individual is given gifts and talents to create entrepreneurial opportunities. Furthermore, in order to experience greater opportunities and foster greater growth, every entrepreneur must be faithful in executing their entrepreneurial duties. Those who do not will lose major opportunities, and God calls those persons lazy!   Those just looking for handouts without acting on their ambition and the willingness to level up from where they are in life are deemed LAZY!

When you teach a man to fish, you are empowering him with a lifelong legacy. But when you continually give a man a fish, you are simply satisfying a temporary need and doing him a disservice.   Furthermore, you are breeding manipulation, control and corruption!

The authorities must begin training the young people for Entrepreneurship, (Proverbs 22: 6), and this should begin at the primary level of Education.   Please note that training goes beyond the ordinary teaching activity.   They have to be taught basic work ethic. They must be made to recognize that body piercing and tattooing are not the new office wear and that the dress code is important for business, locally and internationally.

There are many young people, especially in the area of Visual Arts (Art and Craft), who have such great potential on the international scene.   The curriculum at the Edna Manley College of the Visual and Performing Arts (EMCVPA) needs to be revisited, and an inclusion of Marketing and Tourism programs take place, so that opportunities for export of the skills and talents be afforded the youth in the area of Visual Arts (Art and Craft). They also need to look at expand the Art Programs in the High Schools and Primary level institutions by having more competitions in Art and Craft to bring out the talents of our children and begin to channel their talents in a positive direction; and also offer more enticing rewards as well as greater publicity before, during, and after these competitions.

Factories that have closed down need to be re-opened, and activities such as Embroidery, Sewing (clothes), Fashion Designing, all need to be revived and encouraged in schools and communities and within the nations with a view to export. There is a market for these things in Europe and people will require these things for their bathrooms, living rooms, bedrooms; and items such as baby blankets and clothing will do very well in such places!

Throughout the different nations, factories and warehouses that have been wasted or abandoned have the potential for housing entrepreneurial activities – creating employment opportunities and generating much needed revenue. There are things that have been deemed as garbage which have great potential.

It should be made mandatory for every secondary level student throughout the globe to graduate with at least one proven skill.

Nations are wasting resources in cultural activities and short-term handouts. If we all do not get serious, and begin to create Entrepreneurship, then very shortly we will see different nations being taken over by foreigners – and that is actually the case for many nations today.

Governments need to put politics aside and put people in the positions who are qualified and capable of doing the job. We must all learn our lesson from what happened with Greece in 2010.

New Mind, New Wine, New Business

To deal with the economic crises and other global social issues being faced, as leaders we must always dig deeper each day in the things of God, in order to get the necessary solutions. Time changes, people change, the market demands change – EVERYTHING CHANGES! Even currency rates change – dramatically and quickly! Very shortly, you will see a shortage of foreign exchange in various nations.

Now, if everything changes, but the minds/mindsets of the people do not change, how will that affect the changes in demand and how will nations deal with that? The old order cannot deal with the new order. The mind must be renewed each day that it may be able to accurately discern market in order to prevent loss and further problems in the economy.

The solutions that nations have been carrying out include:

1. Redundancy Exercises

2. Increasing Taxes

3. Capitalizing on Immorality

4. Giving Waivers to Foreign Investors

5. Divesting the Land and Assets of the Nation

6. Borrowing from International Lenders

7. Making Decisions that affect mainly the Small Businesses and the Poor

All these decisions are nothing new and it will only create greater hardship for new businesses, new jobs, new ideas; we must embrace New Wine! It is time for us to try unconventional methods. How about this? The mind of the individual must grow before economy can grow. There is no way locally or globally, we can build on two (2) foundations.

At this juncture, we do not need any more statistics, research and documentation. We need action and results!
We need to ask some pertinent questions:

1. Who controls the Economy?

2. Who decides success or failure?
In the same way that hurdling poverty begins in the mind, likewise economic change must first start in the mind. Before that changes, the mind must change: when the mind changes, the speech will change and when that changes, the environment will change and then our pockets will have more than change!

Without a mind change, regardless of the program we put in place, it is going to fail and put us into further debt.

How Do We Change the Mind?

Before the mind of the people change, the minds of the leaders in every sector and category must change! Changes come through the Word of God, Prayer, Disaster and Adversity! We must look to the One Who controls Change. (Psalms 121).

1. Did the Economic Model ascribed to our nation fit the needs of the nation and the time?

2. Are the programs implemented in our schools fit for the needs of the nation's children and the direction that the nation is headed?

If the mind does not change, rest assured, the sight cannot change.

We must remember a vision is also a function of the heart, not just the eyes, and all nations need a blueprint for economic change. In other words, they need a VISION. If the mind is not renewed, how can it truly identify the value that exists within the nation, catch hold of the vision which is to bring the nation out of its current state, into a place of prosperity and success? What do other countries see existing in our nation that we are not seeing? The old way of learning will not solve the mystery. Neither will there be discernment of what the priorities need to be.

If our minds are not changed, then:

1. What will happen in the next five (5) years regarding Job Creation?

2. In this present economic climate, how will governments collect taxes and at what expense?

3. What will happen to University Students who can no longer afford education? And when they graduate, who will employ them?

4. What will happen in the political arena when politicians employ the same strategies and methods in a changing world?

"The Old Model Is Broken, We Need To Create A New One" – **Ban Ki-Moon, Secretary General of the UN** *(May 17, 2012, New York)*

" 'Worldwide, more than 400 million new jobs will be needed over the next decade. That means that policy-makers must get serious, now, about generating decent employment," said Secretary-General Ban Ki-moon at the high-level thematic debate on The State of the World Economy and Finance and its Impact on Development, held on 17 May. "It is time to recognize that human capital and natural capital are every bit as important as financial capital," he added.'"

We need Vision, lest we perish!

Learn from The Wise Businessman

There is a lot we can learn from those around us that can give us some measure of hope and help to propel us into the greatness that is our future. We must also be willing to learn from the greatest Book ever written – the Holy Bible.

The number one focus of wise businessmen is to build solid foundations for themselves, their households and their generations to come:

1. They are not fussy about brand names, and some even purchase a generic cell phone. They often don inexpensive clothing, such as blazers and jeans.

2. They do not throw money away; they watch every dollar and invest wisely. To them, even the coins have value, so they don't throw coins away either.

3. They are not time wasters: they ascribe great value to time and they know that every second wasted is money down the drain. That is why we have to be disciplined and keep our appointments. For them, performance is key!

4. They do not allow friends and family to manipulate their organizations; they will bring a best friend to lunch and fire him/her on the spot! To them, performance is extremely important and it is a business decision. They appreciate and honor loyalty.

5. They will not be quick to hire someone if they realize that the individual has no longevity. What they want for the organization are assets, not liabilities.

6. While they will compete, it may look like war to the public, but they will not ruin a relationship with their

colleagues or competitors. They know that at the end of the day if they fail, they will need to bail each other out.

7. Remember, their children attend school together, they all attend the same church together and they are all members of the same organizations.

8. The wise businessmen are risk takers. They have faith! They may not recognize it as faith, but they have faith.

9. They are movers and shakers; once the price is right and the circumstances are favorable, there is a deal.

10. They are not tied to any political parties as are the poor. Neither will they willingly grab hold of guns to kill everybody who does not agree with them.

11. They are willing to get involved in the processes necessary to bring success to them.

12. Most of them have no patience, show them the plan and you have to show them how you will finance the plan and what the return(s) on their investments will be.

13. They are not afraid to make tough decisions to survive and remain financially viable during tough times.

14. The wise businessman is not afraid of constructive criticism. They like it when you tell them the truth – even if it makes them angry at first. They use constructive criticism to get ahead and many of them will use the criticism to build new businesses.

15. What the poor sees as garbage, a wise businessman sees as an opportunity for money-making.

16. They are not afraid to borrow in order to expand their organization(s).

17. They are not afraid to take a failing product or business with potential and invest in it. They spend millions on marketing and promotion of whatever they are involved in, so that the public can support it as well.

18. Many will say that such persons are only after profits and they pay cheap; but even Jesus outlines to us that He wants profits and interest on anything with which He entrusts us.

19. Anything that does not bear interest or make a profit in any way will be out of business. (Luke 19: 11 – 27). Otherwise, businessmen would not put any money into a bank that does not give interest. They love trade; and for some it is one of their greatest loves.

20. A wise businessman likes wise debt collectors; even if they know that some of their employees are not to them or the organization, as long as they can bring in a significant portion of the bad debt, they will always have a place in that organization. (Luke 16)

Remember, God is also a wise businessman. He is watching you. He will not give you great wealth if you are not faithful in another man's business. (Luke 16: 12). Be faithful in your organization. Faithfulness/Loyalty is a prerequisite for Promotion. Your reliability is proof of your capacity to properly manage resources.

Learn from the wise businessman what you can, and run with it.

Everything Affects Business

The success of a nation or organization is the ability of those operating it to hear and to obey what God says concerning its plans and operations. When God's influence begins to be a part of your decision-making, then each person will enjoy prosperity. It is not about calling a pastor to have devotion for a few minutes once in a blue moon; it is about making God and His principles a part of our decision-making process on a regular basis.

Millions of resources are being wasted because of man's unwillingness to "seek ye first, the Kingdom of God and His righteousness" so that everything else can be added and fall into place. At the end of everything, God has the final say. The inability of our political parties to seek the Lord has put the nation on the path of loss of all its assets.

When a nation begins struggling and increases its debts, it is on its way to becoming bankrupt in assets. We have never heard a leader say that he/she is going to inquire of the Lord to see what problems caused the initial issues facing the nation. Something broken cannot be fixed unless you know the root cause of the problem is.

Everything, both spiritual and natural, affects business and the economy. You cannot build on a foundation that has cracks; it will ultimately crash! For example, we fail to fix the issues arising in Politics, while pushing to promote Tourism. The political stability of a nation is one of the biggest factors that influence Tourism: if potential tourists catch wind of anything slightly unstable concerning politics and government, then Tourism will be negatively affected in a big way! Watch and see what will happen not long from now concerning Tourism.

Past Problems

Many administrations are guilty of financial injustices against its people. Nations cannot move forward economically until political parties and regimes address the financial injustices that were meted out to the people of the nation. For example, where the US government- afforded bailouts to the wealthy while many of the poor lost their homes and ultimately their families – is something that needs to be made right. Also, in Jamaica, where the FINSAC (Financial Sector Adjustment Company) deals were made to the disadvantage of the poor of the nation, including the divestments of the sugar industry, national airline and its routes, and major properties – are still bearing heavily on the nation – and those things need to be made right before these nations can see the economic growth they desire. Spiritually-speaking it is still weighing the nation down and they must be addressed if nations are to progress economically. Major companies that were once making healthy profits, have fallen behind and experience significant losses, and it is the negative actions/activities that affected their success.

Everything affects business decision-making. That includes who company owners/leaders hire, who they fire, who they rob, how they end relationships with partners and employees, how they carry out their deals, how and with whom they network; even the products they sell/distribute and also the persons they choose to marry.

Looking Beyond Qualifications

Academic qualifications are good, but they should not be the only criteria that create the basis for your hiring decisions. One should look beyond 'qualifications' and look at other qualities such as a gift or 'knack' a person possesses for the job/task/operation. Such persons are blessed with the gift to do the job. (Genesis 30: 27 – 30) Even in hard times, your organization can experience growth and increase if you have the right persons on board; someone gifted to function beyond academics.

Look for persons who are visionaries and team players. They must be good listeners; firm, self-sacrificing and those who are willing to inspect what they expect. A good listener will always be a successful leader, because as they listen to both God and man, solutions will come forth. Such a blessed person can bring peace, unity and growth to the organization even as others fail.

Have you ever seen a thriving organization go down the moment the company removed one (1) employee, or after signing a deal that was never in the original vision? Have you ever seen an organization lose when they merge or takeover another organization or when the lifestyle of one or more members of the organization changes for the worse? Have you ever seen the values and discipline of a school deteriorate once a particular principal leaves?

Everything matters in the success of a business, and everything plays a role. You may have a staff member that you took for granted and thought that he/she was only taking up space. Just the presence of that one person can make a difference in your organization of which you might not even be aware.

Hope for Struggling Businesses

". . . He said to Simon, "Launch out into the deep and let down your nets for a catch." But Simon answered and said to Him, "Master, we have toiled all night and caught nothing; nevertheless, at Your word I will let down the net." And when they had done this, they caught a great number of fish, and their net was breaking. . ." (Luke 5: 5 – 8)

Despite your circumstances today – your business might be struggling, sales are low and slow, the bills are piling up and you are being pressured by lenders – there is always hope for a large catch. In order to receive a miracle that will turn your circumstances around, you need to seek for an instruction - there is always something that you have in possession that can turn things around.

Before one can experience a turnaround within your business or the nation:

1. First, your mindset must begin to change.

2. Second, obedience to instruction is key.

3. Third, you must be willing to be taught by people who are not a part of your profession or even those deemed 'unqualified'. Would an economist take advice from a 'higgler'? Would a doctor take advice from a wholesale owner on how to run successful practice/business? Would a fisherman take instructions from a carpenter on how to be an effective entrepreneur?

In order to turn around your struggling business, you must be willing to do something beyond 'the norm': think deeper, think bigger, increase your faith and be willing to take risks! Even in areas you have failed before, be willing to try again.

Put Local First

There is a dangerous trend that is now coming to the fore in many nations as a result of the financial situations: Nations are now giving citizenship to those who have the monetary substance, and this is a dangerous precedence which has the potential for global security problems.

What nations should be doing is creating an environment for local businesses to thrive! Local businesses provide the opportunities to service the communities. They are the ones who ought to be getting tax breaks, and the alleviation of certain restrictions.

If we desire to see growth in Tourism, we must ensure that we create the environment for locals also to enjoy the beauty of their own country. How many locals can afford to spend a weekend at an All-Inclusive Hotel?

We must engage the principle where we take care of family first! Visitors will always come and go but family will always remain family! We have to believe in ourselves that what we have is of value, and change always begins within, not from the outside.

Nations should not be passing laws because of external influencers; laws must be passed when there is the need for the betterment of the people. Leaders must be willing to engage in self-sacrifice. Leaders cannot expect the people do what they are not willing to do. They must take the time to listen to the people as numerous solutions lie within them.

Cast Your Net and Do Not Give Up

When you cast your net and nothing comes up, do not give up - there are lessons to be learned. You are getting wiser. Your faith is getting stronger. God may be trying to get your attention so that you put your trust in Him. God is trying to change your mindset with the tactics and strategies of fishing. It is not luck or your qualifications that were giving you success in the past. It was in fact God's favor that caused you to succeed all along. God may have a bigger plan for your business. He wants to expand it with new products and ideas. Some people are going through problems because He wants to change their profession and re-route them – getting them into a different geographical area.

Despite how dismal things may seem, there is always something you possess in your physical or spiritual house that can change the game for you. Your situation is not generally as bad as it may seem. In no time, you could go from zero to hero.

Oftentimes, nations tend to focus on improving infrastructure and ignore the invaluable human resources.

When God is going to bless a nation, the vessel He pours into first is the human vessel, who have the ability and capacity to engage change!

I write this to encourage all business owners that are planning to call it a day: DO NOT GIVE UP – launch out into the deep!

Compassion in Business Dealings

There is no doubt that the Bible is the best guide for teaching us how to conduct business transactions in an honest and ethical way. The shaking of the global marketplace is the result of the treatment of the poor and the less fortunate in business transactions by business people and governments. Many do not care, because they believe that regardless of all they do, they will always be in business.

We are all customers in one way or another, hence, if hard times befall a customer, it is imperative that business people carry out business dealings/transactions with compassion. CEOs in various organizations must ensure that when they are recruiting or are placing people in position to deal with the public, their choices must go beyond academic qualifications. If they want their organizations to remain viable, they must put people in place that will show compassion. You cannot allow making a huge profit or the existing laws and guidelines to be excuses given for mistreating their customers/clients and to make judgements.

Any organization or individual within the organization who make decisions without showing mercy or compassion will not last! Before any decisions are made ask yourself this question: "How would I feel if I were on the other side of this situation?"

Many times, the representatives of these organizations smile in the faces of the customers/clients and say – 'I'm sorry but this is a business decision'!

Many people have ended up on the street for something simple, when the organization could have simply worked with them to get back on their feet. There are many organizations that carry out business deals and show no mercy/compassion, leaving many people brokenhearted and bankrupt!

There is no one in this world who has never had a down period or loss! In Life, we all have seasons and different seasons come at different times for different people. (Ecclesiastes 3). Going through a hard season does not mean that the individual is careless. God may just be bringing them through a season of increasing their faith because he wants to increase their business and in the interim, teach them a different level of mercy and compassion. For example, when someone meets in an accident or dies, and the insurance company denies them or their families any form of compensation, the unfair decision-maker will never understand what it is like until it happens to them one day - then they will understand.

Likewise, many of them will never understand what it is like for a person to own their home (or business) for over 40 years – where all their children grew up there and know no other place as home, and when they fall on hard times their place is taken away by the heads of these financial institutions and sold to their friends, instead of extending mercy and work with them, and allow them the opportunity to keep their home.

How about when a husband and wife have retired after over 40 years or more of faithful service, and one spouse dies and the pension that was taken out of the salary of that deceased spouse is stopped instead of going to the household of that remaining spouse to take care of what they built together? Many cannot even get their pension, and are unable to buy the medication they need to live a healthy life!

For so many, every cent is withdrawn from their already small accounts in fees and other charges as a result of the greed of others!

The Bible is clear on how we must operate in business:

1. Do not make the people redundant and not pay them. (Deuteronomy 15: 13)

2. Ensure that within your budget there is always something there for the poor. (Leviticus 23: 22)

3. Pay the people on time when they work. Do not take the money, invest it in something else, and have the people waiting unnecessarily for their earned pay/salary. (Leviticus 23: 22)

4. When someone falls on hard times, do not allow them to be slaves or engage in prostitution. (Leviticus 25: 39)

5. Do not take a bribe and quickly break a contract. (Psalm 15: 1 – 5; Micah 6: 5)

6. Treat both staff and customers with respect. (Leviticus 25: 43)

7. Always conduct your business with integrity. (Proverbs 22: 1; Leviticus 19: 35 – 36)

8. Engage in fair business practices. Give the consumer what you advertise. Do not trick them with the fine print.

9. Write off all the debts after seven (7) years if you want the Lord to bless you in business. Do not sell the debts to other organizations, keeping the people enslaved.

10. Do not repossess or take the people's property away on a weekend or when they have gone to church.

CHAPTER 14

CHANGE THROUGH EDUCATIONAL REFORM

Many people are talking today about the Education System in Jamaica and are purporting various arguments about what went wrong and what we need to do to fix it.

Let it be known that Jamaica still has one of the best Education Systems in the world! Nevertheless, we now need to look at how to improve this system at all levels. Many countries are attempting to model their system by our standards.

Look at the quality of our Teachers! Generally, if the quality of output from our teachers fall, then the quality of what exists in all sectors will fall! The teachers are the ones who mold our children, bring out their purpose and help to direct them on the right career path. Teachers, therefore, shape our children and ultimately shape the society! There is a difference between someone who can teach something and a Teacher. Teaching is a God-given gift that brings out the hidden potential in a person and can cause them to pass a subject at which they were initially doing poorly.

There are a number of persons in the Education system, who are teaching but they are not Teachers. Some are simply persons who have done well in a particular subject area, but are not able to impart it well.

Many times, students who have not acquired the number of subjects they hoped to have, have been encouraged to turn to Teaching as a last resort. On other occasions, some have turned to Teaching because there are no other jobs or options.

Solution

There must be proper screening at the tertiary level at the entry level. Such persons must have a passion and compassion as well as a love for this discipline. They must also have strong discerning to see beyond the physical capabilities and social behavior of each student and identify their potential and as such be willing to work with them to see the realization of such students.

Principals, P.T.A.s and Chairpersons

The politics involved in the selection of Principals must be removed. They should not be selected on the basis of academic achievement only. They must, however, have strong Leadership and Administrative Skills. They must also be good role models and examples within the community. They must command respect, not demand it!

The role of the Parent-Teacher Associations (P.T.A.) must be revisited. They must work in conjunction with all parties involved in the life of the schools for the development of all children. They also need to work along with Guidance Counselors to deal with family issues that play out in the school environment. The Guidance Counselors on the other hand, because of the significant and pivotal role they play in the life of each student, must have strong Christian backgrounds.

The Chairperson of a School Board must be one who walks in integrity, whose lifestyle allows them to be good examples and mentors, not only to the students, but also to the parents as well. His/Her behavior and actions both publicly and privately should be of a high standard.

The Chairperson must be involved in all the activities in the life of the school.

Discipline

This is universal in that it takes not just teachers, but the entire School Community – Parents included – to monitor the Students! No body-piercing, nor tattooing, no pants below the waist, or beltless pants; and no roaming the streets at late hours! They must not be allowed to disrespect teachers in any way. The students should not be allowed to dictate how they are to be disciplined.

Education

The area of Education is broad in its scope and is a key area in any nation. Some perceive that the Governmental Department that governs Education within its nation, only deals with Principal/School Administrators' Assignments, Distribution of Remuneration, and keeping a running list of Grades, Graduates and their Passes, as well as Teachers, Ancillary and Auxiliary Staff. The department of any government that governs Education needs to keep its proverbial ears close to the ground – they need to know what's happening throughout the schools of the nation, have regular meetings not only with the principals, but also with the teachers, students and parents together at different levels. One of their primary goals must be to ensure that the people of the nation achieve at minimum a Secondary level education.

Additionally, the arm of any government that deals with Education needs to utilize the Military and Police Personnel as Volunteer Teachers and Chaplains to instill a certain level of respect, discipline and civic pride among the people starting with the children and youth. Ultimately, all things being equal, it has the potential to facilitate better communities and better nations.

Uniting for Local and Global Change

More and more worldwide, changes are taking place rapidly right before our eyes. Many leaders are stuck in neutral and most are finding it overwhelming - they cannot fix it! We are seeing a domino effect: when they try to fix one area, another issue pops up repeatedly and they are almost at their wit's end. Diplomacy is fast becoming inadequate; it is seemingly all leaders can do to keep it all together and under wraps.

To be quite honest, many of the problems being faced by leaders are the result of poor choices. Are we willing to pay the price to continue this cycle? The only 'solution' that is being executed is that one side is pointing fingers at the other side and vice versa.

In order to be successful leaders, the number one priority must be to please God; He will please the people. Most leaders are using old and familiar political tactics. They are attempting to please party-faithful individuals and other stake holders in order to guarantee success. But they must understand that only God can guarantee success, or anything else for that matter.

Here's a question: Can a leader be popular in the eyes of man, but unpopular with God? Yes indeed! It happens everywhere. For the sake of longevity, leaders must obtain and maintain God's favor, not man's promises. It's not about man's criticism, but about what God says.

Daniel 2: 21 reminds us, *"And He changes the times and the seasons; He removes kings and raises up kings; He gives wisdom to the wise and knowledge to those who have understanding."* (See also Daniel 4: 17, Daniel 5: 21)

1. It does not matter what plans leaders try to implement; there cannot be any success without God's validation.

2. Most leaders will honor gold, silver and bronze even more than they honor Who holds their lives in His hands.

3. There are many political geniuses, orators and strategists worldwide. But God is the Lord of International Politics and He knows all the right moves to make.

A lot is being demanded from leaders regarding Foreign Policies, Economic Policies and Success and Job Creation. But let us get it straight: none of this can be achieved without first seeking God and employing His principles. The nations will not experience economic turnaround even if we were to bring in foreign investors and remove taxes and tariffs. All that will do is totally remove the competitive edge of the local businesses. The money will be sucked out of the country and the debt ceiling will continue to increase.

All on Board

For local or global change, all leaders need to come together – both past and present; and work out a plan to chart the nation ahead. The media also has a role to play. They need to lift the standard. They also have to be willing to help to bring healing to the nation. The number one criterion must be TRUTH!

Many that can help the political process are staying away from it, because they are saying that the media does not care about truth and they are not trustworthy.

A lot of companies, because of the economic situation, are either laying off workers or making them redundant, and these persons cannot get their money. Even those who work on a weekly basis cannot collect a salary. They must remember that they have families and if this matter is not addressed, then it will bring serious repercussions.

Be Vigilant

Leaders and Security Personnel must realize that a leopard never changes its spots. Hence, there is no time for complacency, and all must be vigilant. The enemy is changing his strategy, but he is still an enemy. Furthermore, you must remember that the enemy within is always greater than the enemy without.

It is time for leaders at every level throughout the nations, to unite. There needs to be new thinking, new dialogues. It is time for them to evaluate their inner circle, and understand that times and seasons have changed.

Diplomacy is going through the door and Public Relations strategies out the window, while some are attempting to create a personal legacy. All in all, if we are to truly move ahead, our old habits must surrender to CHANGE.

New Insight for Global Change

It is critical for all stakeholders – whether economic, political, security or the civil society – to seek Divine insight for the nation to move forward.

The key questions for all organizations at this point are: *'How do I prepare my organization for the inevitable change – whether positive or negative - that will take place?'*

'What are the Strengths, Weaknesses, Opportunities and Threats that exist for my organization?'
'What will I need to do to remain in the market?'

'Will I need to retool, revamp or re-structure?'

'What should my main areas of focus be going forward?'

We continually experience global change – some changes happening more rapidly than others. Most organizations usually employ market research to identify market trends. Some even use historical data, profit margin statistics in an effort to determine what is going on; but none of it is helping. Yet they are not trying anything new. A nation cannot run an economy blindly and without going back to the foundation. There are so many with PhDs competing for different political office without offering anything new. Many just oppose valuable suggestions and recommendations for the sake of opposing and without genuinely determining the potential of success for the nation. How can we have change if everyone is applying the same failed system.

Politicians often employ polls, media surveys and historical data to guide their decision-making for the future; but all these can mislead and serve to facilitate poor decision-making. If investors do not change their ways of thinking, they are going to lose millions and some will be out of business.

One will not have the insight needed on Business, Security, Economic/Health Matters or National Direction without reading the Word of God. The advice of Political and Economic pundits is of little value in comparison to the wisdom of God. We need Spirit-filled teachers to prepare the leaders and the nation for what lies ahead.

While age brings wisdom from experience to some extent, God's schooling brings even greater insight. Both young and old must equally seek to hear from God if we are to have a balanced society. (Joel 2: 28). It is very important for advisors at any level and in any capacity to hear from God! (Exodus 24: 9 – 14; 1 Kings 12: 28)

Cyber Revolution

"But you, Daniel, shut up the words, and seal the book until the time of the end; many shall run to and fro, and knowledge shall increase." (Daniel 12: 4)

While knowledge is increasing, most people are downsizing and attempting to increase their technological systems. Even children are being given tablets and iPads! Without the proper levels of integrity and control measures, how will we control Cyber Issues? Are our records and finances really safe? What about school, health or even prison records – are they safe? Should companies be thinking of using manual records and go back to basics as a measure of securing pertinent information, documents and money? Based on Biblical Prophecies (Revelation 13: 16 – 18). Are we seeing the 3-Point Plan as outlined in the Book of Revelation: One-World Currency, One-World Religion and One-World Government, coming together?

We are now seeing clear indications of the Cashless Society coming to the fore where ever almost every financial transaction is being electronically monitored. Will Cyber Crimes affect the sovereignty of a nation, bringing financial hardships on them, forcing them to adopt evil, un-Godly measures to survive?

According to USATODAY.COM on May 9, 2013, *"...an alleged international gang of cyber-thieves managed to steal $45 million from thousands of ATMs in carefully coordinated attacks conducted in a matter of hours..."*

So, it begs the question, "How safe is anything of ours?"

Bitcoins and E-Money are Digital Currencies now rising and are becoming more attractive to payment providers and merchants worldwide. Bitcoins are an experimental currency being tested in several economies today. E-Money is a digital equivalent of cash stored on an electronic device or remotely at a server and can be used to make small payments.

Does this mean that the currencies of the nations will now be put under pressure to the point where they lose value and nations will be forced to accept these new species of money? It is something to think about because it affects every one of us.

Who is safe? What is safe? Where are we and all we own safe? Someone could be a millionaire today and a pauper tomorrow, even more quickly than the traditional 'methods'!

We have seen the movies and heard the possible scenarios and we have laughed at, ridiculed and even ignored them but now it is time to pay attention! These things are real and happening and we can ignore them no longer because we will all be negatively affected.

New insight is needed!

Prepare for Change

Nothing remains the same! Everything is changing including the Earth. Times change! Seasons change. Mankind is the only being that resists change.

Change is inevitable, but there are many who say that everything must be proven and that beyond that, it is either not real or not worth knowing. However, if that is the belief in the season of change, then many will be humbled, and they will no longer experience favor! If what they believe is true, then how do we prove that there is a tomorrow?

Those who plan without God are in fact proclaiming that they are their own masters. Every sector has to prepare for change – politicians, media, church, business investors and every other sector. If persons within these sectors do not plan, then there are going to be great losses and numerous missed opportunities.

Some are praying for God to move, but when God moves, and we are not willing to change our mindsets and follow His leading, then we will miss the mark.

Many nations are suffering because every time they are given the opportunity for change, they make the wrong choices. Choices always bring us either forward or backward. What are you willing to do differently? Are you willing to change your way of thinking? Are you willing to be criticized and to stand alone in order to get the right results?

In order to understand Change, we must be sensitive to His word. It is critical for us to recognize the season we are in and what that season requires. We must ask the question, 'How do I deal with those who resist change?'

Every leader must be sensitive to Times and Seasons. If they are not, then the wise thing to do is to surround themselves with those who do.

Many leaders still think that the old tricks of the trade will always work but they do not. Are we willing to embrace God's principles to help humanity and to bring change? Are leaders willing to implement new strategies and plans, restructure and reform?

Market Conditions

Failure to understand the changes in Market Conditions or even the general marketplace itself is the driving force behind our global problems. Most financial institutions do not understand Times and Seasons and so many of them are caught off-guard, which causes great suffering to humanity.

It is time for the Government and the financial institutions to deal with this issue and change their leadership styles and approach.

Many people and nations often respond to situations after the fact rather than putting plans in place in the event of a situation? This can bring failure, loss and waste. When one does not plan for change, then they get changed!

Countries that do not have an economic blueprint or practical strategies in place, but instead depend on other countries' or organization's policies to drive their nation's economy, need to ask and answer some very critical questions:

1. How will my country (and countrymen) respond to changes that occur within that other nation (or organization)?

2. How will those changes negatively affect my country?

3. What contingency plans have been put in place to deal with major changes and/or fallouts within the other nation?

It is better to build a foundation ahead of time that can deal with the potential changes ahead and expand where necessary, than to attempt a clean up after things have gone awry.

Many things take place in a season of change – a changing of the guard, market change, variety, systems, legislation, monetary policies, prices, climate change, security, shift and people.

Changes can come about through uncommon people and in uncommon places, through uncommon situations. Sometimes, the greatest access we receive comes when we are willing to change according to His Times and Seasons. It is important for us to recognize that the most problematic areas or situations within a nation are where the greatest wealth exists.

We must be willing to embrace and be a part of the change necessary for individual and national development and success; and to do this requires us to prepare ourselves for inevitable change.

Executives Need A Lifestyle Exchange

Politicians and Executives at all levels need to come out of their comfort zones and their current lifestyle and go into one or a few of the developing nations and live with poor in the depressed and deeply poverty-stricken areas for four months, and have first-hand experience of the way of life for people living in these conditions.

It has been previously expressed that to be an effective manager by just staying in the luxury of the air-conditioned office environment with all the amenities, one needs to go into the environment directly and see how other people live, in what conditions they function with the 'resources' they have.

Ask the questions:

1. How many United Nations (UN) personnel at all levels, and World Bank, International Monetary Fund (IMF), politicians and other executives in strategic positions know what it is to be poor?

2. When such persons visit the different developing countries, at which hotels do they sleep?

3. Which airline do they use (if any)?

If they should really take a look at the United Nations reports, or go into the places within these nations where the "common man" goes, they may get a better understanding of what humanity faces on a daily basis, and the effect of policies they formulate and the decisions they make, on the people of the nation. They will see and feel the results of the waste that takes place on a daily basis and will recognize the unequal distribution of resources. They will also see the result of their neglect of the poor.

A simple thing such as high bank charges, how many of the executives can justify their increase? 95% of those who use the bank are the poor. The 5% of the 'haves'/rich that use the bank only do so for the sake of investment loans and daily housekeeping. The majority of their funds are off-shore or in hedge funds which are protected. They only have to pay Management Fee.

Biblical Principles outline that the rich man must pay higher taxes than the poor does. Furthermore, they are to give more as God prospers them.

No Shortage of Money

Regardless of what we hear about money shortage to deal with social issues such as Free Education, Free Health,

Water, Sanitation and Training; or even actively assisting veterans with health care and getting homes in which to live - there is no money shortage!

It is through proper management of the resources and the assurance of its equal distribution among the people that will ensure that everyone is given the opportunity to live a prosperous life, giving them the opportunity to serve in every strata of society. Globally speaking, there is only one set of persons serving on boards and/or benefitting from the current system.

1. If there was money shortage, where are the billions coming from to elect political leaders? Where are the billions coming from the facilitate research that become useless the moment they are completed? Where do they find money to give aid in the time disaster, which incidentally is the only time the poor are remembered?

2. Why are dogs living better than human beings?

3. When new executives are elected, millions are spent to refurbish their offices. Oftentimes the money used to refurbish is more than the value of 'the building. From where did the money come?

Every executive is given favor by God within the position they are place to help humanity. It is not about their intellect, they are placed in authority to help humanity. Many of the executives are racking up unnecessary expenses and the poor are the ones who often foot the bills or pay the consequences.

Time to Cut

The time has come, for them to begin cutting their luxuries and the wastage. We cannot reduce poverty or talk about sustainable development when only one set of persons are being required to make sacrifices.

Make no mistake, many of the executives know that if the poor are given the opportunity to succeed, the profits will decrease. But they must understand, unless the poor of the society are financially strong – that is – if the 'feet' of the society are not moving, then the rest of the body cannot move!

In one country, a great deal of money is being spent to do research on the oddities of a duck's private parts, and millions are being spent on erecting statues. Meanwhile, there are children who cannot afford text books or food. There are many people who are carrying out research when all it takes is simple common sense. For example, to find out the causes of Crime, instead of spending money to do research, simply take a good look – it is lack of employment and social injustices that are the main factors.

Instead of fixing the issues, or going to live in the communities themselves for a period in order to be a better manager, they are passing laws to contain and control.

Millions are being spent to research why a research was implemented.

Change Political Ideology

Everyone wants change within a nation. However, before change can come, the political ideology that currently exists must change.

The natural man – particularly the poor – does not/do not know the system of government for which they are voting. Promises are made during every election season; however, the party's representatives do not state their beliefs or ethical stance so the people vote blindly! But, simply put, because the people do not know the substance of whom they vote for, then the people will continue to vote blindly and make wrong choices.

There are many views on how a nation should be led politically including – Democracy, Liberalism, Socialism, Communism and Theocracy. Each view deals with the kind of government it is believed that should exist within the nation, the type of economy pursued, as well as the moral and ethical blueprint for the nation.

So, in the West, for example, Communism and Socialism are fast becoming obsolete; but now there is a battle between Conservativism, Liberalism and Theocracy.

We have seen a push for liberal views to dominate the globe. Even communists and socialists have now disguised themselves under liberal views! However, let us look into it. For the sake of the normal man such as myself, Liberalism emphasizes the Government as the problem-solver and equality for all. Furthermore, Liberals believe in abortion and that a fetus is not human life. They fund abortion with tax payers' money and believe that everything must be liberalized.

Conservatives speak about personal responsibility, limiting government, a free market, individual liberty and that the role of government is to provide the people with the freedom necessary to do what they need to in order to solve problems.

Theocracy states that men and women are not equal in leadership of the family, and that the man is the head of the household. Everyone is not equal, not even Jesus' disciples were equal. The Biblical view does not embrace handouts – it instead states that each must labor to eat. It also tells us to empower the poor. So, while we feed them as Jesus did, we also must teach them to fish – labor. The Theocratic view also states abstinence from sex before marriage, sex education and responsible parenting.

If the government is going to give rights for everything, it is going to result in chaos! Interestingly, Conservativism, like Theocracy, states that human life begins at conception, abortion is murder and both support the death penalty as long as there is a fair justice system.

The Theocratic view believes in nurturing the gifts and talents of the individual and the development of human resources.

Every ideology – regardless of the political connection – must necessarily embrace the Bible as the blueprint for individuals and nations. The problem is that governments have diverted from that focus. They have created and developed ideologies that hold strong, demonic views and oftentimes their personal views – which are now falling apart and are creating more problems.

Every ideology must have a foundation on which they base their views. Theocracy uses the Bible as the guideline. If a view or idea does not have a solid base, then it will lead to bondage, enslavement, economic failure. This is the year that every ideology and view will be tested to see what stands.

The Liberal view states that God has no place in Government, but God is the one who established Civil Government (Romans 13/14). All authorities are accountable to Him! He rules in the affairs of men! The earth is the Lord's and the fullness thereof!

Theocracy states that there is a level playing field in the marketplace, and promotes protection of the poor from the rich; and also, that people should not get wealth by dishonest gain!

1. No ideology must contradict the Bible and any ideology that does is dangerous.

2. The Bible also promotes affordable energy – oil gas, coal, solar! It does not support monopoly. It supports free healthcare, amnesty and transfer of the wealth of the wicked to the just!

3. The Bible also supports accountability for everyone's stewardship and that the family first is responsible for educating their children.

4. The Bible also states that every man has a right to protect himself and his family!

Regardless of the political party to which a person is affiliated, the true ideologies of the political party needs to be checked; and if those ideologies are not aligned with the Bible, then failure is imminent!

For good government, there must be good laws. God's laws are always perfect! He is an expert in government. Laws must be made by God's guidelines. (Psalm 19: 7). Additionally, let us recognize that the government of God supports the payment of tax by every category of society. Likewise, the government of God requires persons at all levels, including the government of the land, to Tithe and give into the House of God.

CHAPTER 15

CRIME, SPORTS AND HUMAN INVESTMENT

One of the greatest investments is investing in Humans. The reason for global and local economic problems we are now experiencing is Human Neglect. Education, Health, Food, Water and Housing are first priority! There will be no change until we address these issues. Interestingly, for most international lenders, these are not areas of priority. Do not be surprised if you begin to see budgetary cuts in these areas.

Modifying tax is not the number one answer to turning the economy around. Stop neglecting the human aspect, look at the practices and policies and deal with that in order to bring change!

Many times, governments turn to the private sector for solutions, while they neglect the people who are experiencing the problem. They often have the solutions and can give greater insight to bring solutions. What they do not realize is that oftentimes, the solutions are in the muddy places!

The private sector is a unit driven by cost, sales and profit-making. Their decisions do not take persons into consideration; they are driven by numbers.

We need a policy shift now more than ever! The wealth cannot be in one area only. There needs to be a balance if there is going to be people power. Jesus outlined the Role of Society in Human Affairs in His principles. Biblical Economics also suggests, when there is recession, the greater portion of the tax should always be with the rich. This fact is supported by Warren Buffett who is an American business magnate, investor, speaker, philanthropist and as at the time this book was written the third (3rd) wealthiest man in the world - Chairman and CEO of a multi-billion-dollar conglomerate in United States.

Possible Solutions

For local and global change and for balance to take place, we have to look at some of these:

1. Salaries, perks and other benefits for executives. Some of those need to be reduced.

2. Military spending. This should be reduced globally.

3. Unnecessary refurbishing of buildings. This practice should cease.

4. Taxation. Financial Market investments should be taxed.

5. Reduce unnecessary manpower, such as assistants that are assigned to assistants.

These areas must be re-assessed.

Dealing with Crime

The cancer of crime that is eating away at the society cannot be controlled or dealt with unless we are ready to deal with the root. For every problem there is a root cause, in much the same way that the success of an individual or a nation has to deal with obedience. (Deuteronomy 28: 1 – 14)

We have to change our mindset. Most times, policies put in place to control crime, do not affect those who are committing the crime; only the innocent feel it!

It is easy to put plans in place, but oftentimes, those who put policies and laws in place are not subject to those laws. VIPs get VIP treatment and most do not get screened. Most are secured or are heavily guarded!

Ask these questions:

1. Who benefits from crime?

2. What does crime have to do with getting power and staying rich?

3. How does one's actions influence the nation's crime rate from spiritual and natural standpoints?

4. What are we fighting? One cannot win a battle until one knows what he/she is fighting!

5. Why are we playing politics with crime?

6. Why are we afraid to deal with the truth?

7. Why do we blame the security forces only, as if they are telling people to commit the crime?

Most persons within the nation know what to do to reduce crime. But to deal with it from the root will affect all sectors because it influences all sectors.

No one really wants to lose power. Everyone in every sector loves power and it is going to take serious Divine Intervention to send the wakeup call and remind us all who truly has all power.

Dealing with crime has to do with our beliefs and our mindsets, and we have to be willing to accept the truth. As a people within the nation, we do not like the truth. In fact, we hate to hear it. We cannot be doing the same thing each day and expect different results. We must change in order to get different results! We do not need more laws, we each need a new mindset!

Remember, *"Righteousness exalts a nation . . ."*

Does God Have A Place in Sports?

In Sports, everybody wants to be a winner! There are numerous victories, defeats and all the emotions that go along with and surround sports. Everyone who is involved in sporting activities, from the sponsors to the coaches to the fans, want to know that they or the players and athletes they support will win. But it is important for all involved in sports

Jamaica is one Third World nation that stands out among their First World counterparts in the area of sports. Yet there is always room for improvement.

Isaiah 48: 17 says, *"Thus says the LORD, your Redeemer, the Holy One of Israel: 'I am the LORD your God, Who teaches you to profit, Who leads you by the way you should go.'"*

This clearly shows us that applying biblical principles in Sports will bring tremendous profit in every capacity. We cannot leave God out of Sports. In addition to that, God empowered each player, each athlete with the equipment (body), He gave each one the tools with which to formulate the tactics and strategies – the formations, plays, and speed with which to function. Furthermore, He gives the insight and intelligence to achieve great things.

Many times, various persons are selected to join or head the delegations and management teams that work with the various players/athletes. You will even see yoga specialists, health and fitness gurus and doctors, but what is not seen is a Spirit-filled chaplain.

Spiritual Strategies

Some things as simple as Fasting and Prayer can give you great victory. A 21-day Fast releases tactics and strategies. Three-day Fasts release favor against a difficult opponent; hearing from God is the key to victory and will allow you to choose the right team.

Picking a team goes beyond talent and performance; but those who are more focused and favorable will win.

We have seen many persons who have applied God's principles and have been successful – Shelly-Ann Frazer-Pryce, Tim Tebow and Jeremy Lin. Even the Ravens who brought on the upset in the Superbowl 2013 were inspired by Psalms 91.

For the Fiji World Cup Rugby Team, the Croatian World Cup Soccer Team, the Jamaica Reggae Boyz or any other team which chooses to use Biblical Principles to achieve victory and maintain it, they must continually be inspired.

Solutions for Sports

During the tenure of Brazilian Rene Simoes, former coach of Jamaica's International Football (Soccer) Team, he was inspired by the word "Jesus Saves!" As it stands now, the current team needs to have a tag line – something that will inspire them and motivate the team to surpass their own expectations of themselves and propel them into victory. For example, "With God all things are possible!" Also, they need to fast at least two (2) weeks before a game. They can also divide the team into two (2) groups to pray and seek the Lord. They also need to shift the players around.

There needs to be one-on-one sessions on a daily basis with the players to deal with their daily mindset. More player-input along with the tactics and strategies which the team should apply, not just to rely on the manager or court.

The team needs to bond and become a cohesive unit. Furthermore, talent and money cannot be the motivating factors in team selection. There must be a genuine love for the sport and the country. Efforts must be made to promote loyalty to the team, the goals and visions of the team and to the country for which they play.

In order to get greater commitment from them and a greater love among them, apply a different strategy; encourage them to interact with and play against high school teams, prep school teams, and little-known clubs. This will keep stirring a fire within them and it will serve to sharpen their skills, and give them an opportunity not only to be mentors to an upcoming generation, but will also renew their focus and allow them to identify future team members.

The lifestyle of each and every player is important. 1 Corinthians 9: 24 – 27 and Hebrews 12: 1 remind us.

Finally, equal emphasis must be given to all girls' teams. They are equally important and should not be neglected.

The Bible: Your Investment Guide

"However, we speak wisdom among those who are mature, yet not the wisdom of this age, nor of the rulers of this age, who are coming to nothing. But we speak the wisdom of God in a mystery, the hidden wisdom which God ordained before the ages for our glory" (2 Corinthians 2: 6 – 7)

Only the Spiritually mature can understand the Wisdom of God. The wisdom of the world is foolishness compared to the wisdom of God. It is for this reason that the plans and advice of philosophers and advisors, who do not seek God, have come to naught. Many will employ the advice of the various money magazines for investment purposes – stocks, bonds and other investment portfolios. But the Bible is the most accurate tool for investment. It tells the Times and Seasons to invest, in what to invest, where to invest (including other countries) wisdom, integrity and solutions in business. It also gives keys to investment and it is your original blueprint in terms of investment. When one uses the Word of God as a guideline to carry out transactions and abides by these principles, then one will experience growth, prosperity, increase in new investments, job creation, divine protection, abundance as well as reduction in crime, debt and security costs, particularly with guns and ammunition.

The days of wanting to create a prosperous economic environment by ignoring the principle of God – those days are over. Unless investors desire to renew their minds and have a new form of thinking, many businesses, particularly the financial institutions, are going to be seriously affected to the point of closing down. Soon, the number of faithful depositors that come into the branches each day will significantly decrease. While the bank makes its profits from loans, that too will be in jeopardy.

If the social issues within the nation are not addressed for improvement, then not only will the nation lose its basic moral fabric, but gambling, pornography and the sex trade will increase and those elements will not grow the economy. With regards to the dysfunction of the family, this is especially so: matters such as general grooming, etiquette, protocol, communication skills, self-esteem development and basic respect for people in general, especially towards the elders of the society, are not promoted and addressed. In fact, lack of such training will only propel crime, violence and poverty.

Investment Strategies

Acquiring wealth comes as a result of putting vision into action with Divine direction and Biblical guidance. For example, for change to take place in the global economy, there needs to be an expansion of the job market. In order to get this expansion, it means that plans and ideas must be developed within. God requires every man to labor. It is time for every man to check and see their areas of struggle and identify the broken things within their community that need to be fixed. What conversations occur repeatedly on a daily basis? Those issues are either a source of pain or joy. Look around the various places that are being neglected and recognize that those places contain the wealth. Which areas of the general market do people avoid? This is where the wealth exists.

Never invest only in one organization. We have always heard the statement, 'never put your eggs in one basket." Ensure that your financial advisors are able to discern the times and seasons as well as the market conditions. Would you invest in something that has not yet been proven? Always invest in an organization where its managers are performers who are willing to change and learn, and are vigilant. Would you trust putting your money in the hands of profilers?

1. Invest in land. Purchase land and hold on to it, now is not the time to sell!

2. Invest in God-fearing countries and companies and communities that look dilapidated and broken down – it's where the wealth exists.

Finally, there is a shift about to take place within the marketplace. Israel is about to rise and it will become an investment paradise. There are a number of hidden treasures that are about to be revealed.

If the Western nations are wise, then they will recognize that now is the time to foster a relationship with Israel. Such nations will receive mutual benefits. We also need to watch Haiti, Egypt and the African nations. There will be great investment opportunities arising in those areas.

Increasing Sales God's Way

Have you ever been in a season, where regardless of how good your advertising campaigns are, and how much you invest in your media campaigns – social and otherwise – and despite all the giveaways, deals and discounts you offer, the sales still sit way below your hopes and expectations? Have you been in a situation where you are getting pressured from every angle regarding your performance, and the financial institutions continue to pressure you to meet your financial obligations and you just cannot see your way out?

Did you know, that even during what we call a 'low season' God can allow us to experience significant increase?

Psalm 68: 9 says: *"You, O God, sent a plentiful rain, whereby You confirmed Your inheritance, when it was weary."*

God's blessing goes beyond any market condition and trend! As long as we acknowledge that God is the One Who gives us tactics and strategies to make sales and increase profits (Isaiah 48: 17) and gain customer loyalty, then He will also reveal to you the strategies you need to employ to keep your customers satisfied.

First, you must create an environment on a daily basis to increase sales. In the same way that natural laws and procedures exist today that govern what we do and what can happen, there are Spiritual laws that support that. According to His word, the Lord loads us daily with benefits. So there must be instructions that we follow on a daily basis to unlock the benefits for increase in sales!

Something as simple as giving free advertisements to a struggling or small organization, sponsoring a small local church group, community team or activities and so on, in your times of difficulty, will make the difference. Having devotions in your organization on a daily basis, going to a Church Service once a month with your staff to give thanks for the previous month's sales – whether sales were good or not will make the difference! Remember that practicing Biblical principles are not hinged on religion. Biblical principles go beyond our beliefs and philosophies. If God created the business, then He also has the solutions when problems arise. There are simple keys for success. For example, if there is unity within your organization to achieve the company quota, then it can be achieved with surplus if there are no doubters. If you believe that your sales will result in $200M for the month, then write it down on paper and on the board in your office or boardroom, and motivate each person to set a goal toward it – speaking/declaring on a daily basis that is already achieved (even before the time frame), then you are going to achieve it!

Unity is the driving force for success in all organizations. When there is no unity, concerning our policies, targets, goals and objectives, then the company will struggle. Unity, positive thinking and speaking create light, change and increase. It has the capacity to heal the economy which was first created by a spoken word. When organizations fail to honor God's favor for success within their business, sales will decline.

Solutions for Businesses

During the 'low season' of sales, make a vow to God stating what you WILL do when He turns the sales around; and be careful to honor that vow! Vows change the environment and bring promotion and success over your competitors.

Always trust God and ask Him to give you insight to market conditions. Many are paying millions of dollars to get advice from the wrong source, which leads them to make poor decisions and causing them to lose their shirts! Some even change their image and even re-brand with very little benefit or success!

Always pray for the success of your customers. Most just sell. But remember that if your customers do not sell, or are not successful in whatever they are doing, they cannot give you the support and that will in turn affect your success.

Pray against, bad checks, bad debts and counterfeit money coming into your business. Pray for quick collections after sales, and also that God will open your eyes to see new market opportunities! Pray that you will meet delivery schedules and not experience 'out-of-stock' conditions. Pray that production will always be on target and that the staff will experience success also that they can be productive.

Pray that your marketing campaign will be 'children-friendly'.

Remember, always treat all your customers with respect and courtesy and ensure that you treat each person you encounter like a potential customer.

Limit Stress in Your Organization

As times become increasingly difficult, stress is also on the increase. The greatest desires of man today are to be debt-free and at peace. The environment today is tense with stress as many are increasingly concerned about tomorrow! As a result of the increasing stress levels, many people try many different things in order to lay hold of peace.

According to David S. Walonick, Ph.D.in his 1993 paper on Causes and Cures of Stress in Organizations, "… Arnold and Feldman (1986) define stress as "the reactions of individuals to new or threatening factors in their work environment." (p. 459) Since our work environments often contain new situations, this definition suggests that stress in inevitable. This definition also highlights the fact that reactions to stressful situations are individualized, and can result in emotional, perceptual, behavioral, and physiological changes."

Politicians and Legislators add to the stress then put laws in place in order to curtail our response to their oppression.

Jesus outlined in Matthew 26: 25 – 34 that worry (stress) is a distraction and that it was unreasonable, unnatural, unhelpful, unnecessary and unbelieving.

Thus, we are not to become distracted from the substantial issues of life over less important matters such as what we will eat or wear. We are the only creation of God that worries. God provides for the birds and we more valuable than they are. God provides for the needs of His own.

While stress is found in all levels of society, let us look at some occupations that carry extreme levels of stress.

1. Police
2. Doctors

3. Nurses
4. Teachers
5. National Leaders
6. Church Leadership/Clergy
7. Tax Collectors
8. Correctional Officers

In order to have a less stressful environment, it is critical for leaders in every organization to play an active role in the process of reducing stress. They could start by looking at more than just the academic qualifications of an individual to place him or her as one of its customer service representatives, for example, and look also at the person's ability/gift to engage their customers pleasantly, professionally and respectfully.

They must also create the environment that is conducive to a pleasant, experience with the organization, that is, set the right atmosphere so that customers/clients feel comfortable and confident doing business with them, even if they may be under financial pressures.

Rules, Laws and Regulations

All these must be carefully thought out and evaluated before they are even brought to the fore. A customer in default of payments ought not to be treated with less respect than the person who is not, because tough times can hit anyone and you never know when the tables may turn.

Debt Collectors and Loan Officers should not always seek to intimidate those in default. It adds nothing but stress and makes their jobs that much harder. Instead, one of their main strategies could be to encourage and motivate their customers, and where possible, visit them to see how they can help to direct them on that issue. They might be pleasantly surprised to see the solutions that would come out of that!

A manager, sitting in a comfortable chair in the office with the air conditioning making rash or rushed decisions about those outside of his/her reality does not realize that it is not as comfortable for those about whom they make their decisions.

Service

Good customer service and a pleasant and professional environment will bring repeat business to your organization, even if your product is not the best in quality by comparison, or if the prices are by comparison higher. Customers will be back because the service they receive makes a huge difference.

Technology has robbed many organizations of the personal touch that is so important to its customers. Today, when you call many organizations, we are met with the impersonal "Press 1" or "Press 2" message; and after all that you hear, "Message Full" or "Goodbye".

From time to time managers need to pretend to be an external customer and try to call their own offices and see what their Secretaries, Administrative Assistants or Personal Assistants are like to deal with! Then they can see what the experience is like and make adjustments where necessary.

There needs to be some serious adjustment and addition to the curriculum at the training level for the Police Force. They must be taught how to remain composed under pressure; how to treat the general public despite treatment by members of the public; how to respond to people and situations and help to bring positive change.

The Power of Grace

During the Easter Season, while we recognize that not everyone celebrates the significance of the season for various reasons, the key thing is to simply be grateful, appreciative and thankful that Jesus did come and lay His life down for us all!

The main fact that we are alive today is as a result of the fact that He came and extended to us His Grace!

Regardless of the spiritual condition one is in, it is God's grace that allows us hope, and grants us the free favor of God. Even as people ridicule God, and challenge Him to do something drastic to them as proof of His existence, it is the grace of God extended to them that keeps them.

The grace of God allows us to have the Favor and Goodness of God. Have you ever been promoted to a position for which you are not qualified or for which you were not the favorite applicant, but you got the job and are doing well? That was the favor of God!

Many may think that success and prosperity have to do with one's academic qualifications! Think about a company making super-profits and exceed financial forecasts. Then you hear the executives of the organization being interviewed and they would credit their success to their own academic achievements, their Public Relations Team or some other thing without acknowledging God. NOT SO! It is God's grace that allowed them to get profits, wisdom, knowledge, and strategies for their business!

When God's grace and favor are removed from any individual or organization – regardless of a person's level of intelligence and academic qualifications, there is going to be failure. Nothing can stop that if God's grace and favor are removed!

Some will say that God's grace favor and goodness are not fair, but God extends grace to whomever He chooses, whenever He chooses.

There are those lawyers who have never lost a case; athletes who have never lost a race. It is God's grace and favor! It is that same grace and favor that allows a commoner to marry a king! (Esther in the Bible, Kate Duchess of Cambridge, Meghan, Duchess of Sussex) Even for a black man to become president of a nation that was always ruled by white men – that is favor also!

Grace and Leadership

A lot of people – particularly leaders – are failing, because they failed to acknowledge God's grace. It is God's grace that allowed a David to remove a Goliath and stop him from threatening a nation. David used five stones – which symbolized grace – to defeat that giant. We need leaders who are not afraid to use God's principles to remove giants – Debt, Poverty, Crime and Hopelessness!

Walking in God's grace allows us to walk in His presence, His rest, His goodness, His mercy, wisdom, truth and discernment to successfully lead a nation. Even more so, many nation leaders have become extremely stressed, wearied, tired and sometimes sick! More often than not, it is a lack of grace that brings these results!

1. It was the grace of God that brought a nation out of oppression and bondage; and not only brought them out debt-free, but with wealth in hand! (Exodus 3, 11, 12)

2. Grace brings protection of those who are faithful to God from the plagues of life! (Exodus 3)

3. Grace allows those God has called and chosen to carry out His assignment. Even Noah – who God chose – to prepare an ark with the capacity to save many who were willing. The Ark can symbolize the preparation of something that is to bring protection, deliverance, and provision in hard times! An Ark cannot sail on dry land – it is going to take a flood. There are many people still in this earth that God is using to prepare for a time to come! Likewise, light has little effect during the daytime – the light shines in the dark!

4. Not everyone has the same capacity for the same things. Oftentimes, leaders are criticized and compared with others, but grace for the task of leadership is given based on their calling. (Romans 12: 3 & 6)

5. Many times, people take on positions onto themselves because they feel that they can do it; but if a person does not have the grace for the position, they would do well not to touch it!

6. It is God's grace that keeps us fresh and flourishing!

7. It is the grace of God that keeps us from falling. (2 Corinthians 12: 7)

8. It is God's grace that causes us to have the opportunity for the abundant life!

Whether you are an Atheist, Buddhist, Muslim or Christian, it is God's grace that keeps us all alive on a daily basis! Never underestimate the power of Grace!

God Will Not Bless Flex-Week

Biblical Principles outline that it is the duty of each and every sector - whether religious or secular organization, or secular government - to build God's House if they want God to build their house! King Solomon showed us the principles of building God's House before building his house (the government). Many are pushing different government leaders and organizations to have a 7-day work week, ignoring one's Sabbath or Day of Worship. But leaders at all levels must be careful of who is advising them.

Any laws that are put in place to weaken God's House or rob one's day of worship is Russian Roulette; and when the dust settles, you will see what will stand – the Word of God or careless suggestion. The book of Haggai clearly outlined the negative consequences that befall a nation, when one ignores the building of God's House. God was speaking to the religious people concerning their duty to Him and to His House and He was also speaking to the Governor who represented the political sector about their duties. Please note, it is not about the Church losing a few dollars from the offering plate who will feel it; it is the businesses who will feel it. The only reason some companies remain viable is the existence of a few genuine Christians within the company. It is going to be 'lights out' on a lot of organizations when the Christians leave.

In the same way that the Scripture outlines – render unto Caesar that which is Caesar's and to God that which is God's, God requires man to pay taxes to the Government, and He also requires man to give to Him that which is due to Him and that includes Worship and Tithing.

Regardless of the beliefs of an individual – whether they are Christian or non-Christian – God clearly outlines in His word that when a nation fails to build His house, that is, when we are making profits and putting everything else first instead of Him, (Matthew 6: 33), then we will see the effect of that on the cattle, the labor force and man. He said He will also withhold the grain, the new wine and the new oil; the ground will not bring forth. Ultimately there will be no economic growth. As they attempt to remedy one issue, several more will spring forth and eat away the profits. God reminds us that He controls the gold and the silver.

Advancing God's Cause

It is the duty of man to advance God's cause, interests and purpose. When man fails to do that then we have global crisis. Each country should learn from Europe and America about what can happen financially when, having been given the freedom of Worship, they chose to neglect the House of God and the day set apart for worshipping Him.

Surprisingly, we are seeing a shift to countries that many may deem un-Godly, because it is perceived that Christianity is not their primary religion. Yet, there are millions in underground churches, in countries like China and India, who are more righteous than those in the West who have neglected God's House.

When an individual, group or nation disregards the day of rest or worship for the sake of acquiring economic power, then the money/finance becomes the new god. So, as it was in Exodus 32, the bull becomes the new god! (Hosea 4: 16, Jeremiah 7: 11; Exodus 32: 4 & 35; Hosea 10: 5)

Many of them in the airline and shipping industries are failing because they refuse to give to the faith-based organization.

A seven-day flex work-week does not improve the economy, it destroys it and the institution of family as well. Furthermore, it adds to the social and moral problems within a nation.

In Nehemiah 13, Nehemiah had to carry out reforms to improve the economy because the merchants wanted to do the same thing – introducing a 7-day work week. What did he do to stop the 'flex week'? He rebuilt the economy!

Christians Must Open Their Own Businesses

With the threat of the seven-day Flex Week, God-fearing people should take the opportunity to open their own businesses and keep it private. Do not go public; when you keep it private you can call your own shots!

Revelation 18 lets us know that we are about to see a shift from the Babylonian system of which the Flex Week is a part – and to a Kingdom system. This is part of the greatest wealth transfer to take place. We are about to see the God-blessed Businesses vs. the Man-made System. Any system built or established without God's blessing will come down.

We should look at companies like Chick-Fil-A that respect the day of worship, as well as Hobby Lobby, Forever 21 and other companies that operate on Biblical Principles.

CHAPTER 16

THE BENEFITS OF GIVING IN THE RESURRECTION SEASON

Everyone wants solutions, but oftentimes our solutions are found in places that seem foolish to man. The Cross is one such place.

In every situation we undergo, the Cross brings victory. Giving during the Resurrection season allows us to partake of the victory which was won for us many years ago.

In days of old, during the first Passover, each house had to sacrifice a lamb to cover every person within their household. Our Passover Lamb was Jesus Christ and when we partake, we are receiving the benefits of Him shedding His blood as our Sacrificial Lamb. Hence all in our household will be protected.

Resurrection is a time of Thanksgiving, a season when every dead thing in our lives can spring back again. Resurrection is the Christian's Passover, and this is the first of the seven feasts God instructed His people to execute. This feast is called the Feast of the Unleavened Bread, and it is required that His people coming before Him with an Offering at all times and never empty-handed. Deuteronomy 16: 16 – 17, and Exodus 23: 15 which says,

"You shall keep the Feast of Unleavened Bread (you shall eat unleavened bread seven days, as I commanded you, at the time appointed in the month of Abib, for in it you came out of Egypt; none shall appear before Me empty);"

There are three (3) specific times that God requires us to come before Him and give as He has prospered us; the months of April, June and October and it is imperative for us to know and understand the Times and Seasons for breakthrough so that we may walk in true prosperity.

Resurrection/Passover brings a First-fruit blessing when we honor Him. (Proverbs 3: 9 – 10). By observing, partaking and giving during this time, the dead things in your life – your broken family relationships, your health, the lack of the presence of the Lord and the things you gave up on – can be restored. Obstacles will roll away – fear, doubt, sorrow and the cares of life! It is spring time so new hope will spring alive again in you! This season carries with it the potential to break you out of your tomb, and break the cycles in your life that lead to fruitlessness. Most importantly, it means that during this time especially, you can resurrect a stronger connection between you and the Heavenly Father.

For those in business, giving during this season carries with it the potential to revive sales and clientele/customers, and cause you to experience debt-forgiveness. King Hezekiah partook of the Passover season and it resurrected the entire nation's economy.

Paul was saved from shipwreck by doing the same; and Peter was released from prison during this season. (Acts 12; Acts 27; 2 Chronicles 30) David's observation of the Passover season caused the plagues and death during his reign to cease!

Can you imagine if our leaders gave and celebrated this Resurrection Season what positive effects it would have on the nation – particularly in the areas of crime and the economy?

The Benefits of Giving

1. God will assign an angel to you. (Exodus 23: 20 & 23)

2. God will be an enemy to your enemies. (Exodus 23: 22)

3. God will give you prosperity. (Exodus 23: 25)

4. God will take sickness away from you. (Exodus 23: 25)

5. God will give you a long life. (Exodus 23: 26)

6. God will bring increase and inheritance. (Exodus 23: 30)

God will give a special year of blessing, and what the enemy stole will be returned to you and protected by God from being overtaken. (Exodus 23: 29)

If you are desperate for change, give during this season and experience the major, positive changes that will take place in your life!

Giving to Achieve Sustainable Development

One of man's main responsibilities is the act of giving. Giving is the act that declares that we have conquered greed. There should be no discrimination or prejudice or wrong motives when it comes to giving.

Giving creates a better environment – reducing poverty, improving education, health, saving lives and easing the burden of suffering! Jesus even outlined that nations and individuals will be judged as a result of their lack of charity to the suffering and less fortunate. (Matthew 25: 35 – 45)

God's judgement will be based on moral character and the character is revealed by charitable deeds or the lack of them.

All organizations experiencing success – whether small or big – must give. Many corporate organizations would say they do not give to faith-based or religious organizations that are building the communities, while they would gladly give to those organizations that promote and support immorality. This is a dangerous precedence!

Giving must not be based on religion, sexual orientation or race – there should be no discrimination of any kind.

Corporate and Government must be careful of the policies they develop when it comes to charity! If such organizations are not willing to give to faith-based organizations, then it means they are not willing to give to the community – since faith-based organizations consist of and help members of the community. That being said, does this mean that faith-based organizations and ultimately the community should not support them through the purchase of their products?

Regardless of which charitable organization is meeting the needs of the communities, regardless of their size, there should be no discrimination. Most Corporate and Governmental organizations, give to large organizations where most of the money given is going to Administrative costs and are not being filtered down to the people who need it most!

There is nothing wrong with checking to ensure that the organizations are legitimate and are being properly run, but where it is found that the organizations (large or small) are legitimate, then where you can, SUPPORT THEM!

Furthermore, the list of charitable organizations, including churches, that exist within the country should be published and whatever funds they are given should be made public or at the least accessible by the general public. We have heard many times that funds have been given/donated to charities but there is little to no effect within the community and no public information that states how the funds were allocated!

Many corporate organizations are more willing to give to very large and highly publicized charitable organizations, but how much of it is reaching to the poor?

Government should seek to increase waivers and duty-free benefits so that the poor can be helped. Cutting will send millions more into poverty. They should be giving 10% from the revenue they collect if they want to see a change to the nation's economy.

Giving Stops Plagues

When plagues begin to affect a nation – whether it by crime, violence, disaster, disease or any other kind of plague – giving is the only thing that can break the cycle and the curses that are affecting the nations. (1 Chronicles 21: 13 – 25)

If nation leaders begin to give and champion the cause of the poor, and give with no strings attached, then we will experience a positive global change!

Giving brings healing. Many people are becoming sick, but giving can bring the change they need. (Psalm 41)

The number one criterion for giving is Love! Many nations and large organizations give for the wrong reason. A tax write-off should not be basis, or motive for giving – it can be an added benefit, but it should not be the main reason an organization gives!

Additionally, organizations must make the genuine effort to give back to the communities as they prosper; and also, to take care of the people in the communities where in their operations are based! By so doing, they will gain the support of the various communities. Companies may give to politicians because they want to secure and procure contracts in the future, but the key is, take care of the people!

Stand in The Gap for The Next Generation

Ezekiel 22: 30 says, *"So I sought for a man among them who would make a wall, and stand in the gap before Me on behalf of the land, that I should not destroy it; but I found no one."*

Many times, people will criticize the Church and ask what they are doing about the negative happenings within a nation or the world. But we must recognize that WE are the Church – every profession – and WE have a responsibility - individually and collectively - to stand in the gap for nations. We have become nations of people that have become caught up in our own little issues/problems/situations, forgetting that we also have a duty to each other and to our nation. Some of us are so caught up in showing off our latest 'self-improvement' projects – who has the latest clothes or enhanced body parts - and when tragedy strikes, that is when there is concern.

When negative happenings begin – increase in Murder, Rape and Famine, and then Hopelessness sets in, it means that there is a break/breach within the spiritual walls of the nation. If someone breaks into a home, if the owner simply adds a burglar alarm without fixing the breach – the broken window/door – then their efforts are wasted. Hence, God wants persons of every profession at every level to make themselves available to Him to be used to rebuild the walls – not the physical, but spiritual walls. We need to 'Stand in the Gap'.

"Standing in the gap" is a metaphor for committed intercession. When there is a gap between man and God, someone needs to stand in and intercede so that God can repair the breach for us. Hence, we have a responsibility to first identify the breach in every profession and stand in.

When there is a breach in the walls, everything comes in – anything takes place. If we are looking for restoration of the family, a good justice system, good governance and healing within a nation, then it is the responsibility of everyone to stand in the gap that the spiritual barriers will be rebuilt. Regardless of the systems or laws put in place, no change will come if there is a gap in the wall.

Every Profession

In order to be effective, every profession knows its own terminologies and jargon and so, knows the precise words to use as opposed to the ordinary lay person who would not be as knowledgeable in that area. For example, a lawyer knows the jargon and terms that he/she would use for certain matters, like "petition", "counter-petition" "recuse", "abrogate" so they could pray accordingly employing those terms that John Q. Public would not ordinarily know. A person who deals with the economy of a nation need to stand in the gap for the things that of that industry that are affecting the nation – inflation, devaluation of the dollar, fiscal policies and so on. They know the terminologies to use as they pray to stop the negative and ask for the increase of the positive. Doctors would know the diseases that are plaguing the nation and would pray accordingly for them to stop using medical terminologies. They would stand in the gap to minimize sicknesses and diseases that are eating away the nation – cancer, HIV, and others so that God will release medical breakthroughs to heal the nation. Security Forces also need to stand in the gap, they cannot simply focus on the physical, but also the spiritual aspect.

Interestingly, there is a name of God – a name ascribed to God which represents every one of these industries in our society.

Effective intercession brings change within a nation, but each person who stands in the gap must realize that we cannot operate the same way that we operated 20 years ago. 20 years ago, we did not have the technological revolution we now have and now as knowledge has increased, so has the technological warfare. There are now games and software that are designed to pollute the minds of our youth and encourage them to commit crimes and do other things; and this is a breach. We need people to rise up in the Information Technology arena to use the relevant jargon and references as they stand in the gap and fight for our young people and the future of the nations.

Recognize that the mind and eyes are direct links to the soul and as such whoever will control the mind and eyes will control the next generation.

So, it is the responsibility of every profession to stand in the gap that change will take place.

CHAPTER 17

REMOVE THE GUARD - REBUILD THE GATES

When the moral and social fabrics of a nation are being worn away by crime, lack of good governance, lack of solutions, a battered economy and the poor state of our youth, we do not need one more survey or feasibility study, we need action.

The fact of the matter is that the gates have been torn down and that has opened the way for all kinds of adversity and plague to enter and afflict the nation.

Imagine you have a building and there are walls around the building; but neither the entrance nor exit, have any gates! It means that there is free access to the building and there is no sentry or security! It is a free-for-all and anything can come and go! Anything you have in the building – goods, people, assets of any kind, can be swiped/stolen at will.

Now a 'gate' is an opening or entrance to something, such as a building, grounds or city. In Biblical days, business, bargaining, negotiations, politics and justice were conducted at the gates.

When a gate is torn down, regardless of new investments, new infrastructure, new systems put in place, no change will come! Regardless of what different parties talk about new reforms – it's the same old thing unless the gates are put in place.

The people of the nation, those in positions of influence – including the Church that has become lukewarm and have found themselves in bed with the politicians – are now reaping the 'rewards' and foreigners are now ruling over them!

Action to Be Taken by Leaders

The first thing Nehemiah did to rebuild the gates was to **Weep**. He wept of the problem and the poor condition of the nation; in the same way that Jesus wept over Jerusalem. This weeping was a repentance on behalf of the nation's people for the condition in which they had put themselves. He had a deep concern for the state of the people.

The Church needs to weep and cry out in repentance for the spiritual condition of the nation and for the epidemic of crime sweeping through it. It must have a deep concern for the state of the nation and not attempt to distance itself in silence!

The next thing Nehemiah did was **Fast**! The people of the nation and the leaders, believe that our deliverance of the nation lies in witchcraft. Sadly, there are many who prefer to go after those things than to Fast for victory from God. Little do they know that by their actions, they are replacing God with Witchcraft.

Today, almost everybody is wearing a 'guard'. A 'guard' is a tool of witchcraft that people acquire to 'protect' themselves – a ring or pendant any item they dedicate for that purpose. Taxi men have their 'guards', Gunmen have 'guards', politicians have 'guards', Businessmen have their 'guards': some in the refrigerator; some in the brassiere; some on the finger; some around the neck! Witchcraft is not a tool that God uses or encourages us to employ - He is certainly not in that! Question: Who are such persons being guarded from? Who are they guarded by? We know the saying 'two wrongs don't make a right', therefore, EVIL + EVIL = MORE EVIL!

Racism, Classism and Development

Racism and Classism, especially in the workplace, have hindered many from upward mobility and promotion, and in so doing, a significant level of growth and development within the nation has also been hindered.

Let it be clear that no one is born racist – Racism is taught. Furthermore, it is not just about the color of one's skin, it includes one's ethnicity and possibly culture. There are many who make it seem as if it is about the "whites against blacks", but there are many black racists that exist as well. Despite all that, what God wants is forgiveness on both sides of the proverbial fence so that everyone – regardless of race or culture – can move forward to achieve greater.

Racism and Classism are issues of the heart and Civil Rights statements and actions will not solve it. This is something that only God can fix through the willingness of those involved to move past it all.

It starts with us as individuals. Many times, persons will quickly cry out Racism while they themselves practice Classism. The schools they attend embed it in their minds and each person is taught from an early age the tenets of Classism and ultimately Racism. The results of this plays out in crime-fighting. There is a tendency to more readily raid the inner-city community while they turn a blind eye to some of the real culprits living in the hills. Ultimately, people are treated well (or not) based on the color of their skin and their social status. It is even affecting the electoral process – candidates are presented in different areas based on the color of their skin.

Hindering Upward Mobility

Many times, those within the corporate circles struggle for upward mobility; and with all their qualifications and hard work, they are overlooked for promotion in favor of someone else because of the color of their skin or their last name. Sadly, this even evident in church circles where a dark-skinned pastor would be assigned to a community/parish where the persons in the community are lighter-skinned and he/she is rejected or mistreated based on that issue. To this day, some cannot sit at the front of the church or in a certain rows or benches if they do not have a certain last name or are not of a certain race or social standing.

The recent exposure of the slavery of blacks in Libya garnered the silence of nations. There was no general outcry by the nations against it – nothing. But I guarantee they would cry out against issues that are of little to no impact on the growth and development of a nation.

One's color, social status, gender or sexuality should never be used as qualifying factors for a person's promotion. If we want to see equality and fairness in the distribution of resources and opportunities within a nation or organization, then these demons must be dealt with and this heart issue corrected, because all of this is a threat to true democracy.

Even within the church, it has been noticed that there are many single people who want to be married but are hindered by what they have been taught – that they should look for a certain color, hair type and so on. When the right person comes, because of their prejudices, they often push them away.

Every form today that we fill out requires information on each person's ethnic background. Why is this really relevant?

All Sectors Affected

Every sector is significantly affected by Racism and Classism – Entertainment, Sports, Media, and Finance to name a few. Recently Serena Williams and Jennifer Hudson had their share of this issue. Persons thought that the house Jennifer Hudson owned belonged to her white driver and that she was the helper. Even President Obama was once mistaken for a chauffeur. Many black doctors are discriminated against. These days companies have what is called an "At Will" contract, so that if they want to let you go on the basis that your skin color is not in keeping with the expectations/desires of the clientele, they can let you go instantly.

God Has the Cure

It is affecting people so much that they are losing their identity in order to fit in. Skin-bleaching, makeup and hair extensions are the order of the day and those facilitating industries are making billions in revenue. Acts 10: 9 – 16, Galatians 3: 28 and James 2 reveal that Racism and Classism existed then too and God did not like it then and He certainly does not now. God even afflicted Miriam, Moses' sister, as a result of her racist statement.

It is time for us to purge these issues from among us so we can move forward - it can only come about when we ask the Lord God for a new heart.

What Is Your Building Code?

The purpose of the building code is to regulate building construction in order protect health, safety and welfare. It controls all aspects of building – materials, exit strategy, fire safety and structural integrity. With this in mind, Biblical Principles are the perfect code to build your organization. It gives criteria, solutions, protection and safety. It warns you of consequences.

The next two and a half (2 ½) years are going to be critical for all nations and organizations. Your building codes will be tested. If you truly understand the number fifty (50) that the nation is celebrating, there is connection to land, inheritance, freedom, debt write-offs, amnesty and pardon of prisoners. The nation should be cutting back on some of the spending for the celebrations, and channel it to help liberate the people and to deal with the great challenges ahead.

The number one (1) criterion for any nation is to center its activities around the building of its people. It is going to be very costly to all the builders who build without God! Build with those who are gifted and talented in particular areas, not politically. We have to build with the right materials.

Rock or Sand?

Rock represents trust, hope, the Word of God, truth, righteousness, faith and revelation. Sand represents carnality, corruption and selfishness. (Galatians 5; Matthew 7: 24 – 29, Luke 6: 46 – 49)

Every building will be tested – rain, flood and wind! These are the three (3) key elements that will, literally and figuratively, come against a building, a nation or an economy.

Recently, the global economy was blamed for the Housing and Vehicle industry fallouts! If those two (2) industries were so significantly affected by the economic wind, on what were they built?

Very shortly, a number of 'houses' will be tested including media houses, churches and civic organizations.

Let us now take a test to see determine the building code for your organization:

1. What would happen if your organization's main clientele or customers pull out?

2. What would happen if you have a loan to repay and you lose all your contracts?

3. What would happen if you have a mortgage and/or car loan/payment and you lose your job tomorrow?

4. What would happen if the top ten (10) Tithers in your Church walk away and there is a Church loan or mortgage to repay?

5. What would happen if your most trusted employee becomes your competitor?

6. What would happen if your operational costs are exceeded and your sales fall significantly?

7. What would happen if you are depending on a loan to take you out of financial debt only to realize that it takes you into deeper debt?

8. What would you do if the bank in which you have put all your savings collapses tomorrow and you lose all your savings?

While you ensure that your building has an entrance and an exit, ensure that there is also an emergency exit and a safe zone in the building!

While there are certain things we have little or no control over, individuals, organizations and nations that build with the right Building Code will not suffer much loss during the wind, fire or rain that is inevitable during the life of any person, organization or nation.

A builder must be wise. Their foundation must be very deeply rooted in God! Bailouts and Cash for Jewelry cannot be your contingency plan. There is nothing wrong with borrowing loans, but that must go to improving infrastructure and increasing manufacturing space, not to service debts. Furthermore, the fine print must be clearly understood, so that there are no negative repercussions on future generations.

It is time to check our building codes to ensure prosperity, peace, growth, unity, and sustainable development, so that each person will have a better quality of life.

Private Sector: Reform or Become Extinct

Generally speaking, the Private Sector bodies have continued to neglect local development within their nations and have ignored opportunities to invest in their staff. In Third World nations, members of the private sector continue to recruit foreigners who were not contributing anything of value to that nation. If you look at some of the board members of many of those companies today, you will see the problem.

In Jamaica, for example, with the latest report of 1.1 million people in poverty, the Private Sector group – one of the most powerful groups in that nation – will need to reform if they want to remain viable and not become extinct.

It has been said many times that the organizations/companies within Private Sector do not just exist to make profits or to simply compete with each other. The Local Private Sector understands the culture and are a part of the culture. They need to begin reaching out to the community.

Jamaica's Digicel, Scotiabank, Flow and the ICD Group's Multi-Care Foundation are models that other players within the Private Sector need to look at emulating as it relates to servicing the community. The ICD Group, for example, started the Management Trainee Program in Jamaica in the 1980's, and there are several other organizations that have followed suit since.

Instead of the aggressive competition and brand wars in the market, there needs to be greater co-ordination within Private Sector groups for the betterment of their nation. They need to begin focusing on the common threats facing their nation such as Foreign Investors being given an edge over the locals, environmental issues and the problems affecting small businesses!

According to Maria Neira, the World Health Organization's (WHO) public and environmental health chief (2014)

"The biggest pollution-related killers were heart disease, stroke, pulmonary disease and lung cancer. The hardest-hit regions of the globe were what the WHO labels Southeast Asia, which includes India and Indonesia, and the Western Pacific, ranging from China and South Korea to Japan and the Philippines. Together, they accounted for 5.9 million deaths. The global death toll included 4.3 million deaths due to indoor air pollution, chiefly caused by cooking over coal, wood and biomass stoves. The toll from outdoor pollution was 3.7 million, with sources ranging from coal heating fires to diesel engines"

Are we ready to transfer the problems to our shores?

In addition to this:

1. The Private Sector needs to respect people's day of worship if they intend to remain viable. They need to understand and realize that GOD must be their center, therefore employees need their time to worship God on Saturdays/Sundays.

2. Small sector companies need help to survive in this economy - given bail-out schemes - loans not from banking institutions, but from other reliable large companies who have been doing well within the market for over 20 years, allowing much time given for payback of loan (non-payment for a year, then begin payment the following year. This will be for those who are desperate in need (bankruptcy).

3. There needs to be a re-evaluation to determine whether gambling is helping or hurting the nation, how it affects the children and our families. We need to know if it is actually making the nation poorer.

4. Private Sector Organizations need to cut the perks and have the companies each adopt a Primary School.

5. Assist university graduates with setting up their businesses, owing to the fact that many of them are out of jobs for as long as 4-8 years. Set up programs that help to co-ordinate the younger generation, giving them reasons for venturing into certain businesses.

6. The Private Sector needs to have an internal system to police their own people; inspecting them every two (2) weeks, and ensure that they adhere to Consumer Rights programs.

7. Have a team to observe closely small companies to see what products will help them greatly to continue into the market for longer years.

8. Conduct urgent meetings with both parties to discuss these situations for change to come to please God.

9. If our local Private Sector wants to survive, they must rebrand their roles and mandates and revisit their vision to embrace the locals; train our local people! They cannot be like our politicians looking for everything overseas to save us. If our economy is to turn, it is going to happen through our own local people.

10. How many of our people can enjoy the beauty of the land?

11. How many of our people can enjoy a weekend at an all-inclusive hotel?

12. How many of them can visit our beaches and resorts and afford it?

13. How many can gamble and drink at the casinos the Private Sector and Government have been pushing as the nation's economic solution?

14. Which direction are we heading for if the normal man cannot afford what is in his own country?

15. Presently, many are saying that crime is the biggest hindrance to our Tourism Sector and the nation in general. With most of our people focusing on investors coming in to save the day; and with the different cultures and beliefs they carry; in addition to the opening up of our borders, can we deal with the external security threats possible to our nation?

Why Labor in Vain?

"Unless the LORD builds the house, they labor in vain who build it; unless the LORD guards the city, the watchman stays awake in vain." (Psalm 127: 1)

Throughout the global catastrophes and failures that have been occurring in this season economic decline, wars, diseases such as Ebola; injustice and human rights issues and the crisis of ISIS - we see that many of the global leaders are clueless about how to deal with these issues. Some are silent concerning how to deal with ISIS.

All this is the result of leaders and nations building without God. Regardless of how brilliant the plans are, they will come to naught and failure. This will be so because in order to experience real success with any plans, visions and ideas, there has to be total reliance on God. In order to build our families well, build the economy, the justice system, have development there must be a total reliance of God.

When we allow God to build the house, you will have true success. When we trust anything else, we labor in vain.

Unsurprisingly, those who should be making those statements have sunken into silence; hence the state of our country and the moral decline. Many are pushing a Secularist agenda. We are even seeing our nation voting against what they should be supporting!

God is a God of order, and as we all know, there can be no building without order! When we remove God from the media, politics and even Hollywood; when we to develop the Youth without prayer and Godly wisdom, then we are creating a global catastrophe, particularly among the Youth. So we are laboring in vain without Him!

When we build without God, we are wasting time and resources, and duplicating processes. God gives treasures to those who love Him, trust Him and obey Him while they are asleep. The men who toil from early in the morning till late in the evening without God, do so in vain.

1. A person who wants to reduce crime and violence with God's absence from the building process labors in vain.

2. A person who trusts electronic devices – surveillance tools and armed guards – without God in it, labors in vain; and it will bring failure.

3. An economist who wants to manage an economy without God in the building process, will fail. Remember, God created the economy, the earth, as well as Times and Seasons; and there are requirements. The earth cannot yield anything without His command! We cannot truly build without Prayer, without the Word of God, nor without seeking Him for direction and instructions.

When God builds the house, He will direct you concerning Trade partners and partnerships. Look at companies such as Forever 21 – Don and Jing Chang; Jamaica Broilers – Robert Levy.

Both Macro and Micro-economic factors without God will bring great pain and hardship. Look at the state of the Jamaican dollar, for example. At this rate, it would be better for the nation to abandon the local dollar, work with CARICOM and let the EC (Eastern Caribbean) Dollar become the new currency for the region.

Many politicians are depending on their political connections in other countries or the agenda of other nations to help them to be successful. This is a deception! What if they fail? What will happen?

Regardless of whatever leadership styles a nation adopts – Communism, Democracy and so on – if God is not the One Who builds the house, then all the manifestos and plans will fail. For us to be successful – individually or collectively - we have to allow God to build our house to work in us and bring His purpose within us out!

Each individual needs to ask the questions: Are we laboring in vain? Is God in charge of our workforce? Is God the center of my family? Once we can honestly answer these questions, it will allow us to make better choices. It will allow our eyes to open, and we will be able to discern good from evil.

God is looking for leaders in business places who are willing to get into the political, legal and financial sectors – who are not afraid to allow God to build their houses. When they come forward, we will see global change.

Common Sense for Nation-Building

As mentioned in many articles, the things that are now happening globally and locally, particularly with regard to Economics, Crime and other social areas, cannot be solved on a natural level. There needs to be Spiritual insight and vision. Vision will come through Prayer and Repentance. (Joel 1 & 2) Then God will instill in the young and old the vision for nation-building.

It is not about the political problems we see, because regardless of the party, all sides have the same mentality. If there is even a change in the political arena and the mindsets do not change and become renewed, the problem will double and the nation will continue on the same trend.

The old ways of doing business has expired. We are in an era where we have to be Divinely-led. Most countries, particularly the 'Third World' nations, are ignoring their greatest assets – the people and the capacities within them! Most are focusing on other areas. Some of the problems really do not require a PhD to be dealt with, just simple common sense.

What made the business pioneers of the previous eras so great was many of them were high school dropouts! In fact, some had only the basic, academic qualifications, but they built multi-faceted and multi-million-dollar corporations or careers! They had insight and vision way ahead of their time, which still stand!

For example, in looking at one of Forbes' list of millionaires and billionaires, we see Sean 'Jay-Z' Carter, Carl Linder, George Foreman, Simon Cowell, Giselle Bundchen, Tim Clark, Richard Branson, David Murdock. Interestingly, Richard Branson, who owns the Virgin Group, owns over 200 companies in 30 countries. All these persons are High School dropouts! They are involved in businesses such as Music, Entertainment, Arts and Culture, Acting, Modeling, Real Estate, Food and Telecommunications. Please note that this is not advocating dropping out of school; good formal education is invaluable. These examples serve to remind us not to discount anyone who does.

All Third World countries possess natural talents and resources. If we are going to build the economy and become great, we need to build around what we possess. A nation's Education System must be streamlined in such a way that it can bring out those who will not do well academically but can excel technically. Should it be that a nation's human resources be managed by the Financial Ministry of the nation?

Within the Third World countries, what has allowed such nations to be popular are Art, Culture, Culinary Skills, Entertainment, Music, Sports and other natural talents. Why not begin to restore all the buildings within areas that were out of use for years and create programs to edify men, women, and children in those buildings. Engage them in Visual Arts (Arts & Crafts), Music, Indoor Sports, Fashion Designing and Landscaping. Begin to put on International Competitions! We can have our own "Wimbledon" in the Caribbean. We can have our own PGA Tournament and Pebble Beach Tournament for golfers. We can have our own internationally broadcasted Caribbean Culinary Competitions! We can have our own international level Hair/Cosmetology Competition and bring out the talents within the inner-city areas! Furthermore, bring down the top salon owners and operators and host international level hair shows and give our local hairdressers, salon owners/operators and stylists the access to express and show their talents in that area – much of which will blow their minds! We have and can use our climate, beaches and culinary expertise to our advantage as a part of the negotiation to bring in the international heavy-hitters (who may learn a thing or two from our locals)!

Begin to build more Playing Fields, Community Training Centers and cut down on highways and security. Some of the worse gunmen are some of the best footballers, inventors, athletes, actors and even chefs! Give them a direction in which to channel their skills and talents and reduce crime and violence.

We need to stop blaming our security forces when the crime rates are not diminishing, when the nation has not effectively supported positive activities and programs for direct the skills and talents that exist within the nation. When the nation fails to do this, then the people will find other outlets and we all know that these outlets may be less than favorable. When people are hungry or desperate enough, they may succumb to negative activities in order to survive. Some may be able to withstand, but not all! If we are going to reduce crime, we will need to create the environment the facilitate that!

Revolution Needed in The Global Health Sector

The Health Sector, which is comprised of the Pharmaceutical and Insurance industries, has now become the number one modern vampire. Gone are the days when all our doctors would put the health of their patients first. Today, while some still do, many do not and frankly, money talks or you're dead!

Oftentimes, even before patients are discharged, they are getting phone calls from the hospital about the payments. It's all about the money. Greed has seeped into the Health Sector.

The Caribbean should in no way allow international influence to dictate health policies of their nation. That is why the local leadership must take advantage and capitalize on it and be different. The Health Sector has become a set of legalized scammers.

The insurance companies increase their policy prices and when they ought to be giving the people the best quality medication, they introduce and promote generic drugs, and that are slowly harming people. Further to that, if you miss a payment, they cancel your policy and try to fight you out of your claim.

Many people are dying and there are many questions that need to be asked. Each individual is responsible for his or her health and we need to be wiser now:

1. Why is it that the older generation, who did not have the equipment and technology we now have, did not have some of the problems/illnesses that exist today?

2. Is modern technology helping us or destroying us? Phones, cell sites, computers – are they affecting us?

3. Why do so many of our products contain so much sugar?

4. Are our people being educated on Nutritional Facts vs. Ingredients, and what to look at when purchasing a product? For example, sucrose, dextrose and sugar are all sugar.

5. Why is healthcare SO expensive?

6. Are these inferior foods causing more problems?

7. Are our medications helping us or causing greater damage to our bodies? It seems to be all about pushing the medication not curing the people

8. Where is the focus of the Health Sector today? Why is there such a fight and why so many regulations against natural products and the natural way of healing?

Biblical Views on Health

The body is the Temple of the Holy Spirit. God dwells in our temples and He wants us to be healed and whole. There are certain things we have to take by force to have good health. God created everything to sustain man. He even outlined in the Garden of Eden, the things that we should eat versus what we should not. (Genesis 1: 29 – 30; Genesis 9: 3; Psalms 104: 14; Psalm 136: 25; Hosea 2: 8; Genesis 2: 15; Genesis 6: 21). In the Book of Revelation, God clearly outlines that the plants are for the healing of the nation – the herbs and the water.

Third World countries have been continuously warned that what they have is greater than gold. Most First World countries have been investing in divesting the land in the region - this is what they are after – the Natural Resources.

If we are going to talk about economic development, then we should have a plan – especially Jamaica, with so many natural resources. We should not have a problem in finding jobs. Wherever problems lie, that is the area where the greatest solutions can be found and our leaders need to wise up and wake up.

God created man from the ground, surrounded by water. This gives us a clue as to what we need to take into our bodies in order to sustain us and our physical health. We need to get back to basics. For example, we need to go back to using natural fertilizers, not the chemicals that are slowly destroying our bodies. How about the pollution of our oceans? Is our marine life safe from pollution? How do these things affect our health? How is the process of rearing poultry affected by our technological advances?

It is the duty of every individual to begin to educate him/her self about what we are to consume on a daily basis.

Entire generations are slowly dying as a result of the current system of operations globally for the Health Sector and urgent change is needed. We have the internet to our advantage to make our own checks and then ask the questions we need answered so that we can make good choices for the sake of our health.

Nations Need Emotional Healing

We are living in a society that is broken and needs healing. There are many in influential positions within the society that need emotional healing but it cannot be done through/by medical resources, only through Spiritual empowerment and deliverance.

A person who needs spiritual and emotional healing first has to identify the root cause. Then the process starts with Forgiveness, which is key. Many who have suffered emotionally have experienced that suffering through painful circumstances such as rape, absence of parent(s), and verbal/physical abuse in childhood by family members or others. It could even be as a result of negative words spoken by a teacher or schoolmate.

There are many who have been told that they would never amount to anything good. Interestingly, because of this kind of abuse, many persons take on different levels of academic study to prove their naysayers wrong. Some, as a result, become professional students accumulating degree upon degree.

If a person is motivated to achieve success based on negative circumstances, they are still not yet healed from the root issue. Many have chosen careers that God did not intend for them. People who have not yet experienced joy, despite their success, can only receive the level of emotional healing they need through the Holy Spirit. Some will go into many forms of Spiritualism in their pursuit for healing and joy - Yoga, Transcendental Meditation, etc. But they will not find the true joy there – it simply creates a cycle of mood swings, instability and leaves them unable to maintain relationships while blaming others. Some become cold and even abusive at the workplace.

Being Whole

The people of a nation cannot enjoy true prosperity until they are emotionally healed and are whole – body, mind, soul, and spirit. (3 John 2). Why is it that some people try hard drugs, and alcohol, engage in promiscuous, reckless sexual activities, or even become gamblers or workaholics? They know that something is wrong, that there is a void that needs filling and they try all these activities so that they can experience peace.

There are those who, because of the love they did not experience growing up, they try to pour out that love upon their own children, but to the point of yielding to their every request and "spoiling" them – which is just as damaging. They become more of a friend to their children than they are a parent and this creates another set of challenges/issues. This may result in those children being on a path to Classism, Pride/Arrogance and possibly Crime.

Emotional problems are worse than physical problems, because emotional problems cannot be addressed as readily as they are intangible.

Emotional problems influence our choices and behavior and affects the nation on a whole more than we think. Some of these problems are also linked to what takes place with the mother during pregnancy. Contrary to some beliefs, Life begins at Conception. The mother's environment and her experience emotionally affect both her and the child/children she carries. For example, if they smoke or drink or are living in an environment where violence takes place regularly, then it is quite likely that the children they carry will do similarly. Recognize that our very calling and purpose are decided in the womb (Jeremiah 1: 5; Isaiah 49: 1; Luke 1: 39 – 45). Children who also survive attempted abortions grow up with a lot of emotional problems.

God's Presence Heals

The main reason God gives us gifts of Healing, Word of Knowledge, and Word of Wisdom and Discernment is to help to administer emotional healing (Luke 5: 17). God wants us to be emotionally stable so that there is overall stability. A simple environment with songs of worship within the workplace can bring emotional healing. Some may feel peace and have goose pimples – like a distressed Saul did when David played. (1 Samuel 16: 23). It brings refreshing and inner healing. Many would have diagnosed

Saul's problem as a mental problem and medicate/sedate him. But his problem was emotional and spiritual.

We need to stop looking at the "quietness" of an individual as being a mark of emotional stability. A person can be quiet on the surface but have a myriad of emotions swirling within waiting for the button to be pushed.

Divine prosperity is not a momentary phenomenon; it is an on-going, progressing state of success and well-being. It is intended for every area of one's life spiritually, physically, emotionally and materially.

For us to move from Poverty to Prosperity, we can only achieve that (and deal with the crime issue) when we begin to deal with the emotional healing needed, especially by those in influential positions in every sector of our society.

BIBLIOGRAPHY

Damazio, Frank. *The Making Of A Leader* © 1988 Frank Damazio, City Bible Publishing. All Rights Reserved

Hayford, Jack W. Executive Editor, *New Spirit-Filled Life®️ Bible,* (New King James Version) © 2002 Steve Lyston, Thomas Nelson, Inc.

Lyston, Steve. *Tactics And Strategies For The Famine For Individuals, Businesses, Governments & NGOs.* © 2012 Trafford Publishing. All Rights Reserved.

Lyston, Steve., Hutchinson, Doris. *The Prophetic Word To The Nations: A Compilation Of Prophetic Utterances From 2009 – 2017.* © 2017 Lyston Consultancy & Enterprises LLC. All Rights Reserved.

Milligan, Ira L. *Understanding The Dreams You Dream*, First Edition. © 1997 Ira Milligan, Treasure House, An Imprint Of Destiny Image Inc.

Pfeiffer, Charles F., Vos, Howard F., Rea, John. Editors, *Wycliffe Bible Dictionary,* (Seventh Printing) © 2005 Hendrickson Publishers, Inc

Price, Paula A. (PhD). *The Prophet's Dictionary: The Ultimate Guide To Supernatural Wisdom,* © 1999, 2002, 2006 Whittaker House

Strong, James. *The New Strong's Expanded Exhaustive Concordance of the Bible, (Red Letter Edition)* © 1990 Thomas Nelson Publishers

Swaggart, Jimmy. *The Holy Bible. The Expositor's Study Bible*. King James Version. Copyright © 2008, Jimmy Swaggart Ministries. Baton Rouge, Louisiana.

Concise Oxford English Dictionary Eleventh Edition. © 1964, 1976, 1982, 1990, 1995, 199, 2001, 2004 Oxford University Press. All Rights Reserved.

http://citeseerx.ist.psu.edu/viewdoc/download?doi=10.1.1.468.8276&rep=rep1&type=pdf

https://www.ilo.org/wcmsp5/groups/public/---arabstates/---ro-beirut/documents/genericdocument/wcms_229364.pdf

https://www.ilo.org/ipec/Informationresources/WCMS_IPEC_PUB_7447/lang--en/index.htm

https://www.scribd.com/document/336139044/8-Causes-and-Cures-of-Stress-in-Organizations-Www-statpac-org-24-5-2016

https://www.securitymagazine.com/articles/84342-hackers-stole-45-million-in-atm-card-breach

https://www.ucanews.com/news/air-pollution-is-now-worlds-greatest-health-risk-says-who/70555

https://www.unicef.org/mdg/childmortality.html

https://www.who.int/ipcs/features/air_pollution.pdf

https://en.wikipedia.org/wiki/Berkshire_Hathaway

https://en.wikipedia.org/wiki/Warren_Buffett

www.ingramcontent.com/pod-product-compliance
Lightning Source LLC
Chambersburg PA
CBHW061125220326
41599CB00024B/4174